CompTIA®
Security+®
Practice Tests
Exam SY0-701
Third Edition

David Seidl

SYBEX®

A Wiley Brand

This book is dedicated to Mike Chapple, who helped me get my start in the writing field. After most of a decade writing together, this was my first entirely solo project. Mike, as always, thank you for helping me get my start almost a decade ago, for encouraging me along the way, and for continuing to challenge me to do more each time we take on another book.
—David

Acknowledgments

Books like this involve work from many people who put countless hours of time and effort into producing them from concept to final printed and electronic copies. The hard work and dedication of the team at Wiley always shows. I especially want to acknowledge and thank senior acquisitions editor, Kenyon Brown, who continues to be a wonderful person to work with on book after book.

I also greatly appreciate the editing and production team for the book, including Lily Miller, the project editor, who is not only an absolute pleasure to work with, but who also brings deep expertise to all aspects of the effort; Chris Crayton, the technical editor, who provided insightful advice and gave wonderful feedback throughout the book; and Archana Pragash, the production editor, who guided me through layouts, formatting, and final cleanup to produce a great book. I would also like to thank the many behind-the-scenes contributors, including the graphics, production, and technical teams who make the book and companion materials into a finished product.

My agent, Carole Jelen of Waterside Productions, continues to provide me with wonderful opportunities, advice, and assistance throughout our writing careers.

Finally, I want to thank my friends and family, who have supported me through the late evenings, busy weekends, and long hours that a book like this requires to write, edit, and get to press.

About the Author

David Seidl is vice president for information technology and CIO at Miami University, where he is responsible for IT across the institution. During his IT career, he has served in a variety of technical and information security roles, including serving as the senior director for Campus Technology Services at the University of Notre Dame, where he co-led Notre Dame's move to the cloud and oversaw cloud operations, ERP, databases, identity management, and a broad range of other technologies and service. Prior to his senior leadership roles at Notre Dame, he served as Notre Dame's director of information security and led Notre Dame's information security program. He taught information security and networking undergraduate courses as an instructor for Notre Dame's Mendoza College of Business and has written 21 books on security certification and cyberwarfare, including coauthoring *CISSP (ISC)² Official Practice Tests* (Sybex, 2021) as well as the current and previous editions of the *CompTIA CySA+ Study Guide: Exam CS0-003* (Wiley, 2023, Chapple/Seidl) and *CompTIA CySA+ Practice Tests: Exam CS0-003* (Wiley, 2023, Chapple/Seidl).

David holds a bachelor's degree in communication technology and a master's degree in information security from Eastern Michigan University, as well as CISSP, CySA+, Pentest+, GPEN, and GCIH certifications.

About the Technical Editor

Chris Crayton, MCSE, CISSP, CASP+, CySA+, Cloud+, S+, N+, A+, is a technical consultant, trainer, author, and industry-leading technical editor. He has worked as a computer technology and networking instructor, information security director, network administrator, network engineer, and PC specialist. Chris has served as technical editor and content contributor on numerous technical titles for several of the leading publishing companies. He has also been recognized with many professional and teaching awards.

Contents

Introduction

CompTIA® Security+® Practice Tests: Exam SY0-701, Third Edition is the perfect companion volume to the *CompTIA® Security+® Study Guide: Exam SY0-701, Ninth Edition* (Wiley, 2023, Chapple/Seidl). If you're looking to test your knowledge before you take the Security+ exam, this book will help you by providing a combination of over 1,000 questions that cover the Security+ domains along with easy-to-understand explanations of both right and wrong answers.

If you're just starting to prepare for the Security+ exam, we highly recommend that you use the *CompTIA Security+ Study Guide, Ninth Edition* to help you learn about each of the domains covered by the Security+ exam. Once you're ready to test your knowledge, use this book to help find places where you may need to study more or to practice for the exam itself.

Since this is a companion to the *Security+ Study Guide*, this book is designed to be similar to taking the Security+ exam. The book itself is broken up into five domain-centric chapters with questions about each domain.

If you can answer 90 percent or more of the questions for a domain correctly, you can feel safe moving on to the next chapter. If you're unable to answer that many correctly, reread the chapter and try the questions again. Your score should improve.

 Don't just study the questions and answers! The questions on the actual exam will be different from the practice questions included in this book. The exam is designed to test your knowledge of a concept or objective, so use this book to learn the objectives behind the questions.

The Security+ Exam

The Security+ exam is designed to be a vendor-neutral certification for cybersecurity professionals and those seeking to enter the field. CompTIA recommends this certification for those currently working, or aspiring to work, in roles, including:

- Systems administrator
- Security administrator
- Tier II support technician
- IT support manager
- Cybersecurity analyst
- Business analyst

The exam covers five major domains:

- Domain 1.0 General Security Concepts
- Domain 2.0 Threats, Vulnerabilities, and Mitigations
- Domain 3.0 Security Architecture
- Domain 4.0 Security Operations
- Domain 5.0 Security Program Management and Oversight

These five areas include a range of topics, from firewall design to incident response and forensics, while focusing heavily on scenario-based learning. That's why CompTIA recommends that those attempting the exam have both the CompTIA Network+ certification and at least two years of hands-on work experience, although many individuals pass the exam before moving into their first cybersecurity role.

The Security+ exam is conducted in a format that CompTIA calls "performance-based assessment." This means that the exam combines standard multiple-choice questions with other, interactive question formats. Your exam may include multiple types of questions, such as multiple-choice, fill-in-the-blank, multiple-response, drag-and-drop, and image-based problems.

The exam costs $392 in the United States, with roughly equivalent prices in other locations around the globe. More details about the Security+ exam and how to take it can be found here:

www.comptia.org/certifications/security

If you're a student, note that CompTIA provides a student discount if you can provide a valid student ID and an .edu email address.

 This book includes a discount code for the Security+ exam—make sure you use it!

You'll have 90 minutes to take the exam and will be asked to answer up to 90 questions during that time period. Your exam will be scored on a scale ranging from 100 to 900, with a passing score of 750.

You should also know that CompTIA is notorious for including vague questions on all of its exams. You might see a question for which two of the possible four answers are correct—but you can choose only one. Use your knowledge, logic, and intuition to choose the best answer and then move on. Sometimes, the questions are worded in ways that would make English majors cringe—a typo here, an incorrect verb there. Don't let this frustrate you; answer the question and move on to the next one.

CompTIA frequently does what is called *item seeding*, which is the practice of including unscored questions on exams. It does so to gather psychometric data, which is then used when developing new versions of the exam. Before you take the exam, you will be told that your exam may include these unscored questions. So, if you come across a question that does not appear to map to any of the exam objectives—or for that matter, does not appear to belong in the exam—it is likely a seeded question. You never know whether or not a question is seeded, however, so always make your best effort to answer every question.

Taking the Exam

Once you are fully prepared to take the exam, you can visit the CompTIA website to purchase your exam voucher:

    www.comptia.org/testing/exam-vouchers/buy-exam

CompTIA offers both on-site proctored exams and online exams. Online exams are available 24/7 using remote proctoring. If you opt for the online exam, you'll want to make sure your system meets the technical requirements described by Pearson VUE, run a system test, ensure you have a distraction-free test location, and make sure you have appropriate ID ready.

Things can go wrong during an exam, including technical failures and other issues. If something does go wrong, your best bet is to follow up directly with Pearson VUE to determine what can be done to resolve the problem.

CompTIA partners with Pearson VUE's testing centers for in-person exams, so if you intend to take one your next step will be to locate a testing center near you. In the United States, you can do this based on your address or your ZIP code, whereas non-U.S. test takers may find it easier to enter their city and country. You can search for a test center near you at the Pearson Vue website, where you will need to navigate to "Find a Test Center."

    www.pearsonvue.com/comptia

Once you know where you'd like to take the exam, you'll need to create a CompTIA single sign-on account. Once you've done so, you'll be able to follow the link to scheduling exams via Pearson VUE. If you already have an account, you can visit Pearson VUE directly at:

    http://home.pearsonvue.com/comptia/onvue

On the day of the test, take two forms of identification that meet the identification requirements found on the Pearson VUE site, and make sure to show up with plenty of time before the exam starts. Remember that you will not be able to take your notes, electronic devices (including smartphones and watches), or other materials in with you, and that other requirements may exist for the test. Make sure you review those requirements before the day of your test so you're fully prepared for both the test itself, as well as the testing process and facility rules.

After the Security+ Exam

Once you have taken the exam, you will be notified of your score immediately, so you'll know if you passed the test right away. You should keep track of your score report with your exam registration records and the email address you used to register for the exam.

Maintaining Your Certification

CompTIA certifications must be renewed on a periodic basis. To renew your certification, you can pass the most current version of the exam, earn a qualifying higher-level Comp-TIA or industry certification, complete the CompTIA CertMaster CE course, or complete sufficient continuing education activities to earn enough continuing education units (CEUs) to renew it.

CompTIA provides information on renewals via their website at:

www.comptia.org/continuing-education

Information about the CertMaster CE course can be found at:

www.comptia.org/continuing-education/choose/
renew-with-a-single-activity/complete-a-comptia-certmaster-ce-course

When you sign up to renew your certification, you will be asked to agree to the CE program's Candidate Agreement, to pay a renewal fee, and to submit the materials required for your chosen renewal method.

A full list of the industry certifications you can use to acquire CEUs toward renewing the Security+ certification can be found at:

www.comptia.org/continuing-education/choose/
renew-with-a-single-activity/earn-a-higher-level-comptia-certification

Using This Book to Practice

This book is composed of seven chapters with over 1,100 practice test questions. Each of the first five chapters covers a domain, with a variety of questions that can help you test your knowledge of real-world, scenario, and best practices–based security knowledge. The final two chapters are complete practice exams that can serve as timed practice tests to help determine whether you're ready for the Security+ exam.

We recommend taking the first practice exam to help identify where you may need to spend more study time and then using the domain-specific chapters to test your domain knowledge where it is weak. Once you're ready, take the second practice exam to make sure you've covered all the material and are ready to attempt the Security+ exam.

As you work through questions in this book, you will encounter tools and technology that you may not be familiar with. If you find that you are facing a consistent gap or that a domain is particularly challenging, we recommend spending some time with books and materials that tackle that domain in depth. This approach can help you fill in gaps and help you be more prepared for the exam.

> To access our interactive test bank and online learning environment, simply visit www.wiley.com/go/sybextestprep, register to receive your unique PIN, and instantly gain one year of free access after activation to the interactive test bank with two practice exams and hundreds of domain-by-domain questions. Over 1,100 questions total!

> Like all exams, the Security+® certification is updated periodically and may eventually be retired or replaced. At some point after CompTIA® is no longer offering this exam, the old editions of our books and online tools will be retired. If you have purchased this book after the exam was retired or are attempting to register in the Sybex online learning environment after the exam was retired, please know that we make no guarantees that this exam's online Sybex tools will be available once the exam is no longer available.

Exam SY0-701 Exam Objectives

CompTIA goes to great lengths to ensure that its certification programs accurately reflect the IT industry's best practices. They do this by establishing committees for each of its exam programs. Each committee consists of a small group of IT professionals, training providers, and publishers who are responsible for establishing the exam's baseline competency level and who determine the appropriate target-audience level.

Once these factors are determined, CompTIA shares this information with a group of hand-selected subject matter experts (SMEs). These folks are the true brainpower behind the certification program. The SMEs review the committee's findings, refine them, and shape them into the objectives that follow this section. CompTIA calls this process a job-task analysis (JTA).

Finally, CompTIA conducts a survey to ensure that the objectives and weightings truly reflect job requirements. Only then can the SMEs go to work writing the hundreds of questions needed for the exam. Even so, they have to go back to the drawing board for further refinements in many cases before the exam is ready to go live in its final state. Rest assured that the content you're about to learn will serve you long after you take the exam.

CompTIA also publishes relative weightings for each of the exam's objectives. The following table lists the five Security+ objective domains and the extent to which they are represented on the exam.

Domain	% of Exam
1.0 General Security Concepts	12%
2.0 Threats, Vulnerabilities, and Mitigations	22%
3.0 Security Architecture	18%
4.0 Security Operations	28%
5.0 Security Program Management and Oversight	20%

SY0-701 Certification Exam Objective Map

Objective	Chapters
1.0 General Security Concepts	
1.1 Compare and contrast various types of security controls.	1
1.2 Summarize fundamental security concepts.	1
1.3 Explain the importance of change management processes and the impact to security.	1
1.4 Explain the importance of using appropriate cryptographic solutions.	1
2.0 Threats, Vulnerabilities, and Mitigations	
2.1 Compare and contrast common threat actors and motivations.	2
2.2 Explain common threat vectors and attack surfaces.	2
2.3 Explain various types of vulnerabilities.	2
2.4 Given a scenario, analyze indicators of malicious activity.	2
2.5 Explain the purpose of mitigation techniques used to secure the enterprise.	2
3.0 Security Architecture	
3.1 Compare and contrast security implications of different architecture models.	3

Exam objectives are subject to change at any time without prior notice and at CompTIA's discretion. Please visit CompTIA's website (www .comptia.org) for the most current listing of exam objectives.

How to Contact the Publisher

If you believe you have found a mistake in this book, please bring it to our attention. At John Wiley & Sons, we understand how important it is to provide our customers with accurate content, but even with our best efforts an error may occur.

In order to submit your possible errata, please email it to our Customer Service Team at wileysupport@wiley.com with the subject line "Possible Book Errata Submission."

Chapter

1

Domain 1.0: General Security Concepts

THE COMPTIA SECURITY+ EXAM SY0-701 TOPICS COVERED IN THIS CHAPTER INCLUDE THE FOLLOWING:

✓ **Domain 1.0: General Security Concepts**

- 1.1 Compare and contrast various types of security controls
    - Categories (Technical, Managerial, Operational, Physical)
    - Control types (Preventive, Deterrent, Detective, Corrective, Compensating, Directive)
- 1.2 Summarize fundamental security concepts
    - Confidentiality, Integrity, and Availability (CIA)
    - Non-repudiation
    - Authentication, Authorization, and Accounting (AAA) (Authenticating people, authenticating systems, authorization models)
    - Gap analysis
    - Zero trust (control plane, data plane)
    - Physical security (bollards, access control vestibule, fencing, video surveillance, security guard, access badge, lighting, sensors)
    - Deception and disruption technology (honeypot, honeynet, honeyfile, honeytoken)
- 1.3 Explain the importance of change management processes and the impact to security
    - Business processes impacting security operations (approval process, ownership, stakeholders, impact analysis, test results, backout plan, maintenance window, standard operating procedure)

- Technical implications (allow lists/deny lists, restricted activities, downtime, service restart, application restart, legacy applications, dependencies)
- Documentation (updating diagrams, updating policies/procedures)
- Version control
- 1.4 Explain the importance of using appropriate cryptographic solutions
  - Public key infrastructure (PKI) (Public key, private, key, key escrow)
  - Encryption (Level, transport/communication, asymmetric, symmetric, key exchange, algorithms, key length)
  - Tools (Trusted Platform Module [TPM], Hardware security module [HSM], key management systems, secure enclave)
  - Obfuscation (Steganography, tokenization, data masking)
  - Hashing
  - Salting
  - Digital Signatures
  - Key stretching
  - Blockchain
  - Open public ledger
  - Certificates (certificate authorities, certificate revocation lists [CRLs], Online Certificate Status Protocol [OCSP], self-signed, third-party, root of trust, certificate signing request [CSR] generation, wildcard)

1. Felicia wants to deploy an encryption solution that will protect files in motion as they are copied between file shares as well as at rest, and also needs it to support granular, per-user security. What type of solution should she select?

   A. Partition encryption

   B. File encryption

   C. Full-disk encryption

   D. Record-level encryption

2. Valerie wants to use a certificate to handle multiple subdomains for her website, including the `sales.example.com` and `support.example.com` subdomains. What type of certificate should she use?

   A. A self-signed certificate

   B. A root of trust certificate

   C. A CRL certificate

   D. A wildcard certificate

3. What information is analyzed during a gap analysis?

   A. Control objectives and controls intended to meet the objectives

   B. Physically separate networks and their potential connection points

   C. Compensating controls and the controls they are replacing

   D. Security procedures and the policies they are designed to support

4. Susan's team has recommended an application restart for a production, customer-facing application as part of an urgent patch due to a security update. What technical implication is the most common concern when conducting an application restart?

   A. Application configuration changes caused by the restart

   B. Whether the patch will properly apply

   C. Lack of security controls during the restart

   D. The downtime during the restart

5. Using a tool like `git` is most frequently associated with what critical change management process?

   A. Having a backout plan

   B. Stakeholder analysis

   C. Version control

   D. Standard operating procedures (SOPs)

6. Jacob is concerned that the password used for one of his organization's services is weak, and he wants to make it harder to crack by making it harder to test possible keys during a brute-force attack. What is this technique called?

   A. Master keying

   B. Key stretching

   C. Key rotation

   D. Passphrase armoring

7. Log monitoring is an example of what control category?

   A. Technical

   B. Managerial

   C. Operational

   D. Physical

8. Rick wants to make offline brute-force attacks against his password file very difficult for attackers. Which of the following is not a common technique to make passwords harder to crack?

   A. Use of a salt

   B. Use of a pepper

   C. Use of a purpose-built password hashing algorithm

   D. Encrypting password plain text using symmetric encryption

9. Diffie–Hellman and RSA are both examples of what important encryption-related solution?

   A. Rekeying

   B. Certificate revocation protocols

   C. Key exchange algorithms

   D. Key generation algorithms

10. Sally wants to ensure that her change management process includes a procedure for what to do if the change fails. What should she create to handle this possibility?

   A. An impact analysis

   B. A backout plan

   C. A regression test

   D. A maintenance window

11. Theresa is concerned that her scheduled maintenance window may extend beyond the allocated time due to an unexpected issue. What element from the CIA triad is she concerned about?

   A. Criticality

   B. Accessibility

   C. Integrity

   D. Availability

12. Alaina is concerned about vehicles that might impact her organization's backup generator. What should she install to prevent both inadvertent and purposeful vehicle impacts on a generator installed outside her building near a parking lot?

   A. A speed bump

   B. An access control vestibule

   C. Bollards

   D. A chain-link fence

13. Ben has deployed a data loss prevention (DLP) tool that inspects data and flags specific data types for review before emails containing it are sent outside the organization. What control type best describes this type of solution?

A. Managerial

B. Detective

C. Corrective

D. Preventive

14. What type of control is a policy or procedure?

A. Directive

B. Corrective

C. Detective

D. Preventive

15. Murali has deployed a file integrity monitoring tool and has configured alerts to notify him if files are modified. What control type best describes this solution?

A. Preventive

B. Deterrent

C. Directive

D. Detective

16. Charles wants to reduce the threat scope of compromised credentials. What type of the following security controls is best suited to meeting this need?

A. Single sign-on

B. Federation

C. Zero trust

D. Multifactor authentication (MFA)

17. Carol wants to obfuscate data that is contained in her database. She wants to be able to refer to the data elements without having the actual data exposed. What type of obfuscation option should she select?

A. Tokenization

B. Encryption

C. Data masking

D. Data randomization

18. What key is used to decrypt information sent by another individual between two people using public key encryption?

A. The recipient's private key

B. The recipient's public key

C. The sender's private key

D. The sender's public key

19. Selah's organization has recently experienced a breach and the private keys for her organization's certificates were exposed. What should she immediately do?

A. Reissue the certificates with changed hostnames and other details.

B. Replace the certificates with self-signed certificates until they can be replaced by the vendor.

C. Revoke the certificates and place them on a certificate revocation list.

D. Replace the certificates with wildcard certificates.

20. Which of the following is not a major concern related to downtime caused by patching and system updates?

A. Attackers compromising the system or service while it is offline

B. Security systems or functions being offline during restart or shutdown processes

C. Unexpected extended downtime

D. Dependencies between systems or services related to downtime

21. Joanna wants to ensure that the most current version of each component in her application is deployed. What change management process will help the most with this requirement?

A. Dependency mapping

B. Version control

C. Impact analysis

D. Allow and deny lists

22. Greg wants to implement a version control system to ensure that changes are made in ways that will not cause problems for his organization's critical software. Which of the following is not a common feature of version control systems designed for software source code?

A. Atomic operations

B. File locking

C. Regression testing

D. Tagging and labeling

23. Christina wants to implement a physical security control that has the greatest flexibility in how it is applied because she knows that exceptions to security practices may be required at times. Which of the following solutions has the greatest flexibility?

A. Video surveillance

B. Security guards

C. Access badges

D. Access control vestibules

24. Lisa wants to ensure that theft of a device will not lead to exposure of the data contained on the device if the device is locked or turned off. What type of encryption should she select to best ensure this?

A. Volume-level encryption

B. Full-disk encryption

C. File-level encryption

D. Partition-level encryption

25. Mahmoud has been asked to implement an allow list for websites that users at his company can visit. What concern should he bring up to management due to this request?

A. Allow lists cannot be used for websites.

B. Allow lists are overly permissive and are likely to allow unwanted sites to be visited.

C. Using an allow list for websites will take a lot of time to maintain.

D. Using an allow list for websites is easily bypassed.

26. Which of the following change management processes does not commonly directly involve stakeholders outside of the IT organization?

A. Impact analysis

B. Building the backout plan

C. The change approval process

D. Determining the maintenance window

27. What hardware component is used to generate, store, and manage cryptographic keys?

A. A CPU

B. A NSA

C. A TPM

D. A CCA

28. Chris wants to check to see if a certificate has been revoked. What protocol can he use to validate the current status of a certificate?

A. TLS

B. OCRS

C. SSL

D. OCSP

29. Brian's organization uses a process where a secure module boots systems, then monitors them as each boot stage proceeds. It validates each signed boot stage and reports on whether the boot process was correct or not when complete. What is the secure module used to verify these stages called?

A. A secure initiation manager

B. A root of trust

C. A boot hash

D. A cryptographic boot manager

30. A vulnerability scan shows that an embedded device that Alice is responsible for has a vulnerability. She knows the vendor is no longer in business and that there is no updated firmware or software update for the device. To resolve the issue, Alice places a firewall between the device and the rest of the network and creates rules that prevent the vulnerable service from being available to other devices. What type of control has Alice deployed?

A. A directive control

B. A compensating control

C. A detective control

D. A procedural control

31. Jason knows that his Apple system uses a separate portion of its SoC (system on chip) to store keys and biometric information. What is this specialized component called?

    A. A TPM

    B. A HSM

    C. A secure enclave

    D. A screened subnet

32. What change management term is used to describe the processes that an organization uses for each change that is made to ensure that a consistent process is used?

    A. Standard operating procedures

    B. A change plan

    C. Fixed operating procedures

    D. A backout plan

33. Jack knows that there are three common types of database encryption. Which of the following is not a common type of database encryption?

    A. Sensitivity-based encryption

    B. Transparent data encryption

    C. Field-level encryption

    D. Column-level encryption

34. Ujamaa wants to conduct a gap analysis as part of his security efforts. Which of the following best describes what he will analyze?

    A. Which services are not configured properly

    B. Whether current patches are installed on all systems

    C. The security program as implemented versus best practices

    D. Legal requirements versus the security program

35. Brandon wants to deploy a detective control that will help him with physical security threats. Which of the following fits his needs?

    A. Fencing

    B. Lighting

    C. Video surveillance

    D. Bollards

36. Jack has deployed a system that appears to attackers to be a vulnerable system. The system is specifically designed to capture information and data from attacks to allow for later analysis. What type of tool has Jack deployed?

    A. A tarpit

    B. A honeypot

    C. A beehive

    D. An intrusion detection system

37. Renee wants to ensure that her logs support nonrepudiation. What should she do to ensure this?

    A. Encrypt, then hash the logs.

    B. Hash the logs and then digitally sign them.

    C. Digitally sign the log file, then encrypt it.

    D. Hash, then encrypt the logs.

38. Isaac wants to deploy sensors to detect intruders in a facility, but he is concerned about the sensors being overly sensitive. What type of sensor is best suited to detecting intruders in an open office environment without significant expense or issues with sensitivity?

    A. Infrared

    B. Pressure

    C. Microwave

    D. Ultrasonic

39. Wayne wants to allow systems to claim identities as part of his AAA process. Which of the following is most commonly used to identify both individuals and systems?

    A. Tokens

    B. Smartcards

    C. Certificates

    D. Usernames

40. What are considerations like database and network connectivity, authentication system access, and network time availability considered in the context of change management processes?

    A. Allowed services

    B. Standard operating procedures

    C. Denied services

    D. Dependencies

41. What role does the policy engine play in a zero-trust environment?

    A. It creates new administrative policies based on user behavior.

    B. It grants access based on policies created by administrators and based on security systems data.

    C. It enforces policies by monitoring connections between clients and servers.

    D. It suggests new administrative policies based on usage patterns for adoption by the organization.

42. Which of the following is not a common post-change activity found in change management practices?

    A. Updating diagrams

    B. Updating procedures

    C. Updating policies

    D. Updating contracts

43. Which of the following activities should Alaina not restrict as part of her preparation for a change window?

   A. Patching

   B. Scaling clustered systems up or down

   C. Changing hostnames

   D. Modifying database configurations

44. What two key features define blockchain ledgers?

   A. They are immutable and nontransferable.

   B. They are shared and can be modified by a vote among all participants.

   C. They are unique to each participant and are atomic.

   D. They are shared and immutable.

45. Damian issues the following command on his Linux server:

```
openssl req -new -newkey rsa:2048 -nodes -keyout exampleserver.
key -out exampleserver.csr
```

What has he done?

   A. Created a certificate signing request

   B. Created a certificate revocation request

   C. Signed a certificate signing request

   D. Updated the OCSP record for a certificate

46. Nick's organization sets aside Saturday nights from 2 a.m. to 4 a.m. for scheduled maintenance. What is this type of reserved time typically called?

   A. Allocated downtime

   B. A maintenance window

   C. An unscheduled outage

   D. An allowed outage

47. Megan wants to assess the impact of a change as part of her change management process. Which of the following is most likely to help her assess impact?

   A. A backout plan

   B. An estimate of the downtime expected

   C. A list of stakeholders

   D. A list of dependencies for impacted systems

48. Jared wants to estimate the downtime that will result as part of a planned change. Which of the following methods will most effectively help him estimate downtime?

   A. Average the downtime from other recent changes.

   B. Contact the vendor for time estimates for the change.

   C. Perform the change in a test environment.

   D. Use a fixed maintenance window.

49. An encryption method in which all participants have the same key is known as which of the following types of encryption?

    A. Shared hashing

    B. Asymmetric encryption

    C. Symmetric encryption

    D. Universal encryption

50. What important encryption challenge does asymmetric encryption help with by using public keys?

    A. Evil twins

    B. Collision resistance

    C. Key length

    D. Key exchange

51. Rick's cloud provider offers a dedicated hardware security module. Which of the following capabilities is it unlikely to offer?

    A. Validating secure boot processes

    B. Key generation

    C. Encrypting and decrypting data

    D. Creating digital signatures

52. Michelle believes that an image she has discovered in an attacker's directory of files contains additional information that has been hidden in it. What is this type of obfuscation called?

    A. Steganography

    B. Image hashing

    C. PNG warping

    D. Image blocking

53. Which of the following is not a common transport encryption protocol?

    A. TLS

    B. IPSec

    C. SAML

    D. SSH

54. What technology is record-level encryption most commonly associated with?

    A. Stored audio files

    B. Databases

    C. Physical disks

    D. Removable storage

55. Yasmine submits the Windows BitLocker key to a central repository after she encryptions the machine. The central repository allows files to be uploaded, but not read, and is protected with access requiring special permissions. What type of solution is Yasmine's company using?

A. A hardware security module

B. Perfect forward secrecy

C. Key escrow

D. Private keys

56. Valerie wants to authenticate her systems using her AAA system. Which of the following options is best suited to system authentication?

A. Asymmetric authentication

B. Certificate-based authentication

C. Symmetric authentication

D. PIN-based authentication

57. Valentine wants to detect if an intruder has accessed a secured file server. Which of the following techniques will work best with a data loss prevention tool to identify data exfiltration?

A. A honeypot

B. A honeynet

C. A honeyfile

D. A honeytoken

58. Jason has recommended that additional lighting be put in place on the exterior of his building as part of a security upgrade. What type of control is lighting?

A. Operational

B. Deterrent

C. Corrective

D. Technical

59. Which of the following controls is typically the most expensive to implement?

A. Bollards

B. Access control vestibules

C. Security guards

D. Access badges

60. Frankie wants to validate the integrity of a file by comparing it against an original copy. Which of the following solutions both fulfills this requirement and avoids known security issues?

A. Hash the original file and the current file using MD5 and compare the hashes.

B. Hash the original file and the current file using SHA-1 and compare the hashes.

C. Hash the original file and the current file using SHA-256 and compare the hashes.

D. Hash the original file and the current file using AES and compare the hashes.

61. Joanna's organization has a policy that requires a user's password to be immediately reset to lock accounts if the account is determined to have been successfully phished. What type of control is this?

A. A detective control

B. A directive control

C. A compensating control

D. A preventive control

62. Jackie wants to implement an AAA system for her network. What AAA protocol is commonly used for network devices?

A. OpenID

B. SAML

C. RADIUS

D. TANGENT

63. Scott wants to automate policy creation in his zero-trust environment's policy engine. Which of the following is not a typical component for automated data and event-driven policy management?

A. A SIEM

B. Threat feeds

C. Infrared sensor data

D. EDR tools

64. Valerie's organization has deployed a zero-trust solution, and Valerie receives an authentication prompt when she is attempting to access a file server. What component of the zero-trust architecture is she interacting with?

A. A policy enforcement point

B. A policy administrator

C. The policy engine

D. The trust manager

65. Matt is assessing his organization's zero-trust model against the NIST Zero Trust Maturity Model. Which of the following is not a common element of zero-trust systems that would be assessed as part of the model?

A. Identity

B. Business model

C. Networks

D. Devices

66. Quentin wants to deploy a single sign-on system to allow his users to log in to cloud services. Which of the following technologies is he most likely to deploy?

A. OpenID

B. Kerberos

C. LDAP

D. TACACS+

67. Marty wants to deploy a corrective control to deal with a recently compromised system. Which of the following would be considered a corrective control?

   A. Patching the vulnerability that allowed the compromise to occur

   B. Deploying full-disk encryption

   C. Deploying an endpoint detection and response (EDR) tool

   D. Enabling logging and sending logs to a SIEM

68. What important encryption feature is not supported by symmetric encryption?

   A. Confidentiality

   B. Integrity

   C. Nonrepudiation

   D. Authentication

69. Theresa wants to use a cloud-hosted security solution that will allow her to safely store and manage secrets. What type of solution should she select?

   A. A TPM

   B. A CA

   C. A KMS

   D. A CSR

70. Joanna is reviewing her account information on an e-commerce website and sees her credit card number displayed as XXXX-XXXX-XXXX-1234. What type of data obfuscation is in use?

   A. Hashing

   B. Data masking

   C. Field encryption

   D. Tokenization

71. Amanda's organization wants to use a decentralized blockchain to store data. Which of the following is true about a decentralized blockchain?

   A. No individual or group controls the blockchain.

   B. Only cryptocurrency-related data can be stored in a blockchain.

   C. Blockchain data can be changed after being stored by the original submitter.

   D. Blockchain ledgers are stored on central servers chosen by regular elections among blockchain participants.

72. What role does a subordinate CA have in a CA hierarchy?

   A. Subordinate CAs issue certificates based on subdomains.

   B. Subordinate CAs provide control over certificate issuance while avoiding the cost of being a root CA.

   C. Subordinate CAs validate root CA activities to ensure auditability.

   D. Subordinate CAs review certificate signing requests before forwarding them to the root CA.

73. Which of the following sensor types is commonly used to detect footsteps?

    A. Infrared

    B. Pressure

    C. Microwave

    D. Ultrasonic

74. Which of the following is not a managerial control?

    A. Risk assessments

    B. Including security in change management processes

    C. Security planning exercises

    D. Implementing firewalls

75. What purpose do third-party certificates serve for customers of cloud services?

    A. They reduce costs by using bring-your-own certificates.

    B. They allow certificates for domains other than the service provider's domain.

    C. They provide control over cryptographic security for the customer.

    D. They allow more flexibility in TLS version selection.

76. Which of the following is not a common control focused on availability?

    A. Uninterruptible power systems

    B. Redundant Internet connectivity

    C. Disk encryption

    D. Load balancers

77. What term describes a collection of honeypots on a network intended to capture information about cybersecurity threats?

    A. A honeyfarm

    B. A honeynet

    C. A honeycluster

    D. A darknet

78. Skip wants to implement a deterrent control to prevent physical security issues for his organization. Which of the following controls should he select?

    A. A fence

    B. A generator

    C. Access badges

    D. A camera system

79. What holds the position of the root of trust in a certificate chain?

    A. A hardened hardware device

    B. A TPM

    C. A root certificate

    D. A wildcard certificate

80. Jill needs to explain the concept of open public ledgers to her organization as management wants to adopt a blockchain-based system. What should she tell them about access to the ledger?

    A. Members must be added by a vote of all current members.

    B. Anyone can join at any time.

    C. Members must be added by a vote of more than 51 percent of current members.

    D. Ledgers are public but membership is private and controlled by the creator of the ledger.

81. Olivia wants to use a self-signed certificate in her test environment for her organization's services to save money on commercial certificates. What warning should her team give her about the use of self-signed certificates in a test environment?

    A. Certificate root of trust validation attempts will fail if implemented.

    B. Self-signed certificates cannot be used for external users to support SSL.

    C. Self-signed certificates cannot be used for internal users to support SSL.

    D. Browsers will not allow self-signed certificates to be used when browsing sites.

82. Amanda is concerned about issues with dependencies that may be found during her pending change. What practice should she implement to help ensure unexpected dependency issues are not encountered?

    A. Update organizational policies and procedures before the change.

    B. Update functional diagrams before the change.

    C. Validate the change in a test environment.

    D. Document legacy applications that may create dependencies.

83. Lucca has implemented an authentication scheme that relies on ticket-granting tickets as part of the authentication process. What common authentication service has he implemented?

    A. TACACS+

    B. Kerberos

    C. MS-CHAP

    D. EAP

84. Jocelyn wants to select a modern encryption algorithm for use in her organization. Which of the following is a currently recommended encryption algorithm?

    A. AES-256

    B. SHA1

    C. DES

    D. Blowfish

85. Elizabeth wants to classify the following controls by their category. What category best describes lighting, fences, bollards, and access control vestibules?

    A. Technical

    B. Managerial

    C. Operational

    D. Physical

86. Jack wants to ensure the integrity of a file that he is sending to a third party via email. How can he provide the integrity of a file to an organization that he has not done business with before?

   A. Encrypt the file and send it to them.

   B. Digitally sign the file.

   C. Send a hash of the file in a separate email.

   D. Email the file size and original name in a separate email.

87. Annie notices that her browser shows that the certificate for the site she is visiting is not valid. After performing some checks, she sees that the certificate is on the CA's certificate revocation list. Which of the following is not a reason for a certificate to be on a CRL?

   A. The CA is compromised.

   B. The certificate's private key was compromised.

   C. The certificate was signed with a stolen key.

   D. The certificate expired.

88. Mohinder wants to use modern, secure hashing algorithms to validate files against known good originals. Which of the following hashing algorithms should he select?

   A. MD5

   B. SHA-1

   C. AES-256

   D. SHA-256

89. Derrick wants to validate an encrypted and digitally signed message sent using asymmetric encryption. What does he need from the sender to validate the message?

   A. The sender's private key

   B. Derrick's private key

   C. The sender's public key

   D. Derrick's public key

90. The major patch release that Susan's team installed has failed, resulting in a nonworking service. What should her team do according to change management best practices?

   A. Declare an outage.

   B. Follow the documented backout plan.

   C. Restore from backups to the previous version.

   D. Uninstall the patch and validate service function.

91. The web server that Angela's organization manages was recently compromised and the SSL certificate's private key was accessed by attackers. Angela's team has completed remediation and has created a new CSR, including a new private key that they have secured. What type of control type best describes the creation of a new key and certificate in this circumstance?

   A. Corrective

   B. Compensating

   C. Deterrent

   D. Detective

92. Mikayla's zero-trust system has received a request for access with an identity, and the basic criteria for access have been met. What should the system do next before providing access to the resource requested?

A. Check the remote system's security status.

B. Require reauthentication using MFA.

C. Check the user's rights to ensure they can access the resource.

D. Determine its level of confidence in the request.

93. Charles sets up an RDP server on an isolated network segment and places a file on it called `passwords.xlsx`. He then configures his IPS and DLP systems to monitor for that file exiting the network segment. What type of tool has Charles deployed?

A. A honeyfile

B. A SQL trap

C. A red flag

D. A trigger file

94. Lucca is using precomputed rainbow tables to attempt to crack hashed passwords from a data breach. He knows that two users have the same password, but the hashes do not match. What password hash security technique has Lucca most likely encountered?

A. Password encryption

B. Salting

C. Hash rotation

D. Password mismatching

95. What operating system is commonly associated with secure enclaves?

A. Windows

B. iOS

C. Linux

D. Android

96. Isaac is concerned that the passwords that his users are creating are too short and can be easily brute-forced if their hashes were compromised. Rather than make his users remember longer passwords, he would like to implement a technical solution to help make the hashes more resistant to cracking. What solution can he use to help with this?

A. Implement pass-the-hash algorithms.

B. Use a collision-resistant hashing algorithm.

C. Implement key stretching techniques.

D. Encrypt passwords rather than hashing them.

97. Christina wants to implement access badges printed with picture IDs for her organization, but she wants to use a wireless reader. What access badge technology is commonly implemented in scenarios like this?

A. Wi-Fi-enabled access badges

B. RFID access badges

C. Bluetooth-enabled access badges

D. NFC access badges

98. Kendra's vulnerability management team has discovered that Internet of Things (IoT) devices deployed a few years ago to monitor temperatures for critical refrigerated equipment are vulnerable to a new attack. After reviewing the issue, her team has discovered that the devices are no longer supported and that the manufacturer has gone out of business. They suggest moving the devices to an isolated network to help protect them. What type of control has Kendra's team suggested?

A. A corrective control

B. A compensating control

C. A confidentiality control

D. A coordinated control

99. Which of the following is not a common factor in adaptive authentication for zero trust?

A. Where the user is logging in from

B. Whether the user has logged in recently from another device

C. What device the user is logging in from

D. If the device is configured correctly

100. Juan's organization is designing their zero-trust model. Which of the following statements is true for network security zones?

A. All communication is secured, regardless of the network security zone it occurs in.

B. Communication receives additional security in low-trust zones.

C. Communication receives less security in high-trust zones.

D. All zero-trust networks are considered secured zones.

101. What advantage do microwave sensors have over infrared sensors?

A. They can detect heat signatures.

B. They are cheaper than infrared sensors.

C. They can penetrate some types of walls.

D. They do not interfere with sensitive equipment.

102. Isaac is conducting a physical penetration test and wants to bypass an access control vestibule. What must he accomplish?

    A. He needs to persuade an individual to allow him to follow them through a single door.

    B. He needs to acquire an individual's access card.

    C. He needs to persuade an individual to allow him to follow them through two doors in a row.

    D. He needs to acquire the individual's access PIN.

103. Rachel wants to select an obfuscation method that will allow her customer service representatives to validate customer identities without providing full access to customer data. What should she select?

    A. Tokenization

    B. Data masking

    C. Steganography

    D. Hashing

104. Valerie's manager has informed her that version control must be implemented for her development team's work. Which of the following is not a common, security-related reason for version control?

    A. To help with patching

    B. To track each contributor's workload

    C. To ensure the proper version is deployed

    D. To help with change management

105. Jackie's change management process involves reporting functional validation test results to stakeholders. Which of the following is not a common stakeholder or stakeholder group for an application upgrade?

    A. Application administrators

    B. Service owners

    C. System administrators

    D. Auditors

106. How many keypairs are required for four individuals to communicate securely using asymmetric encryption?

    A. 1

    B. 4

    C. 8

    D. 12

107. Michelle wants to store secrets for her organization in a cloud service. She wants to ensure the greatest level of security for her organization, and she is willing to spend more money to provide that security. What solution should she look for?

A. A shared cloud TPM

B. A shared cloud HSM

C. A dedicated hardware cloud TPM

D. A dedicated hardware cloud HSM

108. Murali wants to digitally sign a file. What key does he need to sign it?

A. The recipient's private key

B. His private key

C. The recipient's public key

D. His public key

109. What information is necessary for a certificate to be identified properly in an OCSP request?

A. The domain name

B. The original requestor's name

C. The certificate's serial number

D. The identifier for the open public ledger entry

110. Rick checks the certificate for the site he is viewing and sees that it reads `*.example.com`. What type of certificate is this, and why is it in use?

A. It is a self-signed certificate, and it is used for testing purposes.

B. It is a wildcard certificate and is used for testing purposes.

C. It is a wildcard certificate and is used for multiple subdomains.

D. It is a self-signed certificate and is used for multiple subdomains.

111. John wants to write a procedure that addresses what to do if an employee inadvertently discloses their password due to a phishing attempt. What type of control is John considering?

A. A directive control

B. A proactive control

C. A deterrent control

D. A preventive control

112. Adam has been asked to implement an allow list for websites that his servers can visit. What concern should he raise about the implementation of allow lists?

A. Allow lists can be difficult to manage and cause failures if sites that are needed are not added.

B. Allow lists do not prevent sites from being visited if they are not on the allow list.

C. Allow lists cannot be configured to allow entire domains to be visited, creating significant overhead.

D. Allow lists are prone to error, allowing unwanted sites to be added.

113. Jim wants to implement an authentication framework for his wireless network. Which of the following is most commonly used for wireless network authentication?

A. EAP

B. MS-CHAP

C. Kerberos

D. LDAP

114. Gary is preparing change management documentation for an application restart after patching. What step should immediately follow the application restart?

A. Validation testing

B. Documenting the change occurred

C. Updating version control

D. Vulnerability scanning

115. Anna has been told that her organization has deployed microwave sensors in the organization's warehouses. What are microwave sensors most frequently used to detect?

A. Motion

B. Glass break

C. Heat signatures

D. Pressure

116. When is data on a drive that uses full-disk encryption at the greatest risk?

A. During the system boot process

B. When the system is off

C. When the system is logged in and in use

D. When the system is being shut down

117. Alex has configured full-disk encryption for laptops that his organization issues to employees. What cybersecurity objective does this primarily support?

A. Confidentiality

B. Availability

C. Authenticity

D. Integrity

118. What process reviews control objectives for an organization, system, or service to determine if controls do not meet the control objectives?

A. A penetration test

B. A gap analysis

C. A Boolean analysis

D. A risk analysis

119. Frank configures an access control list to ensure that only specific IP addresses are able to connect to a service. What type of control has he deployed?

    A. Managerial

    B. Physical

    C. Technical

    D. Operational

120. Annie has recently implemented a video surveillance system for her organization. What is the largest driver for new ongoing costs for an unmonitored video surveillance system?

    A. Camera maintenance

    B. The ongoing cost of storage

    C. Security guards

    D. Licensing

121. Henry's organization has recently experienced a ransomware attack and is restoring backups from a secure backup system. What type of security control is Henry using?

    A. A preventive control

    B. A directive control

    C. A compensating control

    D. A corrective control

122. What data obfuscation technique relies on a lookup table that allows you to match the data you want to secure to a randomly generated value to ensure that the actual value is not easily accessible?

    A. Hashing

    B. Tokenization

    C. Randomization

    D. Masking

123. What challenge drives the need for key exchange mechanisms?

    A. The number of keys required for symmetric encryption

    B. The need to determine if a key is public

    C. The need to exchange keys in a way that prevents others from obtaining a copy

    D. The need to securely return keys to their owner after they are traded

124. Jackie is performing an impact analysis prior to a large-scale change her team is preparing to implement. Which of the following groups is not typically part of the impact analysis?

    A. Stakeholders

    B. System administrators

    C. Service owners

    D. Legal counsel

125. Ilya wants to create a certificate signing request. Which of the following is not a typical part of a CSR?

    A. The common name of the server

    B. The organization's legal name

    C. A contact email address

    D. The organization's phone number

126. Before Tony stores a password hash, he appends a string of characters that is unique to each password generated using an algorithm he created. What technique is Tony using to help protect his password hashes?

    A. Tokenization

    B. Steganography

    C. Salting

    D. Key stretching

127. Which of the following is not a step taken when a transaction is entered in a blockchain?

    A. The value of the block is determined.

    B. The transaction is sent to a peer-to-peer network of computers.

    C. The transaction is validated using equations.

    D. A transaction history is maintained as part of the blockchain.

128. Kent wants to encrypt network traffic in transit. What cryptographic protocol is most frequently used to add encryption to existing protocols?

    A. S/MIME

    B. TLS

    C. MPLS

    D. SSH

129. Which of the following is not a common concern in change management processes related to legacy applications?

    A. Lack of vendor support

    B. Lack of patches and updates

    C. Ongoing licensing costs

    D. Availability of third-party or consultant expertise

130. Elaine wants to document the technical concerns that dependencies create as part of her change management process. Which of the following concerns is the most common when dependencies are encountered as part of change management?

    A. Documenting the dependencies to ensure they are addressed

    B. Removing the dependencies as part of the change

    C. Patching the dependencies in addition to the main application

    D. Updating diagrams related to the dependencies

131. Gary has implemented record-level encryption for his database. How many keys will he use in a typical implementation of record-level encryption?

   A. One key per record

   B. One key per column

   C. One key per table

   D. One key per database

132. Justin's laptop is part of his organization's zero-trust architecture. What term is used to refer to a device like a laptop, desktop, or mobile device in a zero-trust design?

   A. A subject

   B. A policy engine

   C. A service provider

   D. A policy application point

133. Susan's organization has deployed a zero-trust architecture. Which of the following zero-trust control plane components uses rules to determine who can access a service based on the security status of their system, threat data, and similar information?

   A. Adaptive authorization

   B. Threat scope reduction

   C. Policy-driven access control

   D. Secured zones

134. Scott wants to implement OCSP as part of an application he is creating. What will he implement?

   A. A corrective control security process

   B. Certificate status checking

   C. Transport encryption

   D. Full-disk encryption

135. Which of the following is not a common reason to implement key escrow?

   A. Regulatory compliance

   B. Providing access to encrypted data for administrative reasons

   C. Providing access to encrypted data in emergencies

   D. Preventing the need for key rotation after a user leaves

136. Yariv discovers that he has exposed his private key to other users in his organization by sending it via email instead of his public key. What should he do?

   A. Ask the other users to delete any copies of his private key that they may have.

   B. Immediately add his key to a CRL and reissue the key.

   C. Create a new keypair and notify others that he has replaced his keypair.

   D. Continue to operate as normal as long as the private key was not used maliciously.

137. What happens if a mistake is made and an incorrect transaction is entered into the open public ledger in a blockchain?

    A. The transaction is reversed once it is discovered, and the original transaction is removed from the record.

    B. A new transaction must be processed, and both transactions remain in the record.

    C. The original transaction is updated and becomes the new record.

    D. An error block must be mined and labeled with the transaction number and error details.

138. Which of the following activities will not typically result in a need to update policies and procedures?

    A. Deploying a new application

    B. Installing patches for an existing application

    C. Conducting a lessons learned exercise after an incident

    D. Changes in regulations

139. Hrant's organization wants to ensure that staff members use both something they know and something they have as part of their physical access control scheme. Which of the following solutions meets that requirement?

    A. Security guards and access badges

    B. Keys and access control vestibules

    C. Access badges and PINs

    D. Security guards and access control vestibules

140. Julia wants to detect if an intruder enters a space using a sensor system. Which of the following is not typically used to detect intruders?

    A. Infrared sensors

    B. Pressure sensors

    C. Microwave sensors

    D. Ultrasonic sensors

141. Which of the following is not true for a secure cryptographic hash system?

    A. Hashes are a one-way function.

    B. Hashes generate a fixed length output.

    C. Hashes may generate the same output for multiple inputs.

    D. Hashes are commonly used to verify the integrity of files.

142. Casey wants to prevent tailgating attacks on her datacenter. What type of physical security solution should she put in place?

    A. Video surveillance

    B. Bollards

    C. An access control vestibule

    D. Access badges

143. As Casey continues to work to secure her datacenter, she decides to deploy access badges. What technique will provide the greatest assurance that a stolen or cloned access badge will not allow an attacker access?

A. Use barcode-based badges.

B. Require a PIN along with the badge.

C. Use RFID-based badges.

D. Include a picture of the user on the badge.

144. What term describes the function of digital signatures related to proving that the signature was provided by the owner of a given private key?

A. Ledger-based validation

B. Nonrepudiation

C. Key stretching

D. Authentication

145. John wants to send his public key to another user. What steps are necessary to do so?

A. The key must be sent using Diffie–Hellman.

B. The key can simply be sent via email or other means.

C. The key must be sent using RSA.

D. The key must be signed, then sent via email or other means.

146. Tracy wants to use the most secure salting solution she can. Which of the following options will provide the most secure salt?

A. Set a salt value and store it in a database.

B. Set a salt value and store it in the program code.

C. Generate a unique salt for each hashed entry.

D. Generate a unique salt value every time a value is used.

147. Bob conducts a periodic risk assessment of his organization. What category of security control is this?

A. Technical

B. Managerial

C. Operational

D. Physical

148. After a breach, Jackie removes malicious software from a server that she is responsible for. What control type should she classify this as?

A. Preventive

B. Corrective

C. Compensating

D. Deterrent

149. What can a root SSL (TLS) certificate do?

   A. Remove a certificate from a CRL

   B. Generate a signing key and use it to sign a new certificate

   C. Authorize new CA users

   D. Allow key stretching

150. Christina wants to authenticate individuals as part of her AAA implementation. What will she need to do to authenticate users?

   A. Match users to roles and ensure that rights are assigned.

   B. Conduct biometric enrollments for every user.

   C. Use identity proofing for each user she creates.

   D. Ensure that users provide an identity and one or more authentication factors.

Chapter 2

Domain 2.0: Threats, Vulnerabilities, and Mitigations

THE COMPTIA SECURITY+ EXAM SY0-701 TOPICS COVERED IN THIS CHAPTER INCLUDE THE FOLLOWING:

✓ **Domain 2.0: Threats, Vulnerabilities, and Mitigations**

- 2.1 Compare and contrast common threat actors and motivations

  - Threat actors (Nation-state, Unskilled attacker, Hacktivist, Insider threat, Organized crime, Shadow IT)

  - Attributes of actors (Internal/external, Resources/funding, Level of sophistication/capability)

  - Motivations (Data exfiltration, Espionage, Service disruption, Blackmail, Financial gain, Philosophical/political beliefs, Ethical, Revenge, Disruption/chaos, War)

- 2.2 Explain common threat vectors and attack surfaces

  - Message-based (Email, Short Message Service [SMS], Instant messaging [IM])

  - Image-based

  - File-based

  - Voice call

  - Removable device

  - Vulnerable software (Client-based vs. agentless)

  - Unsupported systems and applications

  - Unsecure networks (Wireless, Wired, Bluetooth)

  - Open service ports

  - Default credentials

- Supply chain (Managed service providers [MSPs], Vendors, Suppliers)
- Human vectors/social engineering (Phishing, Vishing, Smishing, Misinformation/disinformation, Impersonation, Business email compromise, Pretexting, Watering hole, Brand impersonation, Typo squatting)
- 2.3 Explain various types of vulnerabilities
  - Application (Memory injection, Buffer overflow, Race conditions, Time-of-check [TOC], Target of evaluation [TOE], Time-of-use [TOU], Malicious update)
  - Operating system (OS)-based
  - Web-based (Structured Query Language injection [SQLi], Cross-site scripting [XSS])
  - Hardware (Firmware, End-of-life, Legacy)
  - Virtualization (Virtual machine [VM] escape, Resource reuse)
  - Cloud-specific
  - Supply chain (Service provider, Hardware provider, Software provider)
  - Cryptographic
  - Misconfiguration
  - Mobile device (Side loading, Jailbreaking)
  - Zero-day
- 2.4 Given a scenario, analyze indicators of malicious activity
  - Malware attacks (Ransomware, Trojan, Worm, Spyware, Bloatware, Virus, Keylogger, Logic bomb, Rootkit)
  - Physical attacks (Brute force, Radio frequency identification [RFID] cloning, Environmental)
  - Network attacks (Distributed denial-of-service [DDoS], Amplified, Reflected, Domain Name System [DNS] attacks, Wireless, On-path, Credential replay, Malicious code)

- Application attacks (Injection, Buffer overflow, Replay, Privilege escalation, Forgery, Directory traversal)

- Cryptographic attacks (Downgrade, Collision, Birthday)

- Password attacks (Spraying, Brute force)

- Indicators (Account lockout, Concurrent session usage, Blocked content, Impossible travel, Resource consumption, Resource inaccessibility, Out-of-cycle logging, Published/documented, Missing logs)

- 2.5 Explain the purpose of mitigation techniques used to secure the enterprise

  - Segmentation

  - Access control (Access control list [ACL], Permissions)

  - Application allow list

  - Isolation

  - Patching

  - Encryption

  - Monitoring

  - Least privilege

  - Configuration enforcement

  - Decommissioning

  - Hardening techniques (Encryption, Installation of endpoint protection, Host-based firewall, Host-based intrusion prevention system [HIPS], Disabling ports/protocols, Default password changes, Removal of unnecessary software)

1. Brent's organization is profiling threat actors that may target their infrastructure and systems. Which of the following is most likely a motivation for a nation-state actor?

   A. Financial gain

   B. Blackmail

   C. Espionage

   D. Blackmail

2. Ahmed is a sales manager with a major insurance company. He has received an email that is encouraging him to click on a link and fill out a survey. He is suspicious of the email, but it does mention a major insurance association, and that makes him think it might be legitimate. Which of the following best describes this attack?

   A. Phishing

   B. Social engineering

   C. Spear phishing

   D. Trojan horse

3. You are a security administrator for a medium-sized bank. You have discovered a piece of software on your bank's database server that is not supposed to be there. It appears that the software will begin deleting database files if a specific employee is terminated. What best describes this?

   A. Worm

   B. Logic bomb

   C. Trojan horse

   D. Rootkit

4. The company that Yarif works for uses a third-party IT support company to manage their cloud-hosted web application infrastructure. How can Yarif best address concerns about potential threat vectors via the managed service provider (MSP)?

   A. Conduct regular vulnerability scans.

   B. Use shared incident response exercises to prepare.

   C. Ensure appropriate contractual coverage for issues.

   D. Require the MSP to have an annual pentest.

5. Jill's organization has received an advisory about a flaw that could allow software running on a virtual machine to execute code on the system that is running the VM hypervisor. What type of vulnerability is this?

   A. A resource reuse issue

   B. A VM escape issue

   C. A jailbreaking issue

   D. A sideloading issue

6. Helen is concerned about ransomware attacks against workstations that she is responsible for. Which of the following hardening options is best suited to protecting her organization from ransomware?

A. Installing host-based firewalls

B. Installing endpoint protection software

C. Installing a host-based IPS software

D. Removing unnecessary software

7. The company that Gary works for has deployed a wireless network. Which of the following network options is the most secure?

A. WPA-2 Personal

B. WPA-3

C. WPA-2 Enterprise

D. WPA-4

8. What type of attack depends on the attacker entering JavaScript into a text area that is intended for users to enter text that will be viewed by other users?

A. SQL injection

B. Clickjacking

C. Cross-site scripting

D. Bluejacking

9. Unusual outbound network traffic, geographical irregularities, and increases in database read volumes are all examples of what key element of threat intelligence?

A. Predictive analysis

B. OSINT

C. Indicators of compromise

D. Threat maps

10. Julie wants to conduct a replay attack. What type of attack is most commonly associated with successful replay attacks?

A. SQL injection

B. An on-path attack

C. Brute force

D. A DDoS

11. Valerie is investigating a recent incident and checks /var/log on a Linux system. She finds the audit.log file empty despite the system uptime showing over a month of uptime. What has she most likely encountered?

A. A wiped log

B. A recent reboot

C. A system error

D. Incorrect permissions to view the log

12. Jack purchases ads on a site that staff members of his target organization frequently visit in preparation for a penetration test. Once his ads start to display, he replaces the underlying code with attack code that redirects visitors to a login page that matches the organization's own internal website. What type of attack has Jack attempted?

    A. A misinformation attack

    B. A watering hole attack

    C. A disinformation attack

    D. A business website compromise attack

13. Which of the following is not a common concern related to the hardware vendor supply chain?

    A. Malware preinstalled on hardware

    B. Lack of availability of hardware

    C. Third-party hardware modifications

    D. Malicious firmware modifications

14. Ben wants to conduct a credential replay attack. What should he do first to enable the attack?

    A. Create a phishing email.

    B. Conduct an on-path attack.

    C. Use a brute-force password attack.

    D. Conduct an injection attack.

15. Nick is assessing internal threat actors and considering what motivations are likely to drive them. Which of the following is the most likely motivation for an internal threat actor?

    A. Espionage

    B. Blackmail

    C. War

    D. Political beliefs

16. Yasmine is reviewing the software installed on a client's computer and notices that multiple browser toolbars, weather applications, and social media applications were preinstalled. What term is most commonly used to describe this software?

    A. MSPs

    B. Bloatware

    C. Ransomware

    D. Rootware

17. Ilya is reviewing logs and notices that one of his staff has logged in from his home location in China at 2 p.m., and then logged in from the United Kingdom an hour later. What indicator of compromise should he flag this as?

A. Concurrent session usage

B. Resource inaccessibility

C. Impossible travel

D. Segmentation

18. Adam's organization has deployed RFID badges as part of their access control system. Adam is required to enter a 6-digit PIN when he uses his RFID badge and dislikes the additional step. What type of attack is the PIN intended to stop?

A. Piggybacking

B. On-path

C. Concurrent access

D. Badge cloning

19. Jen recently received an email that appeared to be from one of her vendors asking for a change in the method of payment to another account. She normally works with `mike_smith@example.com`, but noticed that the email was from `mike_smith@example.com` on further review. What type of social engineering attack is this?

A. Vishing

B. Business email compromise

C. Smishing

D. Pretexting

20. What is the primary concern for security professionals about legacy hardware?

A. Its likelihood of failure

B. Lack of patches and updates

C. Lack of vendor support

D. Inability to support modern protocols

21. Coleen is the web security administrator for an online auction website. A small number of users are complaining that when they visit the website it does not appear to be the correct site. Coleen checks and she can visit the site without any problem, even from computers outside the network. She also checks the web server log and there is no record of those users ever connecting. Which of the following might best explain this?

A. Typo squatting

B. SQL injection

C. Cross-site scripting

D. Cross-site request forgery

22. The organization that Mike works in finds that one of their domains is directing traffic to a competitor's website. When Mike checks, the domain information has been changed, including the contact and other administrative details for the domain. If the domain had not expired, what has most likely occurred?

    A. DNS hijacking

    B. An on-path attack

    C. Domain hijacking

    D. A zero-day attack

23. Lucia's organization has adopted open source software provided by a third-party vendor as part of their web application. What concern should she express about her software supply chain?

    A. Lack of vendor support

    B. Lack of code auditability

    C. Lack of control over open source dependencies

    D. Lack of updates

24. Alice wants to prevent server-side request forgery (SSRF) attacks. Which of the following will not be helpful for preventing them?

    A. Removing all SQL code from submitted HTTP queries

    B. Blocking hostnames like 127.0.01 and localhost

    C. Blocking sensitive URLs like /admin

    D. Applying allow list–based input filters

25. Tracy wants to protect desktop and laptop systems in her organization from network attacks. She wants to deploy a tool that can actively stop attacks based on signatures, heuristics, and anomalies. What type of tool should she deploy?

    A. A firewall

    B. Antimalware

    C. HIDS

    D. HIPS

26. Mahmoud is responsible for managing security at a large university. He has just performed a threat analysis for the network, and based on past incidents and studies of similar networks, he has determined that the most prevalent threat to his network are attackers who wish to breach the system, simply to prove they can or for some low-level crime, such as changing a grade. Which term best describes this type of attacker?

    A. Hacktivist

    B. Nation-state

    C. Insider

    D. Unskilled attacker

27. How is phishing different from general spam?

    A. It is sent only to specific targeted individuals.

    B. It is intended to acquire credentials or other data.

    C. It is sent via SMS.

    D. It includes malware in the message.

28. Selah includes a question in her procurement request-for-proposal process that asks how long the vendor has been in business and how many existing clients the vendor has. What common issue is this practice intended to help prevent?

    A. Supply chain security issues

    B. Lack of vendor support

    C. Outsourced code development issues

    D. System integration problems

29. Frank is a network administrator for a small college. He discovers that several machines on his network are infected with malware. That malware is sending a flood of packets to a target external to the network. What best describes this attack?

    A. SYN flood

    B. DDoS

    C. Botnet

    D. Backdoor

30. A sales manager at your company is complaining about slow performance on his computer. When you thoroughly investigate the issue, you find spyware on his computer. He insists that the only thing he has downloaded recently was a freeware stock trading application. What would best explain this situation?

    A. Logic bomb

    B. Trojan

    C. Rootkit

    D. Macro virus

31. What threat actor is most likely to be motivated by political beliefs?

    A. Hacktivists

    B. Organized crime

    C. Unskilled attackers

    D. Insider threats

32. What type of threat actors are most likely to have a profit motive for their malicious activities?

    A. State actors

    B. Hacktivists

    C. Unskilled attackers

    D. Organized crime

33. You have noticed that when in a crowded area, you sometimes get a stream of unwanted text messages. The messages end when you leave the area. What describes this attack?

  A. Bluejacking

  B. Bluesnarfing

  C. Evil twin

  D. Rogue access point

34. Dennis uses an on-path attack to cause a system to send traffic to his system and then forwards it to the actual server the traffic is intended for. What information will be visible from his system as it passed through it?

  A. All traffic meant for remote systems

  B. All traffic meant for local systems

  C. Only unencrypted traffic

  D. Only unencrypted traffic meant for his system

35. Andrea recently received a phone call claiming to be from her bank. The caller asked for information including her account number and Social Security number to validate her identity. What type of social engineering attack was Andrea the target of?

  A. Smishing

  B. Brand impersonation

  C. A watering hole attack

  D. A business email compromise attack

36. Jake's vulnerability scanner reports that the software his organization is running is vulnerable to a cryptographic downgrade attack. What concern should Jake have about this potential issue?

  A. Attackers may be able to force use of a weaker encryption algorithm, making data easier to access.

  B. Attackers may be able to force use of weaker hashing, making it easier to recover passwords.

  C. Attackers may be able to force use of older versions of the software, including previously patched vulnerabilities.

  D. Attackers may be able to force encryption to be turned off, causing information to be sent in plain text.

37. Rick has three major categories of data and applications in use in his virtualization environment: highly sensitive; business sensitive; and unclassified, or public information. He wants to ensure that data and applications of different sensitivity are not compromised in the event of a breach. What mitigation technique is best suited to this type of requirement?

  A. Application allow lists

  B. Monitoring

  C. Least privilege

  D. Segmentation

38. Users in your company report someone has been calling their extension and claiming to be doing a survey for a large vendor. Based on the questions asked in the survey, you suspect that this is a scam to elicit information from your company's employees. What best describes this?

   A. Spear phishing

   B. Vishing

   C. War dialing

   D. Robocalling

39. As part of a zero-trust environment, Quentin is given rights that he needs only when he needs them through a checkout process and they are then removed when he is done. What mitigation technique best describes this solution?

   A. Segmentation

   B. Isolation

   C. Least privilege

   D. Configuration enforcement

40. While performing a scan for wireless networks, Lisa discovers a network that does not use WPA-2 or WPA-3. What network traffic information can she recover from devices using this network?

   A. All network traffic

   B. Network packet headers, but not packet data

   C. Network packet data, but not headers

   D. DNS and DHCP queries, but not network packet data

41. Jared is responsible for network security at his company. He has discovered behavior on one computer that certainly appears to be a virus. He has even identified a file he thinks might be the virus. However, using three separate antivirus programs, he finds that none can detect the file. Which of the following is most likely to be occurring?

   A. The computer has a RAT.

   B. The computer has a zero-day exploit.

   C. The computer has a worm.

   D. The computer has a rootkit.

42. John has discovered that an attacker is trying to get network passwords by using software that attempts a series of passwords with a minor change each time the password is tried. What type of attack is this?

   A. Dictionary

   B. Rainbow table

   C. Brute force

   D. Session hijacking

43. Farès is the network security administrator for a company that creates advanced routers and switches. He has discovered that his company's networks have been subjected to a series of advanced attacks by an attacker sponsored by a government over a period of time. What best describes this attack?

   A. DDoS

   B. Brute force

   C. Nation-state

   D. Disassociation attack

44. What type of information is phishing not commonly intended to acquire?

   A. Passwords

   B. Email addresses

   C. Credit card numbers

   D. Personal information

45. Scott discovers that malware has been installed on one of the systems he is responsible for. Shortly afterward passwords used by the user that the system is assigned to are discovered to be in use by attackers. What type of malicious program should Scott look for on the compromised system?

   A. A rootkit

   B. A keylogger

   C. A worm

   D. None of the above

46. Nick purchases his network devices through a gray market supplier that imports them into his region without an official relationship with the network device manufacturer. What risk should Nick identify when he assesses his supply chain risk?

   A. Lack of vendor support

   B. Lack of warranty coverage

   C. Inability to validate the source of the devices

   D. All of the above

47. Naomi is preparing a laptop for a traveling salesperson who frequently needs to connect to untrusted hotel networks. What hardening technique can she use to provide the greatest protection against network-based attacks on untrusted networks?

   A. Install an endpoint detection and response tool.

   B. Install a host-based firewall.

   C. Install an extended detection and response tool.

   D. Install a disk encryption tool.

48. While conducting a vulnerability scan of her network, Susan discovers that a marketing staff member has set up their own server running a specialized marketing tool. After inquiring about the server, which is vulnerable due to missing patches, Susan discovers that the team set it up themselves because of a need that was not met by existing tools. What type of threat actor has Susan encountered?

A. An unskilled attacker

B. An insider threat

C. Shadow IT

D. A hacktivist

49. Which of the following indicators is most commonly associated with a denial-of-service attack?

A. Resource inaccessibility

B. Impossible travel

C. Missing logs

D. Blocked content

50. Henry wants to decommission a server that was used to store sensitive data. What step should he take to ensure the decommissioning process protects the organization's data?

A. Reformat the drives as part of the decommissioning process.

B. Physically destroy the drives as part of the decommissioning process.

C. Remove the system from organizational inventory as part of the decommissioning process.

D. Physically destroy the entire system as part of the decommissioning process.

51. Renee has a large number of workstations and servers in her corporate environment and wants to more effectively monitor logs for them. What solution from the following list is best suited to identifying and alerting on issues in a large-scale environment?

A. Centralized logging

B. A SIEM

C. An IPS

D. An EDR

52. Patrick is reviewing potential attack surfaces for his small business and recently deployed new networked printers for each of his three locations. What should his first action be to begin to properly secure their web management interfaces?

A. Update the firmware.

B. Change their default IP address.

C. Change the default administrator password.

D. Disable unnecessary services.

53. Paul has performed an nmap scan of a new network connected device. He notices TCP ports 22, 80, and 443 are open. If his hardening guidelines only allow encrypted management interfaces, what port or ports should he disable from this list?

A. 22

B. 80

C. 22 and 80

D. 80 and 443

54. The following graphic shows a network connection between two systems, and then a network-based attack. What type of attack is shown?

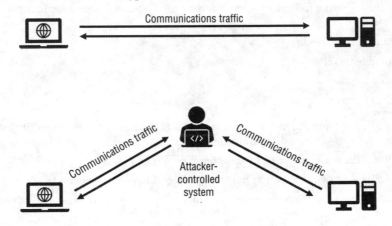

A. A denial-of-service attack

B. A SQL injection attack

C. An on-path attack

D. A directory traversal attack

55. Which of the following protocols is most commonly associated with credential relaying attacks?

A. RDP

B. NTLM

C. SQL

D. TLS

56. After a recent laptop theft, Jaime's organization is worried about data breaches driven by lost devices. What endpoint hardening technique is best suited to preventing this?

A. Encryption

B. Host-based IPS

C. Disabling ports and protocols

D. Changing default passwords

57. Derek wants to conduct a birthday attack against a digital signature. Which of the following best describes the process he would need to take to achieve his goal?

    A. He needs to prepare both a correct and a malicious document and find ways to modify the correct document until its encryption matches the malicious document.

    B. He needs to make sure all dates match in both a correct and a malicious document.

    C. He needs to ensure that the file length and creation date match for both a correct document and a malicious document.

    D. He needs to prepare both a correct and a malicious document, then find ways to modify the malicious document until its hash matches the hash of the correct document.

58. Ashley's organization has recently come under attack and has suffered a DNS outage. As she investigated, she found that requests to her DNS servers were sent to open DNS resolvers using spoofed IP addresses with requests that would result in very large responses from the DNS resolvers to the IP addresses that appeared to be making the request. What type of attack targeted Ashley's organization?

    A. A reflected DDoS

    B. A DNS flood

    C. A mirrored DDoS

    D. A supersized query attack

59. What term is used to describe the problem when two files have the same hash?

    A. A birthday attack

    B. A collision

    C. A bingo

    D. A match-the-hash attack

60. Kara wants to protect against the most common means of firmware-based exploits. Which of the following is not a common firmware defense mechanism for the vendors of devices that use firmware?

    A. Using signed firmware updates

    B. Using input validation for user input

    C. Encrypting firmware

    D. Code review processes for firmware

61. Annie's organization has been facing negative social media campaigns for months and is struggling to address them. Numerous bot posts about the company are providing incorrect information about the company. What type of attack is Annie's company facing?

    A. A misinformation campaign

    B. A pretexting campaign

    C. An impersonation campaign

    D. A disinformation campaign

62. Ines is concerned about messaging through tools like Discord and Slack as attack vectors. What can she do to most effectively limit the attack surface for threats like this?

    A. Deploy EDR tools to all workstations and devices.

    B. Deploy an organizational communication tool or instance instead of using public tools.

    C. Deploy messaging-aware firewalls.

    D. Deploy messaging-aware IPS systems.

63. Ana's vendor has informed her that the hardware her organization uses is considered end-of-life. What should Ana do?

    A. Identify replacement hardware and purchase it immediately.

    B. Purchase an extended support contract from a third-party vendor.

    C. Begin plans to phase out the equipment before it reaches end-of-support.

    D. Install final patches and then isolate the hardware from the network.

64. What threat vector is most impacted by how Windows handles `autorun.inf` files?

    A. Removable devices

    B. Open service ports

    C. Unsecure Wi-Fi

    D. Watering hole attacks

65. Raj wants to reduce the attack surface for a newly purchased laptop. What hardening technique will help him reduce the possibility of remote exploits while also decreasing the amount of ongoing patch management he needs to do for the system?

    A. Encrypt the system's boot drive.

    B. Install EDR software.

    C. Remove unnecessary software.

    D. Change any default passwords.

66. Mary has discovered that a web application used by her company does not always handle multithreading properly, particularly when multiple threads access the same variable. This could allow an attacker who discovered this vulnerability to exploit it and crash the server. What type of error has Mary discovered?

    A. Buffer overflow

    B. Logic bomb

    C. Race conditions

    D. Improper error handling

67. Allan wants to detect brute-force physical attacks. What should he do if he wants to detect the broadest range of physical attacks?

    A. Deploy a monitored security camera system.

    B. Hire a guard to patrol the facility.

    C. Conduct regular inspections of the facility.

    D. Set up an alarm system.

68. Which of the following is not a common threat vector associated with SMS-based attacks?

   A. Malicious links

   B. SMS-based phishing

   C. SMS-delivered images

   D. MFA exploits

69. During a regular review of logs, Jennifer notices that a regularly scheduled script that copies files to another server every hour has run multiple times within the last hour. What indicator of compromise should she categorize this as?

   A. Concurrent session use

   B. Out-of-cycle logging

   C. Missing logs

   D. Impossible travel

70. Pete uses a technique that injects code into memory used by another process to allow him to control what the host program does. What is this technique called for Windows dynamically linked libraries?

   A. WinBuff attacks

   B. DLL injection

   C. A SYRINGE attack

   D. A memory traversal attack

71. Kathleen wants to control network traffic between subnets using her Cisco network devices. What built-in capability can she use to allow or deny traffic based on port, protocol, and IP address?

   A. A HIPS

   B. ACLs

   C. Least privilege lists

   D. VLANs

72. What is the primary purpose of encryption as a control in enterprise environments?

   A. To preserve availability

   B. To support physical security

   C. To preserve least privilege

   D. To preserve confidentiality

73. What type of attack exploits the trust that a website has for an authenticated user to attack that website by spoofing requests from the trusted user?

   A. Cross-site scripting

   B. Cross-site request forgery

   C. Bluejacking

   D. Evil twin

74. Dana wants to use documented and published IoCs as part of her threat-hunting activities. What should she look for to integrate with her SIEM or other security tools?

    A. Threat feeds

    B. A real-time blackhole list

    C. A vulnerability feed

    D. An IP reputation feed

75. The malware that Joseph is working to counter has copied itself to workstations across his environment due to a central, shared fileshare. What type of malware is Joseph most likely fighting?

    A. A Trojan

    B. A virus

    C. A keylogger

    D. A rootkit

76. You are responsible for software testing at Acme Corporation. You want to check all software for bugs that might be used by an attacker to gain entrance into the software or your network. You have discovered a web application that would allow a user to attempt to put a 64-bit value into a 4-byte integer variable. What is this type of flaw?

    A. Memory overflow

    B. Buffer overflow

    C. Variable overflow

    D. Integer overflow

77. The company that Keith works for uses a backoff algorithm that increases the time between when login attempts are allowed after each failed login. Keith has recently attempted to log in and found that his account is not able to log in again for 15 minutes. What should the security administrators at Keith's organization do to find potential indicators of malicious activity?

    A. Review authentication logs.

    B. Interview Keith about his recent logins.

    C. Change Keith's password and check error logs.

    D. Report an incident and start the incident response process.

78. Grayson's organization is concerned about environmental attacks against their datacenter. What type of monitoring is best suited to detecting environmental attacks in a scenario like this?

    A. Video cameras

    B. Intrusion alarm systems

    C. Temperature monitoring sensors

    D. Log analysis

79. Jack's team in HR is paying for an SaaS tool using their HR expense account credit cards without the knowledge of central IT. What type of threat actor does this make Jack's HR team?

A. Shadow IT

B. An inadvertent threat

C. Internal espionage actors

D. An insider threat

80. Amanda is assessing the potential for issues with her organization's recently adopted IaaS vendor. What cloud vulnerability should she worry about if her system administrators do not effectively manage security groups in AWS?

A. Insecure APIs

B. Misconfigurations

C. Malicious insiders

D. MFA-based attacks

81. Jared's organization runs Linux servers, and recent vulnerability scans show that the servers are vulnerable to an issue that is described as follows:

CVE-2018-5703: tcp_v6_syn_recv_sock function in net/ipv6/tcp_ipv6.c in the Linux kernel through 4.14.11 allows attackers to cause a denial of service (slab out-of-bounds write)

What is Jared's best option to remediate a kernel vulnerability like this?

A. Patch the application.

B. Install a HIPS with appropriate rules.

C. Segment the systems away from the Internet to reduce risk.

D. Patch the operating system.

82. What is the likely outcome of a cryptographic collision attack?

A. Attackers can decrypt a file without the private key.

B. Two files that have the same encrypted output but are different files.

C. Two files that both have the same hash but have different contents.

D. Attackers can decrypt the file without the public key.

83. Sarah is working with a small business and noticed that they have a consumer-grade wireless router serving their business. What common hardening checklist item should she validate first as part of securing the device?

A. Removing unnecessary software

B. Running a vulnerability scan

C. Ensuring the default password has been changed

D. Ensuring that unneeded ports have been disabled

84. What technique most effectively prevents resource reuse concerns for storage in a virtual environment?

    A. Firmware updates

    B. Volume encryption

    C. Minimizing cluster size

    D. Reformatting drives

85. Michelle is modeling threat actor motivation for her organization and wants to describe ransomware actors. What motivation is not commonly associated with ransomware?

    A. Data exfiltration

    B. Blackmail

    C. Revenge

    D. Financial gain

86. Which of the following is commonly used in a distributed denial-of-service (DDoS) attack?

    A. Phishing

    B. Adware

    C. Botnet

    D. Trojan

87. Amanda discovers that a member of her organization's staff has installed a remote-access Trojan on their accounting software server and has been accessing it remotely. What type of threat has she discovered?

    A. Zero-day

    B. Insider threat

    C. Misconfiguration

    D. Weak encryption

88. Postings from Russian agents during the 2016 U.S. presidential campaign to Facebook and Twitter are an example of what type of effort?

    A. Impersonation

    B. Disinformation

    C. Asymmetric warfare

    D. A watering hole attack

89. Which of the following threat actors is most likely to be associated with an advanced persistent threat (APT)?

    A. Hacktivists

    B. Nation-state actors

    C. Unskilled attacker

    D. Insider threats

90. Erica wants to conduct an amplified DDoS attack against a system. What key step is required as part of her attack?

   A. Reversing the target's IP address

   B. Spoofing the target's IP address

   C. Conducting an on-path attack to send traffic to the target

   D. Spoofing responses from the amplification system to the target

91. Daryl is investigating a recent breach of his company's web server. The attacker used sophisticated techniques and then defaced the website, leaving messages that were denouncing the company's public policies. He and his team are trying to determine the type of actor who most likely committed the breach. Based on the information provided, who was the most likely threat actor?

   A. A script

   B. A nation-state

   C. Organized crime

   D. Hacktivists

92. Which of the following human vectors are most likely to be part of a voice call-based attack?

   A. A watering hole attack

   B. Pretexting

   C. Disinformation

   D. BEC

93. What is the primary difference in threat vectors between agent client-based and agentless software deployments?

   A. Agentless software does not consume resources and thus cannot result in a resource consumption-based denial-of-service condition.

   B. Client-based software provides a better view of system resources and is able to manage its resource consumption better to avoid issues.

   C. Agentless software does not have an agent that may be potentially vulnerable to attack.

   D. Client-based software allows for greater security because it can be patched.

94. Angela reviews the authentication logs for her website and sees attempts from many different accounts using the same set of passwords. What is this attack technique called?

   A. Brute forcing

   B. Password spraying

   C. Limited login attacks

   D. Account spinning

95. Charles discovers that an attacker has used a vulnerability in a web application that his company runs and has then used that exploit to obtain root privileges on the web server. What type of attack has he discovered?

   A. Cross-site scripting

   B. Privilege escalation

   C. A SQL injection

   D. A race condition

96. Which of the following best describes a zero-day vulnerability?

   A. A vulnerability that the vendor is not yet aware of

   B. A vulnerability that has not yet been breached

   C. A vulnerability that can be quickly exploited (i.e., in zero days)

   D. A vulnerability that will give the attacker brief access (i.e., zero days)

97. You have discovered that there are entries in your network's domain name server that point legitimate domains to unknown and potentially harmful IP addresses. What best describes this type of attack?

   A. A backdoor

   B. An APT

   C. DNS poisoning

   D. A Trojan horse

98. What technique drives image-based threat vectors?

   A. Encryption

   B. Hashing

   C. Forgery

   D. Steganography

99. Eric is conducting a penetration test and wants to release a malicious update for an organization's application. The organization uses public key encryption to sign updates. What does Eric need to deliver an update that systems will accept?

   A. The private key for the signing certificate

   B. A collision with the hashed value of a legitimate update

   C. The public key for the signing certificate

   D. A collision with the hashed value of a malicious update

100. Mike is a network administrator with a small financial services company. He has received a pop-up window that states his files are now encrypted and he must pay .5 bitcoins to get them decrypted. He tries to check the files in question, but their extensions have changed, and he cannot open them. What best describes this situation?

   A. Mike's machine has a rootkit.

   B. Mike's machine has ransomware.

   C. Mike's machine has a logic bomb.

   D. Mike's machine has been the target of whaling.

101. Your company is instituting a new security awareness program. You are responsible for educating end users on a variety of threats, including social engineering. Which of the following best defines social engineering?

- **A.** Illegal copying of software
- **B.** Gathering information from discarded manuals and printouts
- **C.** Using people skills to obtain proprietary information
- **D.** Phishing emails

102. What type of malicious actor will typically have the least amount of resources available to them?

- **A.** Nation-states
- **B.** Unskilled actor
- **C.** Hacktivists
- **D.** Organized crime

103. Jorge wants to brief his organization's leadership on common email threat vectors. Which of the following common threats should not be in his presentation?

- **A.** Phishing
- **B.** Malware sent via email
- **C.** Email spoofing
- **D.** Cross-site scripting

104. Jared has discovered malware on the workstations of several users. This particular malware provides administrative privileges for the workstation to an external hacker. What best describes this malware?

- **A.** Trojan horse
- **B.** Logic bomb
- **C.** Multipartite virus
- **D.** Rootkit

105. Michelle discovers that a number of systems throughout her organization are connecting to a changing set of remote systems on TCP port 6667. What is the most likely cause of this, if she believes the traffic is not legitimate and that the systems are infected with malware?

- **A.** An alternate service port for web traffic
- **B.** Botnet command-and-control via IRC
- **C.** Downloads via a peer-to-peer network
- **D.** Remote-access Trojans

106. Susan performs a vulnerability scan of a small business network and discovers that the organization's consumer-grade wireless router has a vulnerability in its web server. What issue should she address in her findings?

- **A.** Firmware patch management
- **B.** Default configuration issues
- **C.** An unsecured administrative account
- **D.** Weak encryption settings

107. What type of phishing attack occurs via text messages?

    A. Bluejacking

    B. Smishing

    C. Phonejacking

    D. Text whaling

108. John is analyzing a recent malware infection on his company network. He discovers malware that can spread rapidly via vulnerable network services and does not require any interaction from the user. What best describes this malware?

    A. Worm

    B. Virus

    C. Logic bomb

    D. Trojan horse

109. While reviewing web logs for her organization's website, Kathleen discovers the entry shown here:

```
GET http://example.com/viewarticle.php?view=../../../config.txt HTTP/1.1
```

    What type of attack has she potentially discovered?

    A. A directory traversal attack

    B. A web application buffer overflow

    C. A directory recursion attack

    D. A slashdot attack

110. What two files are commonly attacked using offline brute-force attacks?

    A. The Windows Registry and the Linux `/etc/passwd` file

    B. The Windows SAM and the Linux `/etc/passwd` file

    C. The Windows SAM and the Linux `/etc/shadow` file

    D. The Windows Registry and the Linux `/etc/shadow` file

111. You have noticed that when in a crowded area, data from your cell phone is stolen. Later investigation shows a Bluetooth connection to your phone, one that you cannot explain. What describes this attack?

    A. Bluejacking

    B. Bluesnarfing

    C. An evil twin attack

    D. A remote-access Trojan

112. Which of the following situations is not associated with race conditions?

    A. Time-of-check

    B. Time-of-change

    C. Target-of-evaluation

    D. Time-of-use

113. Gabby wants to protect a legacy platform with known vulnerabilities. Which of the following is not a common isolation or segmentation option that could be used to address this issue?

A. Disconnect it from the network.

B. Place the device behind a dedicated firewall and restrict inbound and outbound traffic.

C. Rely on the outdated OS to confuse attackers.

D. Move the device to a protected VLAN.

114. After running nmap against a system on a network, Lucca sees that TCP port 23 is open and a service is running on it. What issue and resolution should he identify?

A. Low ports should not be open to the Internet and should be disabled.

B. Telnet is an insecure protocol and should be disabled.

C. SSH is an insecure protocol and should be disabled.

D. Ports 1–1024 are well-known ports and must be firewalled.

115. Charles sets the permissions on the /etc directory on a Linux system to 777 using the chmod command. If Alex later discovers this, what should he report his finding as?

A. Open or weak permissions

B. Improper file handling

C. A privilege escalation attack

D. None of the above

116. Under what circumstances are concurrent sessions most commonly considered indicators of compromise?

A. When they occur on the same system

B. When they occur on two different systems issued to the same user

C. When they occur in two different locations at the same time

D. When they occur in the same location at the same time

117. During a penetration test, Angela obtains the uniform of a well-known package delivery service and wears it into the target office. She claims to have a delivery for a C-level employee she knows is there and insists that the package must be signed for by that person. What social engineering technique has she used?

A. Impersonation

B. Whaling

C. A watering hole attack

D. Prepending

118. Frank's organization operates in a shared responsibility cloud environment. What can Frank do to determine if he is suffering from a denial-of-service (DoS) attack against his cloud hosting environment?

    A. Nothing; cloud services do not provide security tools.

    B. Call the cloud service provider to have them stop the DoS attack.

    C. Review the cloud service provider's security tools and enable logging and anti-DoS tools if they exist.

    D. Call the cloud service provider's Internet service provider (ISP) and ask them to enable DoS prevention.

119. What is the typical goal intent or goal of hacktivists?

    A. Increasing their reputation

    B. Financial gain

    C. Making a political statement

    D. Gathering high-value data

120. Ryan needs to verify that no unnecessary ports and services are available on his systems, but he cannot run a vulnerability scanner. What is his best option?

    A. Passive network traffic capture to detect services

    B. A configuration review

    C. Active network traffic capture to detect services

    D. Log review

121. John is a network administrator for Acme Company. He has discovered that someone has registered a domain name that is spelled just one letter different than his company's domain. The website with the misspelled URL is a phishing site. What best describes this attack?

    A. Session hijacking

    B. Cross-site request forgery

    C. Typo squatting

    D. Clickjacking

122. Which of the following best describes malware that will execute some malicious activity when a particular condition is met (i.e., if the condition is met, then executed)?

    A. Boot sector virus

    B. Logic bomb

    C. Buffer overflow

    D. Sparse infector virus

123. Una's company is assessing threats to their supply chain and wants to consider the most likely issues that their server hardware supplier may create. Which of the following is not a common concern for organizations assessing hardware providers?

    A. Malicious hardware design

    B. Injection of malicious firmware

    C. Inability to deliver hardware in a timely manner

    D. Malicious software added to default OS images

124. Helen wants to prevent her staff from sideloading applications to their Android devices. What type of tool is best suited to preventing this type of issue without reducing other functionality for the device?

    A. Disable the Google Play store.

    B. Disable the manufacturer's store.

    C. Use an EDR tool.

    D. Use an MDM solution.

125. Tori believes that the system she is investigating may have a rootkit resident on the system. What type of behavior is most likely to indicate a rootkit's presence?

    A. Unusual network traffic

    B. Network scanning

    C. Displaying a ransom notice

    D. Deletion of files

126. Neil wants to deploy a host-intrusion prevention system that will use a third-party threat feed to servers in his datacenter. What concern might his system administrators express about the HIPS that he should consider before he makes the decision?

    A. A HIPS may block traffic, causing an outage or disruption.

    B. A HIPS may prevent least privilege configurations.

    C. A HIPS may bypass application allow lists.

    D. A HIPS may make use of segmentation less effective.

127. Organize the following threat actors by their typical level of sophistication from most sophisticated to least sophisticated:

Hacktivists, Nation-state actors, Organized crime, Shadow IT

    A. Hacktivists, Shadow IT, Organized crime, Nation-state actors

    B. Nation-state actors, Organized crime, Hacktivists, Shadow IT

    C. Organized crime, Hacktivists, Shadow IT, Nation-state actors

    D. Shadow IT, Hacktivists, Organized crime, Nation-state actors

128. What is the most common file-based threat vector?

    A. Phishing

    B. BEC

    C. Malware

    D. XSS

129. Drew wants to address a recent Windows vulnerability that has a CVE rating of 9.6. What should his first step be to address the vulnerability?

    A. Isolate the impacted systems.

    B. Disable the service.

    C. Check to see if a patch is available.

    D. Install a host-based firewall.

130. Clay is decommissioning a server and wants to ensure that the system is properly decommissioned. Once the drives have been wiped or destroyed, what step typically comes next?

    A. Wiping memory

    B. Removing the system from inventory

    C. Removing the system from management

    D. Removing memory

131. Joe recently ran a port scan and found a service running on TCP port 1433. What type of attacks would he expect against this service?

    A. Web-based attacks

    B. Print-server attacks

    C. Oracle database server attacks

    D. Microsoft SQL Server attacks

132. What type of virtualization attack can be prevented by encrypting storage volumes when they are created?

    A. VM escape

    B. Birthday attacks

    C. Pass-the-hash

    D. Resource reuse

133. Tyler discovers that software his organization has deployed sends information about the workstations back to a central server. After capturing network traffic that is being sent, he discovers that it includes the workstation's IP address, operating system, screen resolution, and information about other installed software. What type of malware should Tyler classify this as?

    A. A Trojan

    B. Bloatware

    C. A keylogger

    D. Spyware

134. Eden wants to check errors related to a new security tool installed on her Windows workstation. What log file in Windows contains errors with installed software?

    A. The application log

    B. The security log

    C. The setup log

    D. The system log

135. Trent's company has recently discovered that their DNS information was changed via their registrar. Investigation showed that an administrator's workstation was compromised and that the account details for domain administration were contained on the workstation. What type of DNS-based attack is this?

    A. A DNS-based DoS attack

    B. A DNS hijacking attack

    C. A DNS amplification attack

    D. A DNS-based DDoS attack

136. Giovanni wants to check to see if an impossible travel situation occurred for two logins on a Linux server. What log should he check to confirm or disprove his theory?

    A. `/var/log/messages`

    B. `/var/log/auth.log`

    C. `/var/log/cron.log`

    D. `/var/log/travel`

137. Microsoft's Intune as well as tools like Jamf are examples of tools that provide what sort of mitigation functionality?

    A. Decommissioning

    B. Configuration enforcement

    C. Segmentation

    D. HIPS

138. Nora recently wanted to find information about a scientific discovery and queried an AI large-language model asking for a summary and references. The AI model provided a summary of the discovery and a number of citations. After Nora searched for the articles the AI cited, she discovered that they did not exist. How would this be classified?

    A. As phishing

    B. As misinformation

    C. As disinformation

    D. As brand impersonation

139. Sandeep wants to address the potential for impersonation attacks against her helpdesk. What technique is most likely to prevent impersonation attacks from being successful with her support staff?

    A. Require callers to verify their identity using non-public information.

    B. Avoid publishing the help desk's phone number externally.

    C. Require users to complete awareness training.

    D. Require callers to provide a callback number and call back before completing tasks.

140. Bob is conducting a penetration test against a client's environment and he discovers TCP port 515 exposed to the Internet. What should he report to his client as a potential attack surface?

    A. An exposed Internet connected camera

    B. An exposed print server

    C. An exposed IoT device

    D. An exposed UPS management system

141. Which of the following is not a common cryptographic vulnerability?

    A. Downgrade attacks

    B. Magic key attacks

    C. Collision attacks

    D. Birthday attacks

142. Louis is investigating a malware incident on one of the computers on his network. He has discovered unknown software that seems to be opening a port, allowing someone to remotely connect to the computer. This software seems to have been installed at the same time as a small shareware application. Which of the following best describes this malware?

    A. Trojan

    B. Worm

    C. Logic bomb

    D. Rootkit

143. Which of the following motivations is not commonly associated with advanced persistent threat actors?

    A. Ethical

    B. War

    C. Data exfiltration

    D. Espionage

144. Eve wants to protect against DLL injection attacks. Which of the following practices can help her prevent DLL injection?

A. Do not allow users to run DLLs.

B. Avoid using DLLs.

C. Use fully qualified paths for DLLs instead of searching paths.

D. Use a DLL vulnerability scanner.

145. Mackenzie wants to protect her organization from firmware vulnerabilities. What practice is most effective at preventing malicious firmware from being inadvertently downloaded and installed?

A. Only use digitally signed and validated firmware.

B. Scan firmware with an antivirus tool.

C. Only use encrypted firmware.

D. Avoid updating firmware and only use original firmware.

146. Zoie wants to check for instances of concurrent session usage for her web application. Where should she look for these indicators?

A. Her firewall logs

B. Her antivirus (AV) logs

C. Her authentication logs

D. Her web application server logs

147. Valerie knows that a system in her environment has been compromised and wants to take immediate action. Which of the following options should she select if she is worried about the system impacting other hosts on the network?

A. Deploy antimalware tools to the system and scan it.

B. Immediately isolate the system.

C. Immediately deploy any missing patches to the system.

D. Change default passwords and check for unexpected user accounts.

148. Casey is worried about downgrade attacks against her Apache web servers. What should she do to most effectively prevent downgrade attacks?

A. Prevent TLS fallback.

B. Require current web browsers.

C. Run the most current version of Apache.

D. Use an IDS.

149. What type of attack is based on sending more data to a target variable than the data can actually hold?

A. Bluesnarfing

B. Buffer overflow

C. Bluejacking

D. Cross-site scripting

150. Which of the following is an attack that seeks to attack a website, based on the website's trust of an authenticated user?

   A. XSS

   B. XSRF

   C. Buffer overflow

   D. Directory traversal

151. Mary wants to harden workstations she is responsible for against malware attacks. Which of the following is not a common solution to this?

   A. Installing EDR

   B. Limiting administrative access

   C. Installing antivirus

   D. Using disk encryption

152. Spyware is an example of what type of malware?

   A. Trojan

   B. Unwanted programs

   C. RAT

   D. Ransomware

153. Olivia has provisioned a new virtual machine in a cloud environment and is conducting forensic exercises to practice cloud forensic activities. She discovers data on her newly provisioned drive when she begins to analyze the drive. What issue has Olivia encountered?

   A. A VM escape issue

   B. Improper chain of custody

   C. A resource reuse issue

   D. Improper legal hold

154. Chuck wants to help his organization protect against business email compromise (BEC) attacks. Which of the following is not a common best practice to defend against BEC?

   A. Delete all attachments from emails.

   B. Use two-factor authentication.

   C. Review suspicious email carefully for typos and other indicators.

   D. Don't click URLs in unsolicited emails—visit URLs manually.

155. A penetration tester calls a staff member for her target organization and introduces herself as a member of the IT support team. She asks if the staff member has encountered a problem with their system, then proceeds to ask for details about the individual, claiming she needs to verify that she is talking to the right person. What type of social engineering attack is this?

   A. Pretexting

   B. A watering hole attack

   C. Phishing

   D. Shoulder surfing

156. What type of attack targets a specific group of users by infecting one or more websites that group is specifically known to visit frequently?

    A. A watercooler attack

    B. A phishing net attack

    C. A watering hole attack

    D. A phish pond attack

157. When a multithreaded application does not properly handle various threads accessing a common value, and one thread can change the data while another thread is relying on it, what flaw is this?

    A. Memory leak

    B. Buffer overflow

    C. Integer overflow

    D. Time-of-check/time-of-use

158. Geoff believes that a workstation on his network may have been the target of an on-path attack. What indicator is most likely to indicate this type of attack on a local network segment?

    A. External DNS resolution shows an improper result.

    B. The ARP table shows an alternate address for the gateway.

    C. Encrypted traffic has been forced to use a less secure algorithm.

    D. A website's URL has been modified.

159. Kathleen's IPS flags traffic from two IP addresses as shown here:

```
Source IP: 10.11.94.111
http://example.com/home/show.php?SESSIONID=a3fghbby
Source IP: 192.168.5.34
http://example.com/home/show.php?SESSIONID=a3fghbby
```

What type of attack should she investigate this as?

    A. A SQL injection attack

    B. A cross-site scripting attack

    C. A session replay attack

    D. A server-side request forgery attack

160. Andy is an end user in an organization that uses an application allow list to control what applications are used on workstations. What does Andy need to do if he wants to install an application on his workstation?

    A. Download the application, then run the installer using an administrator account.

    B. Manually add the application installer to the allow list for his workstation.

    C. Request that the application be added to the allow list and have it installed by his organization's administrators.

    D. Use a jailbreak to install the application.

161. Frank is traveling and wants to connect to an unsecure wired network in his hotel. Which of the following is not a common threat he should consider how to prevent while on an unsecured hotel wired network?

A. Network packet capture

B. Network-based attacks

C. Evil twins

D. Worms

162. An attacker is trying to get access to your network. He is sending users on your network a link to a new game with a hacked license code program. However, the game files also include software that will give the attacker access to any machine that it is installed on. What type of attack is this?

A. Rootkit

B. Trojan horse

C. Spyware

D. Boot sector virus

163. Rae's company recently received an email from a former employee threatening to release company data that they copied before they left the organization if the organization does not pay them a severance package. What threat actor motivation should she categorize this as?

A. Espionage

B. Revenge

C. Blackmail

D. Service disruption

164. Jack wants to sideload applications to his Android phone. What does he need to do first to allow this?

A. Jailbreak the phone.

B. Transfer the files to the phone.

C. Install a package manager.

D. Disable antimalware protection.

165. Jill is conducting a penetration test and uses the following query against a vulnerable web application. What data will she see if it succeeds?

```
SELECT * FROM users WHERE category = 'customers' OR 1=1--'
```

A. A list of all customers

B. A list of all customers whose userID is 1 or larger

C. A list of all customers whose userID is 1

D. A list of all users

166. Greg's checklist for securing new Linux-based devices includes disabling unneeded ports and protocols. What primary purpose does this serve?

    A. It speeds up port scans.

    B. It reduces the number of logged events.

    C. It prevents using up default ports.

    D. It reduces the device's attack footprint.

167. Nathaniel's organization has recently deployed multifactor authentication (MFA), which requires both a password and an MFA code to be provided to authenticate to critical services. Despite this, an attacker has recently logged into an administrative console using a password and MFA code belonging to a user. Which of the following types of malware is most likely to allow an attacker to successfully undertake this type of attack?

    A. A virus

    B. A worm

    C. A logic bomb

    D. A keylogger

168. Which of the following is not a common attribute of organized crime threat actors?

    A. Internal

    B. Well resourced

    C. Sophisticated

    D. External

169. Darryl is showing Valerie his iPhone and explains that his niece installed a package manager called Cydia on the device that allows him to install applications that are not available via the Apple App Store. What does Valerie know about his iPhone?

    A. It has been infected with malware.

    B. It can be remotely controlled via SSH.

    C. It can be remotely controlled via a web interface.

    D. It is jailbroken.

170. Isaac is reviewing IPS rules used by his organization and notices rules that block the use of ' as well as OR 1=1 in HTTP queries. What type of attacks is Isaac's organization attempting to stop?

    A. Buffer overflow attacks

    B. SQL injection attacks

    C. Replay attacks

    D. Directory traversal attacks

171. Vicki is reviewing common BEC attack methods with her team. Which of the following is not a common BEC technique?

  A. Using compromised email accounts

  B. Using slightly modified spoofed email addresses

  C. Sending email from the user's personal email account

  D. Using malware to access email accounts

172. Craig wants to control the applications employees can install on the laptops they are issued. If he wants the greatest level of control and is not concerned about flexibility or overhead to manage his solution, which of the following will best meet his needs?

  A. An access control list

  B. Application allow list

  C. An application deny list

  D. Segmentation

173. Ron wants to prevent users from using SSH between two network segments. Which of the following ACLs will prevent users in a segment 10.10.10.0/24 from using SSH to connect to the 10.10.20.0/24 network segment?

  A. PERMIT IP 10.10.10.0/24 * 10.10.20.0/24 22

  B. DENY IP 10.10.10.0/24 * 10.10.20.0/24 22

  C. PERMIT IP 10.10.20.0/24 * 10.10.10.0/24 22

  D. DENY IP 10.10.20.0/24 * 10.10.10.0/24 22

174. Sam's organization uses a DNS black hole to prevent access to known malicious sites. The organization relies on a reputation service feed that is used to add the known malicious domains and IP addresses. DNS lookups that would go to those sites is sent to an internal redirect site that lets users know the site is inaccessible. Sam reviews the logs to determine if a system is trying to access those blocked sites regularly. What type of indicator of compromise is Sam looking for?

  A. Blocked content

  B. Resource inaccessibility

  C. Missing logs

  D. Published or documented indicators

175. Christina is reviewing a Linux system that she is responsible for, and notices that the /usr filesystem is 80 percent full. After review, she notices that a single user's home directory has hundreds of files in it that were recently added. What type of indicator of compromise should she categorize this as?

  A. Resource inaccessibility

  B. Blocked content

  C. Impossible travel

  D. Resource consumption

176. What term is used to describe the unwanted but generally harmless programs that are commonly installed on consumer computers when they are purchased?

- **A.** Spyware
- **B.** Bloatware
- **C.** Logic bombs
- **D.** Firmware

177. Michael is performing a forensic analysis of a compromised workstation and discovers a copy of `cmd.exe` in the `\system32` folder on a Windows workstation that does not match the real `cmd.exe` file. When he looks at the file, he discovers that it is capable of running as an administrator. What type of attack has he discovered?

- **A.** A buffer overflow attack
- **B.** A Trojan attack
- **C.** A privilege escalation attack
- **D.** A replay attack

178. While reviewing logs, Chris sees an Apache web log that includes the following entry:

`https://www.example.com/viewer.php?filename=../../../etc/passwd%00.png`

What type of attack has Chris most likely uncovered, and what file will it return?

- **A.** A replay attack, `password00.png`
- **B.** A directory traversal attack, `password00.png`
- **C.** A replay attack, `passwd`
- **D.** A directory traversal attack, `passwd`

179. What common mitigation technique relies on VLANs to separate systems?

- **A.** Encryption
- **B.** Segmentation
- **C.** Impossible travel
- **D.** HIPS

180. Mark's coworker recently discovered that he can use the Linux `su` command to run programs as one of his peers. What type of attack is this?

- **A.** A replay attack
- **B.** A vertical privilege escalation attack
- **C.** A horizontal privilege escalation attack
- **D.** A forgery attack

181. Jason is monitoring his network and notices that hundreds of different IP addresses are sending requests to one of his organization's servers. The requests are small, and when he inspects them he sees a simple HTTP GET command for a file. When the server responds, it sends back a very large response. What type of attack is likely occurring, and what is it attempting to accomplish?

    A. A DoS attack and exploiting a vulnerable service

    B. A DDoS and a buffer overflow

    C. A DDoS and resource exhaustion

    D. A DoS attack and an on-path attack

182. Dan was recently troubleshooting a web server and deployed a firewall rule to his organization's datacenter firewall at the beginning of the ruleset. The rule reads:

    ALLOW FROM ANY:TCP 80 TO ANY:ANY

    What type of vulnerability should the security team at Dan's workplace label this as?

    A. A jailbreak

    B. A race condition

    C. A misconfiguration

    D. An injection attack

183. Brian wants to protect files that are regularly sent via email as part of his organization's business practice. What type of encryption is best suited to this type of usage?

    A. Full-disk encryption

    B. File-level encryption

    C. Volume encryption

    D. Transport encryption

184. Olivia has deployed Microsoft's Intune for her environment. What capability has she gained for her devices?

    A. Malware detection and response

    B. Configuration enforcement

    C. Code versioning

    D. Web application firewalling

185. Jill is concerned about supply chain attacks against her organization's service providers. Which of the following should be her most significant concern about her software-as-a-service (SaaS) service provider as she documents her supply chain risks?

    A. Compromise of the SaaS vendor, leading to access to her data

    B. Attacks against the SaaS vendor, leading to hours of downtime

    C. Lack of availability of hardware from her SaaS vendor for delivery

    D. Software vulnerabilities in tools provided by the vendor

186. Elizabeth is investigating a network breach at her company. She discovers a program that was able to execute code within the address space of another process by using the target process to load a specific library. What best describes this attack?

A. A logic bomb

B. Session hijacking

C. Buffer overflow

D. DLL injection

187. Annie wants to prevent a TOC/TOU issue that occurs with her organization's business application. The issue occurs when scripts run as part of the application access a shared data file. Sometimes one instance of the script opens the file, checks that inventory is sufficient to meet customer needs, then waits for the customer's interaction. At the same time, another instance of the script checks, sees that there is sufficient inventory, and also provides that information to another customer. If both customers place orders, Annie's organization is unable to meet demand. If Annie wants to continue to grow her business's use of the application, which of the following options is the best way to prevent this issue?

A. Delete the resource after each use.

B. Only run one instance of the process.

C. Make multiple copies of the resource so each process has its own.

D. Lock the resource until the process is done with it.

Chapter 3

Domain 3.0: Security Architecture

THE COMPTIA SECURITY+ EXAM SY0-701 TOPICS COVERED IN THIS CHAPTER INCLUDE THE FOLLOWING:

✓ **3.1 Compare and contrast security implications of different architecture models**

- Architecture and infrastructure concepts
    - Cloud (Responsibility matrix, Hybrid considerations, Third-party vendors)
    - Infrastructure as code (IaC)
    - Serverless
    - Microservices
    - Network infrastructure (Physical isolation, Air gapped, Logical segmentation, Software-defined networking [SDN])
    - On-premises
    - Centralized vs. decentralized
    - Containerization
    - Virtualization
    - IoT
    - Industrial control systems (ICS)/supervisory control and data acquisition (SCADA)
    - Real-time operating system (RTOS)
    - Embedded systems
    - High availability
    - Considerations (Availability, Resilience, Cost, Responsiveness, Scalability, Ease of deployment, Risk transference, Ease of recovery, Patch availability, Inability to patch, Power, Compute)

✓ **3.2 Given a scenario, apply security principles to secure enterprise infrastructure**

- Infrastructure considerations
    - Device placement
    - Security zones
    - Attack surface
    - Connectivity
    - Failure modes (Fail-open, Fail-closed)
    - Device attribute (Active vs. passive, Inline vs. tap/monitor)
    - Network appliances (Jump server, Proxy server, Intrusion protection system, [IPS]/intrusion detection system [IDS], Load balancer, Sensors)
    - Port security (802.1X, Extensible Authentication Protocol [EAP])
    - Firewall types (Web application firewall [WAF], Unified threat management [UTM], Next-generation firewall [NGFW], Layer 4/Layer 7)
- Secure communication/access
    - Virtual private network (VPN)
    - Remote access
    - Tunneling (Transport Layer Security [TLS], Internet protocol security [IPSec])
    - Software-defined wide area network (SD-WAN)
    - Secure access service edge (SASE)
- Selection of effective controls

✓ **3.3 Compare and contrast concepts and strategies to protect data**

- Data types
    - Regulated
    - Trade secret
    - Intellectual property

- Legal information
- Financial information
- Human- and non-human-readable
- Data classifications
  - Sensitive
  - Confidential
  - Public
  - Restricted
  - Private
  - Critical
- General data considerations
  - Data states (Data at rest, Data in transit, Data in use)
  - Data sovereignty
  - Geolocation
- Methods to secure data
  - Geographic restrictions
  - Encryption
  - Hashing
  - Masking
  - Tokenization
  - Obfuscation
  - Segmentation
  - Permission restrictions

✓ **3.4 Explain the importance of resilience and recovery in security architecture**

- High availability
  - Load balancing vs. clustering
- Site considerations
  - Hot
  - Cold

- Warm
  - Geographic dispersion
- Platform diversity
- Multi-cloud systems
- Continuity of operations
- Capacity planning
  - People
  - Technology
  - Infrastructure
- Testing
  - Tabletop exercises
  - Fail over
  - Simulation
  - Parallel processing
- Backups
  - On-site/off-site
  - Frequency
  - Encryption
  - Snapshots
  - Recovery
  - Replication
  - Journaling
- Power
  - Generators
  - Uninterruptible power supply (UPS)

1. Nancy wants to adopt a backup strategy that will meet her organization's desires about the amount of data that could be lost in a scenario where a restoration from backup was required and also wants to establish guidelines for how long a restoration should take. What two key objectives should she set?

    A. An RPO and an RTO

    B. An RFBT and an RPO

    C. An RPO and an MTBF

    D. An MTBF and an RFBT

2. John is running an IDS on his network. Users sometimes report that the IDS flags legitimate traffic as an attack. What describes this?

    A. False positive

    B. False negative

    C. False trigger

    D. False flag

3. Enrique is concerned about backup data being infected by malware. The company backs up key servers to digital storage on a backup server. Which of the following would be most effective in preventing the backup data being infected by malware?

    A. Place the backup server on a separate VLAN.

    B. Air gap the backup server.

    C. Place the backup server on a different network segment.

    D. Use a honeynet.

4. What type of system is used to control and monitor power plant power generation systems?

    A. IPG

    B. SEED

    C. SCADA

    D. ICD

5. Geoff wants to establish a contract with a company to have datacenter space that is equipped and ready to go so that he can bring his data to the location in the event of a disaster. What type of disaster recovery site is he looking for?

    A. A hot site

    B. A cold site

    C. A warm site

    D. An RTO site

6. Olivia needs to ensure an IoT device does not have its operating system modified by third parties after it is sold. What solution should she implement to ensure that this does not occur?

    A. Set a default password.

    B. Require signed and encrypted firmware.

    C. Check the MD5sum for new firmware versions.

    D. Patch regularly.

7. Maria is a security engineer with a manufacturing company. During a recent investigation, she discovered that an engineer's compromised workstation was being used to connect to SCADA systems while the engineer was not logged in. The engineer is responsible for administering the SCADA systems and cannot be blocked from connecting to them. What should Maria do to mitigate this threat?

    A. Install host-based antivirus/antimalware software on the engineer's system.

    B. Implement account usage auditing on the SCADA system.

    C. Implement an NIPS on the SCADA system.

    D. Use FDE on the engineer's system.

8. Mike is a security analyst and has just removed malware from a virtual server. What feature of virtualization would he use to return the virtual server to a last known good state?

    A. Sandboxing

    B. Hypervisor

    C. Snapshot

    D. Elasticity

9. Which of the following is not an advantage of a serverless architecture?

    A. It does not require a system administrator.

    B. It can scale as function call frequency increases.

    C. It can scale as function call frequency decreases.

    D. It is ideal for complex applications.

10. Which of the following is the most important benefit from implementing SDN?

    A. It will stop malware.

    B. It provides scalability.

    C. It will detect intrusions.

    D. It will prevent session hijacking.

11. Derek has been asked to implement his organization's service-oriented architecture as a set of microservices. What does he need to implement?

    A. A set of loosely coupled services with specific purposes

    B. A set of services that run on very small systems

    C. A set of tightly coupled services with custom-designed protocols to ensure continuous operation

    D. A set of services using third-party applications in a connected network enabled with industry standard protocols

12. Abigail is responsible for datacenters in a large, multinational company. She has to support multiple datacenters in diverse geographic regions. What would be the most effective way for her to manage these centers consistently across the enterprise?

    A. Hire datacenter managers for each center.

    B. Implement enterprise-wide SDN.

    C. Implement infrastructure as code (IaC).

    D. Automate provisioning and deprovisioning.

13. Naomi wants to secure a real-time operating system (RTOS). Which of the following techniques is best suited to providing RTOS security?

    A. Disable the web browser.

    B. Install a host firewall.

    C. Use secure firmware.

    D. Install antimalware software.

14. Ben has been asked to explain the security implications for an embedded system that his organization is considering building and selling. Which of the following is not a typical concern for embedded systems?

    A. Limited processor power

    B. An inability to patch

    C. Lack of authentication capabilities

    D. Lack of bulk storage

15. Madhuri has configured a backup that will back up all of the changes to a system since the last time that a full backup occurred. What type of backup has she set up?

    A. A snapshot

    B. A full backup

    C. An incremental backup

    D. A differential

16. Devin is building a cloud system and wants to ensure that it can adapt to changes in its workload by provisioning or deprovisioning resources automatically. His goal is to ensure that the environment is not overprovisioned or underprovisioned and that he is efficiently spending money on his infrastructure. What concept describes this?

    A. Vertical scalability

    B. Elasticity

    C. Horizontal scalability

    D. Normalization

17. Nathaniel wants to improve the fault tolerance of a server in his datacenter. If he wants to ensure that a power outage does not cause the server to lose power, what is the first control he should deploy from the following list?

    A. A UPS

    B. A generator

    C. Dual power supplies

    D. Managed power units (PDUs)

18. George is a network administrator at a power plant. He notices that several turbines had unusual ramp-ups in cycles last week. After investigating, he finds that an executable was uploaded to the system control console and caused this. Which of the following would be most effective in preventing this from affecting the SCADA system in the future?

    A. Implement SDN.

    B. Improve patch management.

    C. Place the SCADA system on a separate VLAN.

    D. Implement encrypted data transmissions.

19. Mia is a network administrator for a bank. She is responsible for secure communications with her company's customer website. Which of the following would be the best for her to implement?

    A. SSL

    B. PPTP

    C. IPSec

    D. TLS

20. Nora has rented a building with access to bandwidth and power in case her organization ever experiences a disaster. What type of site has she established?

    A. A hot site

    B. A cold site

    C. A warm site

    D. A MOU site

21. Mike is concerned about data sovereignty for data that his organization captures and maintains. What best describes his concern?

    A. Who owns the data that is captured on systems hosted in a cloud provider's infrastructure?

    B. Can Mike's organization make decisions about data that is part of its service, or does it belong to users?

    C. Is the data located in a country subject to the laws of the country where it is stored?

    D. Does data have rights on its own, or does the owner of the data determine what rights may apply to it?

22. What are the key limiting factors for cryptography on low-power devices?

    A. There are system limitations on memory, CPU, and storage.

    B. The devices cannot support public key encryption due to an inability to factor prime numbers.

    C. There is a lack of chipset support for encryption.

    D. Legal limitations for low-power devices prevent encryption from being supported.

23. Elaine wants to adopt appropriate response and recovery controls for natural disasters. What type of control should she use to prepare for a multi-hour power outage caused by a tornado?

   A. A hot site

   B. A generator

   C. A PDU

   D. A UPS

24. Tim wants to ensure that his web servers can scale horizontally during traffic increases, while also allowing them to be patched or upgraded without causing outages. What type of network device should he deploy?

   A. A firewall

   B. A switch

   C. A horizontal scaler

   D. A network load balancer

25. Nathaniel has deployed the control infrastructure for his manufacturing plant without a network connection to his other networks. What term describes this type of configuration?

   A. Screened subnet

   B. Air gap

   C. Vaulting

   D. A hot aisle

26. Chris is preparing to implement an 802.1X-enabled wireless infrastructure. He knows that he wants to use an Extensible Authentication Protocol (EAP)-based protocol that does not require client-side certificates. Which of the following options should he choose?

   A. EAP-MD5

   B. PEAP

   C. LEAP

   D. EAP-TLS

27. Olivia is implementing a load-balanced web application cluster. Her organization already has a redundant pair of load balancers, but each unit is not rated to handle the maximum designed throughput of the cluster by itself. Olivia has recommended that the load balancers be implemented in an active/active design. What concern should she raise as part of this recommendation?

   A. The load balancer cluster cannot be patched without a service outage.

   B. The load balancer cluster is vulnerable to a denial-of-service attack.

   C. If one of the load balancers fails, it could lead to service degradation.

   D. The load balancer cannot handle the throughput due to having two active nodes.

28. Mark is responsible for managing his company's load balancer and wants to use a load-balancing scheduling technique that will take into account the current server load and active sessions. Which of the following techniques should he choose?

    A. Round-robin

    B. Weighted response time

    C. Least connection

    D. Source IP hashing

29. Ramon is building a new web service and is considering which parts of the service should use Transport Layer Security (TLS). Components of the application include:

    1. Authentication

    2. A payment form

    3. User data, including address and shopping cart

    4. A user comments and reviews section

    Where should he implement TLS?

    A. At points 1 and 2, and 4

    B. At points 2 and 3, and 4

    C. At points 1, 2, and 3

    D. At all points in the infrastructure

30. Which device would most likely process the following rules?

    ```
    PERMIT IP ANY EQ 443
    DENY IP ANY ANY
    ```

    A. NIPS

    B. HIPS

    C. Content filter

    D. Firewall

31. Charles wants to use IPSec and needs to be able to determine the IPSec policy for traffic based on the port it is being sent to on the remote system. Which IPSec mode should he use?

    A. IPSec tunnel mode

    B. IPSec PSK mode

    C. IPSec IKE mode

    D. IPSec transport mode

32. What two connection methods are used for most geofencing applications?

    A. Cellular and GPS

    B. USB and Bluetooth

    C. GPS and Wi-Fi

    D. Cellular and Bluetooth

33. Jason wants to implement a remote access virtual private network (VPN) for users in his organization who primarily rely on hosted web applications. What common VPN type is best suited to this if he wants to avoid deploying client software to his end-user systems?

A. A TLS VPN

B. An RDP (Remote Desktop Protocol) VPN

C. An Internet Control Message Protocol (ICMP) VPN

D. An IPSec VPN

34. Binary data is an example of what type of data?

A. Non-human-readable

B. Encrypted

C. Human-readable

D. Masked

35. What IP address does a load balancer provide for external connections to connect to web servers in a load-balanced group?

A. The IP address for each server, in a prioritized order

B. The load balancer's IP address

C. The IP address for each server in a round-robin order

D. A virtual IP address

36. Matt has enabled port security on the network switches in his building. What does port security do?

A. Filters by MAC address

B. Prevents routing protocol updates from being sent from protected ports

C. Establishes private VLANs

D. Prevents duplicate MAC addresses from connecting to the network

37. Tom is responsible for VPN connections in his company. His company uses IPSec for VPNs. What is the primary purpose of AH in IPSec?

A. Encrypt the entire packet.

B. Encrypt just the header.

C. Authenticate the entire packet.

D. Authenticate just the header.

38. Abigail is responsible for setting up a network-based intrusion prevention system (NIPS) on her network. The NIPS is located in one particular network segment. She is looking for a passive method to get a copy of all traffic to the NIPS network segment so that it can analyze the traffic. Which of the following would be her best choice?

A. Using a network tap

B. Using port mirroring

C. Setting the NIPS on a VLAN that is connected to all other segments

D. Setting up a NIPS on each segment

39. Janice is explaining how IPSec works to a new network administrator. She is trying to explain the role of IKE. Which of the following most closely matches the role of IKE in IPSec?

   A. It encrypts the packet.

   B. It establishes the SAs.

   C. It authenticates the packet.

   D. It establishes the tunnel.

40. Emily manages the IDS/IPS for her network. She has a network-based intrusion prevention system (NIPS) installed and properly configured. It is not detecting obvious attacks on one specific network segment. She has verified that the NIPS is properly configured and working properly. What would be the most efficient way for her to address this?

   A. Implement port mirror/monitor mode for that segment.

   B. Install a NIPS on that segment.

   C. Upgrade to a more effective NIPS.

   D. Isolate that segment on its own VLAN.

41. You are responsible for an e-commerce site. The site is hosted in a cluster. Which of the following techniques would be best in assuring availability?

   A. A VPN concentrator

   B. Aggregate switching

   C. An SSL accelerator

   D. Load balancing

42. Ryan is concerned about the security of his company's web application. Since the application processes confidential data, he is most concerned about data exposure. Which of the following would be the most important for him to implement?

   A. WAF

   B. TLS

   C. NIPS

   D. NIDS

43. Claire has been notified of a zero-day flaw in a web application. She has the exploit code, including a SQL injection attack that is being actively exploited. How can she quickly react to prevent this issue from impacting her environment if she needs the application to continue to function?

   A. Deploy a detection rule to her IDS.

   B. Manually update the application code after reverse-engineering it.

   C. Deploy a fix via her WAF.

   D. Install the vendor-provided patch.

44. Christina wants to ensure that session persistence is maintained by her load balancer. What is she attempting to do?

   A. Ensure that all of a client's requests go to the same server for the duration of a given session or transaction.

   B. Assign the same internal IP address to clients whenever they connect through the load balancer.

   C. Ensure that all transactions go to the current server in a round-robin during the time it is the primary server.

   D. Assign the same external IP address to all servers whenever they are the primary server assigned by the load balancer.

45. Next-generation firewalls include many cutting-edge features. Which of the following is not a common next-generation firewall capability?

   A. Geolocation

   B. IPS and/or IDS

   C. Sandboxing

   D. SQL injection

46. Patrick has been asked to identify a UTM appliance for his organization. Which of the following capabilities is not a common feature for a UTM device?

   A. IDS and or IPS

   B. Antivirus/antimalware

   C. MDM

   D. DLP

47. Theresa implements a network-based IDS. What can she do to traffic that passes through the IDS?

   A. Review the traffic based on rules and detect and alert about unwanted or undesirable traffic.

   B. Review the traffic based on rules and detect and stop traffic based on those rules.

   C. Detect sensitive data being sent to the outside world and encrypt it as it passes through the IDS.

   D. All of the above.

48. Murali is building his organization's container security best practices document and wants to ensure that he covers the most common items for container security. Which of the following is not a specific concern for containers?

   A. The security of the container host

   B. Securing the management stack for the container

   C. Insider threats

   D. Monitoring network traffic to and from the containers for threats and attacks

49. Fred sets up his authentication and authorization system to apply the following rules to authenticated users:

    Users who are not logging in from inside the trusted network must use multifactor authentication.

    Users who have logged in from geographic locations that are more than 100 miles apart within 15 minutes will be denied.

    What type of access control is Fred using?

    A. Geographic restrictions

    B. Time-based logins

    C. Supervisory control

    D. Role-based access

50. Maria is responsible for security at a small company. She is concerned about unauthorized devices being connected to the network. She is looking for a device authentication process. Which of the following would be the best choice for her?

    A. CHAP

    B. Kerberos

    C. 802.11i

    D. 802.1X

51. Jason is considering deploying a network intrusion prevention system (IPS) and wants to be able to detect advanced persistent threats (APTs). What type of IPS detection method is most likely to detect the behaviors of an APT after it has gathered baseline information about normal operations?

    A. Signature-based IPS detections

    B. Heuristic-based IPS detections

    C. Malicious tool hash IPS detections

    D. Anomaly-based IPS detections

52. Mila wants to generate a unique digital fingerprint for a file, and needs to choose between a checksum and a hash. Which option should she choose and why should she choose it?

    A. A hash, because it is unique to the file

    B. A checksum, because it verifies the contents of the file

    C. A hash, because it can be reversed to validate the file

    D. A checksum, because it is less prone to collisions than a hash

53. Mila gives her team a scenario, and then asks them questions about how they would respond, what issues they expect they might encounter, and how they would handle those issues. What type of exercise has she conducted?

    A. A tabletop exercise

    B. A walk-through

    C. A simulation

    D. A drill

54. Jerome needs to explain the key difference between high availability and fault tolerance to his management. What is the major difference between the two?

   A. High availability is designed to avoid service interruptions almost entirely, whereas fault-tolerant environments have minimal service disruptions.

   B. High availability provides services, whereas fault tolerance handles issues.

   C. High availability focuses on data, whereas fault tolerance focuses on infrastructure.

   D. High availability has minimal service interruptions, whereas fault-tolerant environments are designed to avoid service interruptions almost entirely.

55. What element of the CIA triad is geographic dispersion intended to help with?

   A. Confidentiality

   B. Integrity

   C. Assurance

   D. Availability

56. Valentine wants to choose an appropriate obfuscation method to allow her customer service representatives to validate credit card numbers without exposing the full number to the staff member. What obfuscation method should she select?

   A. Masking

   B. Tokenization

   C. Steganography

   D. Hashing

57. Mateo wants to conduct a fail over test for his datacenter. What will he need to do to accomplish this?

   A. Turn off all systems in his datacenter.

   B. Simulate what would occur during a datacenter outage.

   C. Force a fail over using his network or other systems.

   D. Cause an outage of a critical system.

58 Casey's organization has proprietary information models that they use to analyze the market that they operate in. What data type best describes this information?

   A. Trade secret

   B. Regulated

   C. Financial information

   D. Public information

59. Nicole wants to protect her SMTP email exchanges from being read by others while on the wire. What can she implement to protect SMTP?

   A. SPF

   B. TLS

   C. DKIM

   D. EXIF

60. Brandon deploys a server in a VLAN used for IoT devices. He then creates firewall rules that allow users in a system administration network to SSH to that server so that they can manage systems in the protected network segment. What type of solution has Brandon deployed?

   A. A UTM

   B. A jump server

   C. An ICS server

   D. A VPN

61. What protocol is commonly used to allow for secured tunnels between corporate networks through untrusted networks?

   A. RTOS

   B. SHA-1

   C. IPSec

   D. RSA

62. Asher's organization has created a list of potential customers based on an analysis of their use of their site, buying habits, and ability to spend money on new products. What type of data is a list like this?

   A. Legal information

   B. Trade secrets

   C. Regulated data

   D. Classified data

63. Eva wants to deploy a network security device that will provide firewall services as well as IPS and email filtering. Which device should she deploy?

   A. A UTM

   B. An FWSM

   C. A WAF

   D. An ELB

64 Ramon wants to conduct an exercise for his organization with the least potential to cause disruption. Which of the following testing methodologies is least likely to cause potential issues with service delivery?

   A. Tabletop exercises

   B. Fail over exercises

   C. Simulation exercises

   D. Parallel processing exercises

65. Cassandra is considering transitioning from an on-premises to a hybrid cloud environment. Which of the following concerns will she need to consider that would not have been required in a single on-premises datacenter previously?

   A. RPOs

   B. Data sovereignty

   C. RTOs

   D. Power resilience

66. Nick wants to protect Microsoft Excel files in transit across a network. Which of the following is not a method he could use to protect data in transit?

A. TLS

B. VPN

C. File encryption

D. Disk encryption

67. Dani wants to protect HTTP traffic that is sent from SCADA devices on her network to a cloud-hosted controller. The devices don't natively support an HTTPS connection. What could she do to transparently protect the data?

A. Set up a VPN connection from each SCADA device to the remote server.

B. Set up a TLS-enabled proxy between the devices and the server.

C. Set up SD-WAN.

D. Install X.509 certificates on each SCADA device.

68. Selah's organization is conducting a simulation exercise. Which of the following is not a common element of a simulation?

A. Testing of notification processes

B. Testing of procedures

C. Testing of fail over capabilities

D. Testing of communication systems

69. Which of the following is not a common practice used to secure data in transit?

A. Encryption

B. TLS

C. Geolocation

D. VPN

70. Olivia wants to deploy a new firewall. What type of firewall should she select if the ability to operate at layer 7 is important to her?

A. A WAF

B. An NGFW

C. A stateful firewall

D. A packet filter

71. Marcellus wants to ensure that his organization has sufficient capacity to handle the failure of a web server. What type of technology could he deploy to ensure that individual web server failures are handled gracefully without using an overly complex solution?

A. Platform diversity

B. A multi-cloud system

C. A load balancer

D. A warm site

72. What failure mode is typically preferred for in-line network taps?

  A. Fail-open

  B. Fail over

  C. Fail-closed

  D. Fail-reset

73. What key network technology is the core of an SASE implementation?

  A. TLS

  B. VLANs

  C. IPSec

  D. SD-WAN

74. Mikayla wants to prevent unauthorized users from plugging network devices into her wired network. What control would be most effective for this if she needs Ethernet jacks to be available in publicly accessible spaces for her staff to plug devices in as they move around the facility, but also wants to ensure those devices are secure?

  A. NAC

  B. Port security

  C. IPS

  D. Jump servers

75. Mark's organization is preparing to move to an infrastructure as code model. He's worried about what to do if a change in code causes issues. What common IaC practice will help the most with this?

  A. Threat modeling

  B. Least privilege

  C. Version control

  D. Artifact signing

76. The company that Alex works for is preparing to adopt a platform as a service tool for their customer relationship management needs. Alex knows that third-party vendors are responsible for some, but not all, security in a PaaS environment. Which of the following is the PaaS vendor responsible for?

  A. Network security

  B. Endpoint security

  C. User account security

  D. Application security

77. Nick's organization houses tape-based backups for their critical data in their primary datacenter. What resilience issue could result in the event of a major disaster?

  A. The tapes may not have been validated and might not be able to be restored.

  B. A single disaster could destroy both the facility and the tapes.

  C. The tapes may not last for the expected lifetime of the backups.

  D. Tapes are relatively slow and may not allow for timely restoration.

78. Charles wants to adopt an encryption tool. What encryption standard should he look for the tool to support to ensure that he is using a current secure standard to protect his data?

    A. AES-512

    B. AES-256

    C. AES-128

    D. AES-192

79. Which of the following is not a common security concern with real-time operating systems?

    A. Inability to install security tools

    B. Lack of updates or patches

    C. Likelihood of malware infection

    D. Vulnerability concerns

80. Chris wants to create a token to substitute for data in a database. Which of the following is not a common attribute for tokens?

    A. They don't have exploitable meaning themselves.

    B. They are easily reversible to identify the original data, even without the tokenization scheme.

    C. They frequently rely on one-way hash functions.

    D. Tokens must be mapped to matching original data.

81. Pete's organization has had a system fail and Pete wants to recover from backup. Which of the following backup methods will typically result in the fastest restoration timeframe?

    A. Snapshots

    B. Replication

    C. Journaling

    D. Tape backup

82. Henry accesses a database server from his workstation. What data state best describes the data while it is on the network?

    A. Data at rest

    B. Data in use

    C. Data on the wire

    D. Data in transit

83. Theresa's organization operates in multiple countries. She knows that there are different laws that apply to her organization's use of data in each country they operate in. What concept describes this?

    A. Obfuscation

    B. Legal hold

    C. Data sovereignty

    D. Geographic restrictions

84. Hrant is deploying a network tap that supports an IPS for monitoring. If he wants to ensure that his organization's security remains the same even if the tap and IPS fails, and prefers downtime to a lack of monitoring, what type of failure mode and monitoring deployment should he select?

 A. In-line, fail-closed

 B. In-line, fail-open

 C. Tap, fail-closed

 D. Tap, fail-open

85. Troy wants to physically isolate a device. What does he need to do to accomplish this?

 A. Move it to a secure VLAN.

 B. Implement 802.1X.

 C. Create a physical air gap.

 D. Unplug the device from power and the network.

86. Yasmine wants to ensure that her organization has appropriate connectivity as part of their infrastructure design for their primary site. Which of the following concerns should she review to ensure that physical disasters do not disable her company's operations?

 A. Service provider path diversity

 B. Ensuring both fiber and copper connectivity are used

 C. Implementing SD-WAN

 D. Geographic dispersion

87. Carlos uses a remote desktop tool to connect to a server through a firewall that protects his organization's database servers. He then uses software on the server to manage the database servers. What type of solution is Carlos using?

 A. A network tap

 B. SASE

 C. SD-WAN

 D. A jump server

88. Alaina is planning how to staff her warm site in the case of a natural disaster that disables her primary site. What concern is most likely to impact her capacity planning for staff in this scenario?

 A. Whether staff will be able to reach the site

 B. Whether staff will be impacted by the disaster

 C. Whether the site will be impacted by the disaster

 D. Whether generator fuel will be available

89. Which of the following is not a common type of incident response exercise?

 A. Drills

 B. Simulations

 C. Tabletop

 D. Walk-throughs

90. Jack wants to ensure that files have not changed. What technique can he use to compare current versions of the files to an original copy?

   A. Encryption.

   B. Check the file size.

   C. Check the file metadata.

   D. Compare hashes of the files.

91. Yuri wants to use an off-site backup location. What challenge can off-site backup locations create for organizations?

   A. It is difficult to validate the integrity of the backups.

   B. Retrieving the backups may slow down recovery.

   C. The backups cannot be easily updated.

   D. Off-site backups may be impacted by the same disaster.

92. Which of the following is a common part of technology capacity planning for resilience?

   A. Cross-training staff

   B. Using load balancers

   C. Using multiple geographically diverse datacenters

   D. Deploying uninterruptible power supplies

93. Which of the following data types best describes data covered by the European Union's GDPR?

   A. Trade secrets

   B. Intellectual property

   C. Regulated data

   D. Legal information

94. What is the biggest downside of using journaling as part of a backup restoration process?

   A. Larger volumes of data may be lost.

   B. The time it takes to restore from a journal.

   C. Journals cannot be encrypted for security.

   D. Journaling does not support live databases.

95. Jill wants to design her organization for high availability. Which of the following design elements best supports power resilience for a high-availability environment for an on-site datacenter?

   A. Using generators

   B. Using UPS systems

   C. Using UPS systems backed up by generators

   D. Using a warm site on a separate power grid

96. Valerie is concerned that the data obfuscation technique that her organization is using to ensure customer data is not visible to staff members who do not need to see it for their jobs may be vulnerable to client-side tampering. Which of the following techniques is most likely to be vulnerable to client-side tampering resulting in de-obfuscation?

A. Masking

B. Tokenization

C. Encryption

D. Hashing

97. Which of the following is not a commonly used business data classification?

A. Sensitive

B. Confidential

C. Top Secret

D. Public

98. Malia is reviewing potential considerations for her ICS deployment. Which of the following is typically not a consideration that Malia can control or change for embedded devices?

A. Ease of deployment

B. Patch availability

C. Risk transference

D. Compute

99. What layer is Layer 7 in the OSI model?

A. The physical layer

B. The application layer

C. The transport layer

D. The session layer

100. Network connected devices built into washing machines, microwaves, and other household appliances are examples of what type of network device?

A. ICS

B. SCADA

C. Embedded systems

D. Virtualization

101. What term best describes a set of loosely coupled, fine-grained services that communicate via lightweight protocols, allowing organizations to easily build new services without additional dependencies or infrastructure?

A. Containerization

B. IoT

C. Software-defined infrastructure

D. Microservices

102. What type of backup is done to update a full backup with changes made after the full backup occurred?

   A. Incremental

   B. Partial

   C. Daily

   D. Snapshots

103. As part of an exercise for her organization, Sharon calls a team member and asks them to check the status of critical systems. The team member, who is aware of the exercise, does not actually validate the systems but responds that specific systems are down based on the scenario. What type of exercise is Sharon most likely part of?

   A. A tabletop exercise

   B. A fail over exercise

   C. A simulation exercise

   D. A parallel processing test

104. Zhuri wants to ensure that her organization's datacenter remains online during an extended power outage. What power resilience option is best suited to extended outages?

   A. Generators

   B. Solar

   C. UPS

   D. PDUs

105. Cesar wants to ensure that his organization's SCADA and ICS devices remain secure. What is the most effective way to ensure that network attacks cannot impact his operation's critical infrastructure?

   A. Separate VLANs

   B. TLS

   C. Physical isolation

   D. SDN

106. What key data element is used to validate which systems are allowed to use Ethernet ports where port security is enabled?

   A. Their IP address

   B. The network card's manufacturer

   C. The user's password

   D. Their MAC address

107. Which of the following is not a common concern for extended power outages where generators are providing power to a datacenter they were designed to support during outages?

   A. Fuel availability

   B. Generator maintenance

   C. Generator capacity

   D. Physical redundancy

108. Rafael wants to protect his data from being accessed by unauthorized users. Which of the following is not well suited to preventing attacks by insider threats?

   A. Encryption

   B. Geographic restrictions

   C. Tokenization

   D. Permission restrictions

109. Malia wants to protect data in use. Which technique is not a good solution to ensuring that data in use is protected?

   A. Encryption

   B. Control access to the data

   C. Hashing data

   D. Limiting where data is processed

110. Lisa wants to ensure that her organization's datacenter can properly handle short power disruptions and temporary undervoltage events. What power resilience solution is best suited to her needs?

   A. Generators

   B. UPS systems

   C. PDUs

   D. Solar power

111. Valentine has containerized her applications. What will not be part of the container?

   A. The operating system

   B. The application

   C. Needed libraries

   D. Configuration files

112. Jaime wants to manage connectivity, including both MPLS and broadband Internet services, for her organization. What technology should she select to enable her to manage multiple connection types using a software-based control system?

   A. SASE

   B. SDN

   C. SD-WAN

   D. VSAN

113. Cassandra wants to deploy a network security device that can detect and stop attacks. What type of network security device should she use if she wants to stop attacks based on behaviors and threat feeds?

   A. An IDS

   B. A proxy server

   C. An IPS

   D. A jump server

114. Contracts, NDAs, and SOWs are all examples of what type of data?

    A. Legal information

    B. Trade secrets

    C. Regulated

    D. Financial

115. Jackson has deployed a next-generation firewall. Which of the following features is most likely to help him prevent new attacks without having to create individual rules to stop them?

    A. Threat feeds

    B. Application awareness

    C. Deep packet inspection

    D. High throughput

116. Which of the following is not provided by an IPSec VPN?

    A. Confidentiality

    B. Authentication

    C. Availability

    D. Integrity

117. What technologies are most frequently used to help enforce geographic restrictions?

    A. Wi-Fi and Bluetooth

    B. GPS and Wi-Fi

    C. GPS and encryption

    D. DNS and GPS

118. In the cloud responsibility matrix, what three areas is the provider always responsible for in an IaaS environment?

    A. Data, devices, and accounts

    B. Identities, applications, and network controls

    C. Operating systems, applications, and physical hosts

    D. Datacenters, networks, and physical hosts

119. Kirk's organization contracts with a cloud service provider. Kirk is concerned about third-party vendors that his cloud service provider uses. How can Kirk best address these concerns?

    A. Through direct contracts with the third-party vendors

    B. By requiring regular audits of third-party vendors

    C. Through the contract with his cloud service provider

    D. By performing vulnerability scans of the third-party vendors

120. Frankie wants to connect two remote sites so that they appear to be on the same local network segment. What type of solution is best suited to this requirement if she wants traffic sent between the locations to be secure despite traversing the public Internet?

A. Establish a VLAN between the two locations.

B. Use TLS to encapsulate each service provided between the two locations.

C. Set up a VPN tunnel between the two locations.

D. Reclassify the data as public and send the data as normal.

121. Which of the following best describes replication as a resilience strategy?

A. It makes a complete backup copy of live data that can be restored from media if needed, then journaled changes can be replayed to catch up to the moment of failure.

B. It creates a continuous copy of live data either asynchronously or synchronously.

C. It uses a series of snapshots to provide disaster recovery for virtual machines.

D. It requires high-speed media to keep up with live data.

122. Sade works for a large organization that wants to ensure that their connectivity is properly secured. What type of security device should she select if throughput and advanced security capabilities are both important factors in selection?

A. A UTM device

B. An NGFW device

C. A WAF

D. A proxy server

123. Barb's organization has a recovery point objective of 6 hours. At least how often should Barb conduct incremental backups to meet this RPO?

A. Once every hour

B. Once every 6 hours

C. Once every 12 hours

D. Once a day

124. Geoff's data is stored in a cloud service's database. What data state is the data in?

A. It is at rest.

B. It is in transit.

C. It is in use.

D. It is sovereign.

125. Tara's web development team has written code that allows sensitive customer information to be hidden from users who do not have the right permissions. When individuals who do not have the proper rights to view sensitive information use the application, the data is displayed as a series of asterisks:

Account number: ****-******-**

What data obfuscation technique has Tara's team employed to help protect her organization's data?

- **A.** Encryption
- **B.** Data classification
- **C.** Hashing
- **D.** Masking

126. Ed is building a continuity of operations plan (COOP) for his organization. What three scenarios does a COOP address?

- **A.** Loss of personnel, loss of systems, loss of availability
- **B.** Natural disasters, human-made disasters, mistakes or errors
- **C.** Loss of access to a facility, damage to a facility, natural disasters
- **D.** Loss of access to a facility, loss of personnel, and loss of services

127. Which of the following properly describes a SPAN port configured on a switch or router for monitoring?

- **A.** Active and inline
- **B.** Passive and inline
- **C.** Active and a monitor
- **D.** Passive and a monitor

128. Renee wants to choose a control that will protect her organization against SQL injection attacks. Which of the following is likely to be the most effective control for attacks that are announced without prior notice and that require a very quick response?

- **A.** Web application penetration testing
- **B.** A WAF
- **C.** Static code review
- **D.** SASE

129. Maria wants to deploy a web application firewall that will stop new attacks against her organization. What should she do to make sure that her web application firewall rules are as current as possible?

- **A.** Manually add new rules based on email updates.
- **B.** Deploy rules based on the OWASP Top 10.
- **C.** Subscribe to a threat feed and deploy rules based on the feed.
- **D.** Subscribe to the vendor's managed WAF rule service.

130. Gary's organization provides Wi-Fi network connectivity for customers, employees, and IoT building automation devices. What should he implement if he needs each of the three groups to have access to the same resources at times without the three groups of users being able to connect to each other?

- **A.** Fail-closed networks
- **B.** Security zones
- **C.** Data classification
- **D.** Fail-open networks

131. Kendra is designing a web application infrastructure and wants to use a load balanced cluster. Which of the following considerations is not directly addressed by using a load balancer?

    A. Availability

    B. Responsiveness

    C. Scalability

    D. Risk transference

132. Angie is logging in to a server. What data state is her authentication information in?

    A. Data in storage

    B. Data at rest

    C. Data in validation

    D. Data in use

133. Patrick wants to deploy a virtual private networking (VPN) technology that is as easy for end users to use as possible. What type of VPN should he deploy?

    A. An IPSec VPN

    B. An SSL/TLS VPN

    C. An HTML5 L2TP VPN

    D. An SAML VPN

134. Servers in redundant clusters are typically not placed in the same server rack in case of a water leak or other issue that impacts the rack. What consideration describes this type of design decision?

    A. Connectivity

    B. Geographic dispersion

    C. Device placement

    D. Attack surface

135. Akio is considering a decentralized model to manage her organization's multiple datacenters. What key advantage could this provide for her organization?

    A. Reductions in cost

    B. Increased resilience

    C. Reductions in complexity

    D. Increased complexity

136. Kim's organization operates a cloud-hosted IaaS environment and uses an infrastructure as code model to deploy systems. A vulnerability has been found in the web server software that the organization uses. What process should her team use to remediate the vulnerability?

    A. Manually patch each web server.

    B. Update the underlying base image for the servers and redeploy the web servers.

    C.   Add the patch to the code repository for the servers, transfer the load to other servers, and replace unpatched servers with patched versions by reinstantiating them.

    D.   Update the underlying base image, drain the load from working servers, and replace with new instances.

137. Jason's organization wants to classify data that the organization regularly uses. The data is customer data, and could cause harm to the company if it was released. Which of the following data classifications best fits this type of data?

    A.   Confidential

    B.   Restricted

    C.   Critical

    D.   Public

138. Which of the following is not a common consideration for legacy devices?

    A.   Cost

    B.   Ease of recovery

    C.   Patch availability

    D.   Inability to patch

139. Which of the following is not a common service provided by a UTM device?

    A.   Firewall

    B.   SD-WAN

    C.   IPS

    D.   Antivirus/antimalware

140. Nick wants to enable remote access for his organization and wants users to have a simple experience without significant overhead when connecting. What type of solution should he implement?

    A.   A TLS VPN

    B.   SD-WAN

    C.   SDN

    D.   An IPSec VPN

141. Jaime has deployed smart lighting and thermostats to her new buildings. What technique will have the largest impact if she wants to harden the devices?

    A.   Applying an industry standard baseline configuration

    B.   Moving the devices to a separate security zone

    C.   Fully patching the devices when they are deployed

    D.   Vulnerability scanning, then remediating the devices on a regular basis

142. Chuck has deployed a cloud-based security environment that combines SD-WAN, zero trust, cloud access security broker (CASB), and firewall services to replace traditional VPNs. What sort of service has Chuck deployed?

A. SaaS

B. SASE

C. SONET

D. SCM

143. Lucca wants to fully validate his organization's hot site's ability to perform as needed in the event of an outage. What type of testing should he run to ensure that the hot site is completely tested as though an actual disaster has occurred?

A. Fail over

B. Simulation

C. Tabletop

D. Parallel processing

144. Christina's organization has purchased a remote facility that they intend to use in case of a major disaster. The building has basic utilities, including Internet connectivity, but no other preparation has been made. What type of site is this?

A. A warm site

B. A hot site

C. A cold site

D. A dispersion site

145. Which of the following is not commonly part of a tabletop exercise?

A. A discussion of roles

B. A discussion of likely actions

C. Simulated calls to resources

D. A guided conversation

146. Helen has deployed both Cisco and Juniper routers in her organization to ensure that a vulnerability in one vendor's products does not result in a complete outage of her organization. What is this type of design called?

A. Platform agnostic

B. Platform diversity

C. Multi-cloud

D. Parallel processing

147. Kaito has deployed a system that accepts traffic from web browsers and distributes it to systems based on the number of connections that each server has. He has assigned each server a rating based on how powerful it is. Each time a new request comes in, requests are sent to the system with the lowest number of connections after taking into account the relative rating of each server. What type of load balancing is Kaito using?

A. Source IP hashing

B. Resource-based

C. Weighted least connection

D. Round-robin

148. Jessica has port-scanned a multifunction printer and has discovered that the device provides services on ports 80, 443, 515, and 9100. Which of the following terms best describes this?

A. The printer's attack surface

B. The printer's security zone

C. The printer's scalability

D. The printer's resilience

149. Geoff is considering whether to deploy on-premises infrastructure or cloud-hosted infrastructure. His most important requirements in order are:

Ease of scalability

Management overhead

Cost

If Geoff wants to run a containerized service that can handle very large loads, what model should he select?

A. SaaS

B. PaaS

C. IaaS

D. On-premises

150. Bank account numbers, credit card numbers, and invoice information are all examples of what type of data?

A. Intellectual property

B. Financial

C. Public

D. Trade secrets

151. John has deployed three servers that all respond as though they're the same device to provide service he runs. What term best describes this configuration?

A. Load balancing

B. Clustering

C. Fail-open

D. Fail-closed

152. Alaina's organization is required to comply with the PCI DSS standard. What type of data is she most likely dealing with?

    A. Intellectual property

    B. Trade secrets

    C. Financial information

    D. Regulated information

153. Theresa wants to back up her virtualization environment. What backup scheme is most frequently used for virtual machines?

    A. Journaling

    B. Snapshots

    C. Replication

    D. Grandfather/Father/Son

154. What is the primary reason an organization might choose a parallel processing testing scenario over a fail over testing scenario?

    A. Parallel processing allows for more throughput.

    B. Fail over does not fully test redundant systems.

    C. Fail over requires organizations to create a significant issue to allow for the fail over to occur.

    D. Parallel processing typically handles issues without outages.

155. Brent wants to monitor traffic using an IPS. He needs to prevent attack traffic from impacting his datacenter and wants to minimize the amount of traffic that the IPS device has to filter. Where should he place the device to best match these requirements based on the following figure?

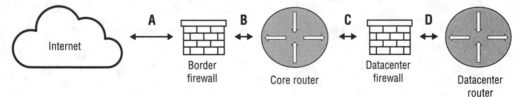

    A. Position A

    B. Position B

    C. Position C

    D. Position D

156. Marco is preparing to brief his organization's leadership about challenges that may result from adopting a hybrid cloud design. Which of the following is the primary concern that he should highlight?

    A. Jurisdictional challenges

    B. Increased complexity

    C. Increased cost

    D. Regulatory challenges

157. Julia is designing her organization's external connectivity as part of infrastructure capacity planning. She knows that the organization typically uses approximately 7 gigabits per second of connectivity from their primary site. Julia has the following connectivity options, what should she select?

A. A 10 Gbps primary and a 5 Gbps secondary connection

B. A 5 Gbps primary and a 5 Gbps secondary connection

C. A 100 Gbps primary and a 10 Gbps secondary connection

D. A 10 Gbps primary and a 10 Gbps secondary connection

158. Daria wants to establish a disaster recovery site that can immediately take over for her organization's primary datacenter in the event of a disaster. What sort of site should she build out?

A. A hot site

B. A warm site

C. A cold site

D. A dispersion site

159. Cathy wants to build a high-availability infrastructure for her midsize company's headquarters building network. Which of the following is not a common element for a high-availability network core?

A. Redundant routers

B. Generators

C. Geographic dispersion

D. Multiple connectivity providers

160. The GDPR, HIPAA, FERPA, and the GLBA all impact what type of data?

A. Intellectual property

B. Classified data

C. Regulated data

D. Trade secrets

161. Jacob is concerned about attacks against his virtual machines that would target the hypervisor. What term describes this type of attack?

A. VM escape

B. Hypervisor escalation

C. VM shell attacks

D. Container breaches

162. Jill knows that IPSec uses a number of common protocols. Which of the following is not a key IPSec protocol?

A. AH

B. ISA

C. ESP

D. IKE

163. An IDS is an example of what type of network device?

    A. Active

    B. Air gapped

    C. Fail-closed

    D. Passive

164. Why can't hashing be used to securely store data that needs to be accessed in its original form?

    A. Hashing takes too long to reverse.

    B. Hashing uses symmetric encryption.

    C. Hashing uses a one-way function.

    D. Hashing uses asymmetric encryption.

165. Jerome wants to use an obfuscation method to protect data in his database. His organization works with sensitive customer data and does not want to run the risk of that data being exposed via their web application, but still wants to use the rest of their customer data in the application. What obfuscation process or tool should he use to ensure that the data can be matched to customers while remaining secure?

    A. Use a steganographic program to modify the data, then use that data for the web application.

    B. Use a masking algorithm to completely mask the data, then use a single database.

    C. Tokenize the data and use the tokenized data in a database set up for the web application.

    D. Hash the data in the original database, then use the database for the web application.

166. Jules is planning a SCADA deployment for her organization. Which of the following is most likely to be a major concern over the lifetime of the SCADA system?

    A. Cost

    B. Scalability

    C. Inability to patch

    D. Availability

167. Susan has deployed a network using software-defined networking. What part of her network is most critical to secure as part of this architecture?

    A. The routers

    B. The switches

    C. The SDN controller

    D. The SD-WAN connections

168. The ability to obtain third-party support for a device or system is an example of which consideration?

    A. Availability

    B. Risk transference

    C. Compute

    D. Responsiveness

169. Yarif wants to create security zones in his network. Which of the following technologies is best suited to doing this based on roles and user identities?

   A. NAC and VLANs

   B. 802.1X and containerization

   C. SDN and MAC address filtering

   D. SD-WAN and VLANs

170. Elle is conducting an exercise for her organization and wants to run an exercise that is as close to an actual event as possible. What type of event should she run to help her organization get this type of real-world practice?

   A. A simulation

   B. A tabletop exercise

   C. A walk-through

   D. A wargame

171. What security advantage does a serverless model provide?

   A. Cost savings

   B. No need to patch infrastructure

   C. No vulnerable functions

   D. No need to log events

172. Laura is planning for continuity of operations. What personnel concern should she plan to handle for her hot site in the event of a large-scale natural disaster in the area where her primary facility is?

   A. Lack of facility power

   B. Inability to authenticate personnel

   C. Insider threats

   D. Lack of available personnel

173. Which of the following is not a common means of enforcing segmentation on a network?

   A. ACLs

   B. VLANs

   C. Firewalls

   D. Air gaps

174. Binary files are an example of what type of data?

   A. Human-readable

   B. Restricted

   C. Non-human-readable

   D. Confidential

175. Erin uses a journaling backup scheme for her database. After a system outage she needs to restore from her backups. If her organization uses a daily backup scheme that runs at midnight, and the issue occurred at 2 a.m., how much data is Erin likely to lose?

A. Two hours of data

B. One day and two hours of data

C. One week of data

D. Little or no data

176. Which of the following is typically used to manage an ICS?

A. SDN

B. SCADA

C. Active Directory

D. SD-WAN

177. Maria's organization uses a cloud backup provider and performs encrypted backups for their IaaS infrastructure and data. If the data needs to be restored, what will Maria need to do?

A. Ask the vendor for the recovery key.

B. Provide the recovery key.

C. Restore the recovery key from backup and use it.

D. Generate a new recovery key and restore from backup.

178. What two major differences separate backups and replication?

A. Replication is periodic, but does not require restoration processes before data is able to be used.

B. Backups are continuous but require restoration processes before data is able to be used.

C. Backups are periodic and do not require restoration before data is able to be used

D. Replication is continuous and does not require restoration processes before data is able to be used.

179. Erin's organization uses a backup schedule that creates a full backup once a week, then creates differential backups once a day on all other days. If the full backup was done four days ago, and Erin needs to restore from it, how many backups will she have to restore in total?

A. One

B. Two

C. Three

D. Four

180. What advantage does an IPSec VPN have over a TLS VPN when protecting traffic?

A. It operates at the network layer rather than the transport layer.

B. It supports stronger encryption types.

C. It does not rely on tunneling.

D. It does not provide advantages over TLS, and TLS should be used instead when possible.

181. Vera wants to manage multiple commercial Internet services for her organization to ensure connectivity. What technology should she select to manage and maintain this?

   A. SASE

   B. SDN

   C. IPSec

   D. SD-WAN

182. Katie is considering deploying embedded devices. Which of the following limitations is most commonly associated with embedded devices?

   A. Compute limitations

   B. Responsiveness limitations

   C. Availability issues

   D. Cost issues

183. What term best describes intangible assets created by staff members of a company like designs and concepts?

   A. Trade secrets

   B. Sensitive data

   C. Intellectual property

   D. Trademarks

184. Jaime is concerned about the volume of logs that her new application may create. What capacity planning item should she focus on?

   A. Compute

   B. Power

   C. Storage

   D. People

185. Henry's organization relies on remote workers in multiple regions. Each region has an office where workers work part-time, and the organization's core services rely on a variety of SaaS providers. What network model best describes this type of usage model?

   A. Centralized

   B. Decentralized

   C. On-premises

   D. Logically segmented

186. Tom wants to use geographic restrictions as part of his security design. What type of tool is commonly used to manage geographic restrictions for mobile devices?

   A. EDR

   B. MDM

   C. 802.1X

   D. VPNs

187. Jack has deployed a load balancer for his organization. When a new connection is made, the load balancer assigns the connection to the next server in a list, moving through the list over time as it distributes connections. What type of load balancing algorithm is in use?

    A. Capacity-based

    B. Round-robin

    C. Least load

    D. User pinning

188. What is the best way to protect data at rest?

    A. Classification

    B. Segmentation

    C. Encryption

    D. Hashing

189. Kathleen wants to monitor her datacenter's environmental status. What solution should she invest in to meet this need?

    A. An HVAC system

    B. UPS systems

    C. Environmental sensor appliances

    D. A load balancer

190. Danielle's organization has experienced a total power outage. The datacenter is currently running on its UPS. What concern should Danielle have if the UPS is her organization's only power resilience control?

    A. The generator may not start.

    B. The UPS batteries may run out before the outage is over.

    C. The generator may run out of fuel in a long outage.

    D. The UPS may not handle the surge when power resumes.

191. Valerie wants to connect one of her company's remote locations back to the organization's main network. What type of solution can she use for a persistent connection between the networks that will securely tunnel data across a commodity Internet connection?

    A. A TLS VPN

    B. A web proxy

    C. An IPSec VPN

    D. An 802.1X tunnel

192. What does port security use to determine what machines or devices can connect to a network port?

    A. A list of userIDs

    B. A multifactor token code for each user

    C. A list of MAC addresses

    D. A list of IP addresses

193. Valerie wants to provide remote access to her organization's applications to users who are traveling or working remotely. She wants to ensure that users have a secure way to work with organizational data, but also wants to provide the simplest and easiest secure means of access. What should Valerie implement?

- **A.** An IPSec VPN
- **B.** A jump server
- **C.** A TLS VPN
- **D.** An SD-WAN controller

194. Which of the following is not available as part of a snapshot?

- **A.** The underlying hypervisor's configuration
- **B.** The virtual machine's power state
- **C.** The virtual machine's memory state
- **D.** The virtual machine's disks

195. What role does geolocation play in considerations related to data?

- **A.** It determines if data is at rest.
- **B.** It impacts data sovereignty concerns.
- **C.** It determines if data is in use.
- **D.** It determines the data's criticality.

196. Dane works for an energy provider that manages devices throughout a large geographic region using a control system that monitors and controls power infrastructure. The system operates from a central command center and uses cellular, broadband, and other connectivity methods to connect devices to the control center. What type of system is Dane's company using?

- **A.** RTOS
- **B.** Embedded systems
- **C.** IoT
- **D.** SCADA

197. Jorge wants to assess his organization's Internet-accessible attack surface. Which of the following methods is most likely to provide a complete understanding?

- **A.** Open source intelligence (OSINT) review
- **B.** Threat feeds
- **C.** Vulnerability scanning
- **D.** Penetration testing

198. Brent has deployed multiple brands of IoT devices across his organization to ensure that if an issue with one type of device or device vendor occurs others will still function. What is the largest concern he should address with this design that focuses on platform diversity?

- **A.** Complexity of management
- **B.** Availability
- **C.** Resilience
- **D.** Ease of deployment

199. Mark wants to protect data in use. Which of the following options should he select to protect data in use?

A. Hashing

B. A secure enclave

C. Containerization

D. Tunneling data

200. The following figure shows two simplified design concepts. What security architecture is shown in Model 2?

Model 1
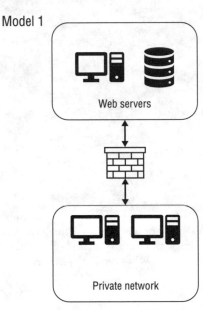
Web servers

Private network

Model 2
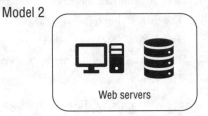
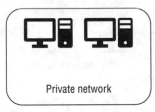
Web servers

Private network

A. Logical segmentation

B. Air gapped

C. Serverless

D. On-premises

201. Masking, encryption, and tokenization are all examples of what?

A. Data encryption methods

B. Data classification methods

C. Data obfuscation methods

D. Data tagging methods

202. Liana wants to deploy a load balancer and wants to ensure that if a session is interrupted users have the highest chance of being reconnected to the same server. What algorithm should she select?

A. Round-robin

B. IP hash

C. Weighted least connection

D. Resource-based

203. Kyle wants to authenticate users who plug into his network, then assign them to a VLAN based on their role. What technology could he use to do this?

A. 802.1X

B. Port security

C. VLAN tagging

D. EAP

204. Using VLANs is an example of what type of segmentation?

A. Air gapping

B. Logical segmentation

C. Physical segmentation

D. Physical isolation

205. Lucca has deployed an SD-WAN controller. Which of the following types of connectivity will not typically be managed with an SD-WAN solution?

A. Wi-Fi

B. MPLS

C. Broadband

D. LTE

206. The information that is found on Kirk's company's Internet-facing website needs to be classified as part of his organization-wide data classification process. What classification should he apply?

A. Public

B. Internal

C. Confidential

D. Restricted

207. Jim wants to design his network for high availability (HA). What first step is commonly taken in HA designs for networks?

A. Configure a hot site.

B. Purchase redundant hardware.

C. Identify single points of failure.

D. Implement clustering.

208. Theo wants to ensure that artifacts in his IaC environment have not been tampered with. What should he require as part of his version control check-in system?

    A. Artifact signing

    B. Container image scanning

    C. Dependency checks

    D. Static analysis

209. Angela is considering using encryption as part of the security controls applied to her backups. In the event of a major disaster, what concern should she address about having encrypted backups?

    A. Time to decrypt the backups

    B. Cost of encrypting the backups

    C. Ensuring the key is recoverable in a disaster

    D. The amount of space that the encryption adds to the backups

210. Which of the following is not a common security issue with IoT devices?

    A. Insecure communication

    B. Data leaks

    C. Ransomware

    D. Device vulnerabilities

211. Jack is worried about outages that may disrupt service from his IaaS vendor's cloud environment. Which of the following options provides the greatest likelihood of avoiding service disruptions from an outage from his current IaaS vendor?

    A. Deploying to multiple availability zones (AZs)

    B. Deploying to multiple regions

    C. Deploying to multiple cloud vendors

    D. Requiring contractual terms around uptime

212. Chuck is responsible for an on-site datacenter. He wants to ensure that the datacenter has appropriate network connectivity to ensure resilience and performance. Which of the following will have the greatest impact on meeting that requirement?

    A. Contract for a higher bandwidth connection from a single vendor.

    B. Deploy a UPS.

    C. Contract with two separate network service providers.

    D. Install a generator.

213. Ben has grouped his data based on use cases and sensitivity and has applied different security practices based on those groupings. What data security technique is he using?

    A. Segmentation

    B. Obfuscation

    C. Masking

    D. Tokenization

214. Monica wants to prevent users from sharing data and cares more about control than flexibility. What type of access control model is best suited to ensuring central control over file access?

   A. Role BAC

   B. DAC

   C. MAC

   D. Rule BAC

215. Tara is monitoring web traffic to her organization's website from a local public library and notices that all of the logins seem to come from the same IP address. She knows that the library provides multiple workstations for public use as well as public Wi-Fi. What type of network appliance might be in use?

   A. A jump server

   B. A proxy server

   C. A load balancer

   D. A DLP system

216. What three responsibilities are typically shared in PaaS environments according to the cloud responsibility matrix?

   A. Identity infrastructure, applications, and network controls

   B. Data, devices, and accounts

   C. Physical hosts, physical networks, and physical datacenters

   D. Operating systems, applications, and data

217. Marco wants to build a set of services for financial transactions for his company. The services need to be capable of scaling quickly to very large numbers of transactions, and need to be able to operate without major dependencies on other components of the architecture. What architecture should he select to best meet these needs?

   A. Containerization

   B. Virtualization

   C. Microservices

   D. SCADA

218. What major advantage does a monitoring port have over an inline network tap?

   A. It is easier to configure.

   B. It has higher performance.

   C. It is more secure.

   D. If it fails, it will not impact the network.

219. Which of the following is not typically true of embedded systems?

    A. They provide the ability to install additional software.

    B. They have a long lifespan.

    C. They have memory and CPU constraints.

    D. They are not designed for end-user configuration and control.

220. Naomi wants to be able to easily move her application between cloud service providers and to use automation to allow for deployment of the application. What technology best allows for applications to be bundled with the libraries and other components they need without requiring additional overhead like an operating system?

    A. Containerization

    B. Snapshots

    C. Embedded systems

    D. Segmentation

221. What term describes the right of countries to pass laws that control the use of data within their borders?

    A. Data classification

    B. Treaty obligations

    C. Treaty rights

    D. Data sovereignty

222. Ian's organization uses a root certificate authority that only allows certificate signing locally. All certificates are transferred via USB drives because the system is not connected to the network. What type of security design is in use?

    A. Port security

    B. An air gapped design

    C. Defense-in-depth

    D. A zero-trust design

223. The company that Jayne works for has moved their web application infrastructure to a serverless model. Jayne's security team has informed her that they believe the application is undergoing a large-scale resource exhaustion-based distributed denial-of-service attack. If the application is running in Microsoft's serverless Azure environment, what is the most critical concern Jayne should have about the attack?

    A. Loss of data

    B. Cost of the resource usage

    C. Inability to review logs

    D. Vulnerabilities in the application

224. Elaine knows that prior to 802.1X enabling a port, only EAP traffic is allowed through the port. What does this permit?

A. Vulnerability scanning

B. Authentication

C. Port scanning

D. System security status validation

225. Tristan deploys the network device shown in the following figure. The organization's web browsing traffic is directed through it and the traffic is filtered as described in the image. What type of network appliance is shown?

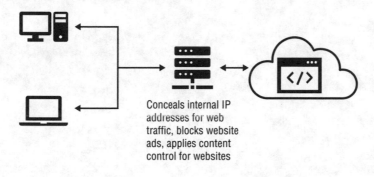

Conceals internal IP addresses for web traffic, blocks website ads, applies content control for websites

A. A web application firewall

B. A proxy server

C. A jump server

D. A load balancer

226. Parvati wants to configure her web application firewall to prevent basic SQL injection attacks. Which of the following rules could she use to accomplish this?

A. Filter out all OR statements.

B. Filter out single quotes.

C. Block all SQL statements.

D. Block all AND statements.

Chapter

4

Domain 4.0: Security Operations

THE COMPTIA SECURITY+ EXAM SY0-701 TOPICS COVERED IN THIS CHAPTER INCLUDE THE FOLLOWING:

✓ **4.1 Given a scenario, apply common security techniques to computing resources**

- Secure baselines
  - Establish
  - Deploy
  - Maintain
- Hardening targets
  - Mobile devices
  - Workstations
  - Switches
  - Routers
  - Cloud infrastructure
  - Servers
  - ICS/SCADA
  - Embedded systems
  - RTOS
  - IoT devices
- Wireless devices
  - Installation considerations
    - Site surveys
    - Heat maps
- Mobile solutions
  - Mobile device management (MDM)

- Deployment models
  - Bring your own device (BYOD)
  - Corporate-owned, personally enabled (COPE)
  - Choose your own device (CYOD)
- Connection methods
  - Cellular
  - Wi-Fi
  - Bluetooth
- Wireless security settings
  - Wi-Fi Protected Access 3 (WPA3)
  - AAA/Remote Authentication Dial-In User Service (RADIUS)
  - Cryptographic protocols
  - Authentication protocols
- Application security
  - Input validation
  - Secure cookies
  - Static code analysis
  - Code signing
- Sandboxing
- Monitoring

✓ **4.2 Explain the security implications of proper hardware, software, and data asset management**

- Acquisition/procurement process
- Assignment/accounting
  - Ownership
  - Classification
- Monitoring/asset tracking
  - Inventory
  - Enumeration

- Disposal/decommissioning
  - Sanitization
  - Destruction
  - Certification
  - Data retention

✓ **4.3 Explain various activities associated with vulnerability management**

- Identification methods
  - Vulnerability scan
  - Application security
    - Static analysis
    - Dynamic analysis
    - Package monitoring
  - Threat feed
    - Open-source intelligence (OSINT)
    - Proprietary/third-party
    - Information-sharing organization
    - Dark web
  - Penetration testing
  - Responsible disclosure program
    - Bug bounty program
  - System/process audit
- Analysis
  - Confirmation
    - False positive
    - False negative
  - Prioritize
  - Common Vulnerability Scoring System (CVSS)
  - Common Vulnerability Enumeration (CVE)
  - Vulnerability classification

- Exposure factor
- Environmental variables
- Industry/organizational impact
- Risk tolerance
- Vulnerability response and remediation
  - Patching
  - Insurance
  - Segmentation
  - Compensating controls
  - Exceptions and exemptions
- Validation of remediation
  - Rescanning
  - Audit
  - Verification
- Reporting

✓ **4.4 Explain security alerting and monitoring concepts and tools**

- Monitoring computing resources
  - Systems
  - Applications
  - Infrastructure
- Activities
  - Log aggregation
  - Alerting
  - Scanning
  - Reporting
  - Archiving
  - Alert response and remediation/validation
    - Quarantine
    - Alert tuning

- Tools
    - Security Content Automation Protocol (SCAP)
    - Benchmarks
    - Agents/agentless
    - Security information and event management (SIEM)
    - Antivirus
    - Data loss prevention (DLP)
    - Simple Network Management Protocol (SNMP) traps
    - NetFlow
    - Vulnerability scanners

✓ **4.5 Given a scenario, modify enterprise capabilities to enhance security**

- Firewall
    - Rules
    - Access lists
    - Ports/protocols
    - Screened subnets
- IDS/IPS
    - Trends
    - Signatures
- Web filter
    - Agent-based
    - Centralized proxy
    - Universal Resource Locator (URL) scanning
    - Content categorization
    - Block rules
    - Reputation
- Operating system security

- Attestation
- Access controls
  - Mandatory
  - Discretionary
  - Role-based
  - Rule-based
  - Attribute-based
  - Time-of-day restrictions
  - Least privilege
- Multifactor authentication
  - Implementations
    - Biometrics
    - Hard/soft authentication tokens
    - Security keys
  - Factors
    - Something you know
    - Something you have
    - Something you are
    - Somewhere you are
- Password concepts
  - Password best practices
    - Length
    - Complexity
    - Reuse
    - Expiration
    - Age
  - Password managers
  - Passwordless
- Privileged access management tools

- Just-in-time permissions
- Password vaulting
- Ephemeral credentials

✓ **4.7 Explain the importance of automation and orchestration related to secure operations**

- Use cases of automation and scripting
  - User provisioning
  - Resource provisioning
  - Guard rails
  - Security groups
  - Ticket creation
  - Escalation
  - Enabling/disabling services and access
  - Continuous integration and testing
  - Integrations and Application programming interfaces (APIs)
- Benefits
  - Efficiency/time saving
  - Enforcing baselines
  - Standard infrastructure configurations
  - Scaling in a secure manner
  - Employee retention
  - Reaction time
  - Workforce multiplier
- Other considerations
  - Complexity
  - Cost
  - Single point of failure
  - Technical debt
  - Ongoing supportability

✓ **4.8 Explain appropriate incident response activities**

- Process

    - Preparation

    - Detection

    - Analysis

    - Containment

    - Eradication

    - Recovery

    - Lessons learned

- Training

- Testing

    - Tabletop exercise

    - Simulation

- Root cause analysis

- Threat hunting

- Digital forensics

    - Legal hold

    - Chain of custody

    - Acquisition

    - Reporting

    - Preservation

    - E-discovery

✓ **4.9 Given a scenario, use data sources to support an investigation**

- Log data

    - Firewall logs

    - Application logs

    - Endpoint logs

    - OS-specific security logs

- IPS/IDS logs
- Network logs
- Metadata
- Data sources
  - Vulnerability scans
  - Automated reports
  - Dashboards
  - Packet captures

1. John wants to harden his organization's routers. If there are no currently known vulnerabilities or issues with the device, which of the following hardening options will provide the biggest benefit?

   A. Moving their administrative interfaces to a protected VLAN

   B. Disabling unnecessary services

   C. Installing the most current patch level for the OS

   D. Enabling SNMP-based logging

2. Jackson is reviewing his organization's logs and discovers multiple new user accounts created after business hours using administrative credentials. What term describes searching for potential issues like this?

   A. IoC creation

   B. Threat hunting

   C. Root cause analysis

   D. Eradication

3. Cynthia is concerned about attacks against an application programming interface (API) that her company provides for its customers. What should she recommend to ensure that the API is only used by customers who have paid for the service?

   A. Require authentication.

   B. Install and configure a firewall.

   C. Filter by IP address.

   D. Install and use an IPS.

4. Greg wants to gain admission to a network which is protected by a network access control (NAC) system that recognized the hardware address of systems. How can he bypass this protection?

   A. Spoof a legitimate IP address.

   B. Conduct a denial-of-service attack against the NAC system.

   C. Use MAC cloning to clone a legitimate MAC address.

   D. None of the above.

5. Melissa's organization has deployed a firewall that uses three interfaces to provide services. The first interface connects to the Internet, the second to a network where the organization's web servers reside, and the third to a secured network where the organization's workstations are connected. What type of firewall architecture has Melissa's organization deployed?

   A. An ACL

   B. A screened subnet

    C. A binary firewall

    D. A multihomed, multiroute NGFW

6. CVE is an example of what type of feed?

    A. A threat intelligence feed

    B. A vulnerability feed

    C. A critical infrastructure listing feed

    D. A critical virtualization exploits feed

7. Amanda scans a Red Hat Linux server that she believes is fully patched and discovers that the Apache version on the server is reported as vulnerable to an exploit from a few months ago. When she checks to see if she is missing patches, Apache is fully patched. What has occurred?

    A. A false positive

    B. An automatic update failure

    C. A false negative

    D. An Apache version mismatch

8. Telnet, RSH, and FTP are all examples of what?

    A. File transfer protocols

    B. Unsecure protocols

    C. Core protocols

    D. Open ports

9. What term describes data that is collected from publicly available sources that can be used in an intelligence context?

    A. OPSEC

    B. OSINT

    C. STIX

    D. IntCon

10. Patrick has subscribed to a commercial threat intelligence feed that is only provided to subscribers who have been vetted and who pay a monthly fee. What industry term is used to refer to this type of threat intelligence?

    A. Proprietary threat intelligence

    B. OSINT

    C. ELINT

    D. Corporate threat intelligence

11. Susan receives $10,000 for reporting a vulnerability to a vendor who participates in a program to identify issues. What term is commonly used to describe this type of payment?

    A. A ransom

    B. A zero-day disclosure

    C. A bug bounty

    D. A payday

12. Ben runs a vulnerability scan using up-to-date definitions for a system that he knows has a vulnerability in the version the web server is running. The vulnerability scan does not show that issue when he reviews the report. What has Ben encountered?

    A. A silent patch

    B. A missing vulnerability update

    C. A false negative

    D. A false positive

13. Angela reviews bulletins and advisories to determine what threats her organization is likely to face. What type of activity is this associated with?

    A. Incident response

    B. Threat hunting

    C. Penetration testing

    D. Vulnerability scanning

14. Frank is using the cloud hosting service's web publishing service rather than running his own web servers. Where will Frank need to look to review his logs to see what types of traffic his application is creating?

    A. Syslog

    B. Apache logs

    C. The cloud service's web logs

    D. None of the above

15. The following graphic shows a report from an OpenVAS vulnerability scan. What should Charles do first to determine the best fix for the vulnerability shown?

ID: f64e51b3-7448-4e95-a6a4-cb11861360b5
Created: Mon Apr 27 00:10:10 2020
Modified: Mon Apr 27 00:10:10 2020
Owner: securityplus

Result: PHP-CGI-based setups vulnerability when parsing query string parameters from php files.

Vulnerability	✱	Severity	⊙	QoD	Host	Location	Actions
PHP-CGI-based setups vulnerability when parsing query string parameters from php files.		7.5 (High)		95%	10.0.2.4	80/tcp	

Summary
PHP is prone to an information-disclosure vulnerability.

Vulnerability Detection Result
Vulnerable url: http://10.0.2.4/cgi-bin/php

Impact
Exploiting this issue allows remote attackers to view the source code of files in the context of the server process. This may allow the attacker to obtain sensitive information and to run arbitrary PHP code on the affected computer. Other attacks are also possible.

Solution
Solution type: ▢ VendorFix

PHP has released version 5.4.3 and 5.3.13 to address this vulnerability. PHP is recommending that users upgrade to the latest version of PHP.

Vulnerability Insight
When PHP is used in a CGI-based setup (such as Apache's mod_cgid), the php-cgi receives a processed query string parameter as command line arguments which allows command-line switches, such as -s, -d or -c to be passed to the php-cgi binary, which can be exploited to disclose source code and obtain arbitrary code execution.

An example of the -s command, allowing an attacker to view the source code of index.php is below:

http://example.com/index.php?-s

Vulnerability Detection Method
Details: PHP-CGI-based setups vulnerability when parsing query string parameters from ph... (OID: 1.3.6.1.4.1.25623.1.0.103482)

Version used: 2019-11-08T10:10:55+0000

References

CVE: CVE-2012-1823, CVE-2012-2311, CVE-2012-2336, CVE-2012-2335

A. Disable PHP-CGI.

B. Upgrade PHP to version 5.4.

C. Review the vulnerability descriptions in the CVEs listed.

D. Disable the web server.

16. Ian runs a vulnerability scan, which notes that a service is running on TCP port 8080. What type of service is most likely running on that port?

A. SSH

B. RDP

C. MySQL

D. HTTP

17. Carolyn runs a vulnerability scan of a network device and discovers that the device is running services on TCP ports 22 and 443. What services has she most likely discovered?

A. Telnet and a web server

B. FTP and a Windows file share

C. SSH and a web server

D. SSH and a Windows file share

18. Susan is responsible for application development in her company. She wants to have all web applications tested before they are deployed live. She wants to use a test system that is identical to the live server. What is this called?

A. A production server

B. A development server

C. A test server

D. A predeployment server

19. Alexandra is preparing to run automated security tests against the code that developers in her organization have completed. Which environment is she most likely to run them in if the next step is to deploy the code to production?

A. Development

B. Test

C. Staging

D. Production

20. Chris wants to limit who can use an API that his company provides and be able to log usage of the API uniquely to each organization that they provide access to. What solution is most often used to do this?

A. Firewalls with rules for each company's public IP address

B. User credentials for each company

C. API keys

D. API passwords

21. Angela wants to ensure that IoT devices in her organization have a secure configuration when they are deployed and that they are ready for further configuration for their specific purposes. What term is used to describe these standard configurations used as part of her configuration management program?

A. A baseline configuration

B. An essential settings list

C. A preinstall checklist

D. A setup guide

22. Chris is following the CIS Windows Server 2022 benchmark and notices that it recommends that Computer Configuration\Policies\Administrative Templates\Windows Components\Search\Allow indexing of encrypted files is set to disabled. What potential issue would this help to prevent?

    A. Data leakage

    B. Denial of service

    C. Insecure service

    D. Dark web access

23. Elizabeth wants to implement a cloud-based authorization system. Which of the following protocols is she most likely to use for that purpose?

    A. OpenID

    B. Kerberos

    C. SAML

    D. OAuth

24. Tony wants to implement a biometric system for entry access in his organization. Which of the following systems is likely to be most accepted by members of his organization's staff?

    A. Fingerprint

    B. Retina

    C. Iris

    D. Voice

25. What is the primary threat model against static codes used for multifactor authentication?

    A. Brute force

    B. Collisions

    C. Theft

    D. Clock mismatch

26. Nadine's organization stores and uses sensitive information, including Social Security numbers. After a recent compromise, she has been asked to implement technology that can help prevent this sensitive data from leaving the company's systems and networks. What type of technology should Nadine implement?

    A. Stateful firewalls

    B. OEM

    C. DLP

    D. SIEM

27. Social login, the ability to use an existing identity from a site like Google, Facebook, or a Microsoft account, is an example of which of the following concepts?

    A. Federation

    B. AAA

    C. Privilege creep

    D. Identity and access management

28. Charles has configured his multifactor system to require both a PIN and a password. How many effective factors does he have in place once he presents both of these and his username?

    A. One

    B. Two

    C. Three

    D. Four

29. Naomi is designing her organization's wireless network and wants to ensure that the design places access points in areas where they will provide optimum coverage. She also wants to plan for any sources of RF interference as part of her design. What should Naomi do first?

    A. Contact the FCC for a wireless map.

    B. Conduct a site survey.

    C. Disable all existing access points.

    D. Conduct a port scan to find all existing access points.

30. Charlene wants to provision her organization's standard set of marketing information to mobile devices throughout her organization. What MDM feature is best suited to this task?

    A. Application management

    B. Remote wipe

    C. Content management

    D. Push notifications

31. Denny wants to deploy antivirus for his organization and wants to ensure that it will stop the most malware. What deployment model should Denny select?

    A. Install antivirus from the same vendor on individual PCs and servers to best balance visibility, support, and security.

    B. Install antivirus from more than one vendor on all PCs and servers to maximize coverage.

    C. Install antivirus from one vendor on PCs and from another vendor on the server to provide a greater chance of catching malware.

    D. Install antivirus only on workstations to avoid potential issues with server performance.

32. Madhuri's web application converts numbers that are input into fields by specifically typing them and then applies strict exception handling. It also sets a minimum and maximum length for the inputs that it allows and uses predefined arrays of allowed values for inputs like months or dates. What term describes the actions that Madhuri's application is performing?

    A. Buffer overflow prevention

    B. String injection

    C. Input validation

    D. Schema validation

33. You're outlining your plans for implementing a wireless network to upper management. What wireless security standard should you adopt if you don't want to use enterprise authentication but want to provide secure authentication for users that doesn't require a shared password or passphrase?

    A. WPA3

    B. WPA

    C. WPA2

    D. WEP

34. You are the chief security officer (CSO) for a large company. You have discovered malware on one of the workstations. You are concerned that the malware might have multiple functions and might have caused more security issues with the computer than you can currently detect. What is the best way to test this malware?

    A. Leave the malware on that workstation until it is tested.

    B. Place the malware in a sandbox environment for testing.

    C. It is not important to analyze or test it; just remove it from the machine.

    D. Place the malware on a honeypot for testing.

35. Isaac is reviewing his organization's secure coding practices document for customer-facing web applications and wants to ensure that their input validation recommendations are appropriate. Which of the following is not a common best practice for input validation?

    A. Ensure validation occurs on a trusted server.

    B. Validate all client-supplied data before it is processed.

    C. Validate expected data types and ranges.

    D. Ensure validation occurs on a trusted client.

36. Isaac wants to prevent corporate mobile devices from being used outside of his company's buildings and corporate campus. What mobile device management (MDM) capability should he use to allow this?

    A. Patch management

    B. IP filtering

    C. Geofencing

    D. Network restrictions

37. Sophia wants to test her company's web application to see if it is handling business logic properly. Which testing method would be most effective for this?

    A. Static code analysis

    B. Fuzzing

    C. Baselining

    D. Version control

38. Endpoint detection and response has three major components that make up its ability to provide visibility into endpoints. Which of the following is not one of those three parts?

   A. Data search

   B. Malware analysis

   C. Data exploration

   D. Suspicious activity detection

39. Carl has been asked to set up access control for a server. The requirements state that users at a lower privilege level should not be able to see or access files or data at a higher privilege level. What access control model would best fit these requirements?

   A. MAC

   B. DAC

   C. RBAC

   D. SAML

40. Jack wants to deploy a network access control (NAC) system that will stop systems that are not fully patched from connecting to his network. If he wants to have full details of system configuration, antivirus version, and patch level, what type of NAC deployment is most likely to meet his needs?

   A. Agentless, preadmission

   B. Agent-based, preadmission

   C. Agentless, postadmission

   D. Agent-based, postadmission

41. Eric wants to provide company-purchased devices, but his organization prefers to provide end users with choices among devices that can be managed and maintained centrally. What mobile device deployment model best fits this need?

   A. BYOD

   B. COPE

   C. CYOD

   D. VDI

42. Claire is concerned about an attacker getting information regarding network devices and their configuration in her company. Which protocol should she implement that would be most helpful in mitigating this risk while providing management and reporting about network devices?

   A. RADIUS

   B. TLS

   C. SNMPv3

   D. SFTP

43. Eric is responsible for his organization's mobile device security. They use a modern mobile device management (MDM) tool to manage a BYOD mobile device environment. Eric needs to ensure that the applications and data that his organization provides to users of those mobile devices remain as secure as possible. Which of the following technologies will provide him with the best security?

    A. Storage segmentation

    B. Containerization

    C. Full-device encryption

    D. Remote wipe

44. Tara is concerned about staff in her organization sending email with sensitive information like customer Social Security numbers (SSNs) included in it. What type of solution can she implement to help prevent inadvertent exposures of this type of sensitive data?

    A. FDE

    B. DLP

    C. S/MIME

    D. POP3S

45. Mason is responsible for security at a company that has traveling salespeople. The company has been using ABAC for access control to the network. Which of the following is an issue that is specific to ABAC and might cause it to incorrectly reject logins?

    A. Geographic location.

    B. Wrong password.

    C. Remote access is not allowed by ABAC.

    D. Firewalls usually block ABAC.

46. Darrell is concerned that users on his network have too many passwords to remember and might write down their passwords, thus creating a significant security risk. Which of the following would be most helpful in mitigating this issue?

    A. Multifactor authentication

    B. SSO

    C. SAML

    D. LDAP

47. Frank is a security administrator for a large company. Occasionally, a user needs to access a specific resource that they don't have permission to access. Which access control methodology would be most helpful in this situation?

    A. Mandatory access control (MAC)

    B. Discretionary access control (DAC)

    C. Role-based access control

    D. Rule-based access control

48. Oliver needs to explain the access control scheme used by both the Windows and Linux filesystems. What access control scheme do they implement by default?

A. Role-based access control

B. Mandatory access control

C. Rule-based access control

D. Discretionary access control

49. Stefan just became the new security officer for a university. He is concerned that student workers who work late on campus could try to log in with faculty credentials. Which of the following would be most effective in preventing this?

A. Time-of-day restrictions

B. Usage auditing

C. Password length

D. Credential management

50. Chloe has noticed that users on her company's network frequently have simple passwords made up of common words. Thus, they have weak passwords. How could Chloe best mitigate this issue?

A. Increase minimum password length.

B. Have users change passwords more frequently.

C. Require password complexity.

D. Implement single sign-on (SSO).

51. A companywide policy is being created to define various security levels. Which of the following systems of access control would use documented security levels like Confidential or Secret for information?

A. RBAC

B. MAC

C. DAC

D. BAC

52. Users in your network are able to assign permissions to their own shared resources. Which of the following access control models is used in your network?

A. DAC

B. RBAC

C. MAC

D. ABAC

53. Cynthia is preparing a new server for deployment, and her process includes turning off unnecessary services, setting security settings to match her organization's baseline configurations, and installing patches and updates. What is this process known as?

- **A.** OS hardening
- **B.** Security uplift
- **C.** Configuration management
- **D.** Endpoint lockdown

54. John is performing a port scan of a network as part of a security audit. He notices that the domain controller is using secure LDAP. Which of the following ports would lead him to that conclusion?

- **A.** 53
- **B.** 389
- **C.** 443
- **D.** 636

55. Which of the following access control methods grants permissions based on the user's position in the organization?

- **A.** MAC
- **B.** RBAC
- **C.** DAC
- **D.** ABAC

56. Gary is designing his cloud infrastructure and needs to provide a firewall-like capability for the virtual systems he is running. Which of the following cloud capabilities acts like a virtual firewall?

- **A.** Security groups
- **B.** Dynamic resource allocation
- **C.** VPC endpoints
- **D.** Instance awareness

57. Henry is an employee at Acme Company. The company requires him to change his password every three months. He has trouble remembering new passwords, so he keeps switching between just two passwords. Which policy would be most effective in preventing this?

- **A.** Password complexity
- **B.** Password history
- **C.** Password length
- **D.** Multifactor authentication

58. Tracy wants to limit when users can log in to a stand-alone Windows workstation. What should Tracy do to meet this requirement?

- **A.** Set login time restrictions.
- **B.** Turn the system off automatically during hours it should not be used.

    C. Hire security guards to monitor the space.

    D. Disable remote login during the hours the system should not be used.

59. Lucas is looking for an XML-based open standard for exchanging authentication information. Which of the following would best meet his needs?

    A. SAML

    B. OAuth

    C. RADIUS

    D. NTLM

60. Murali is preparing to acquire data from various devices and systems that are targets in a forensic investigation. Which of the following devices is the least volatile according to the order of volatility?

    A. Backups

    B. CPU cache

    C. Local disk

    D. RAM

61. What phase of the incident response process should be placed at point A in the following image?

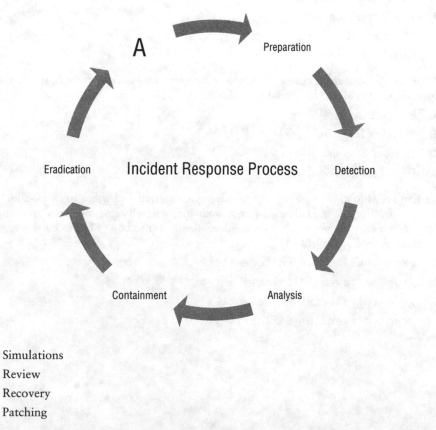

    A. Simulations

    B. Review

    C. Recovery

    D. Patching

62. Brent wants to use a tool to help him analyze malware and attacks and wants to cover a broad range of tactics and tools that are used by adversaries. Which of the following is broadly implemented in technical tools and covers techniques and tactics without requiring a specific order of operations?

A. The CIS Benchmark

B. The Dark Web Analysis Project

C. The MITRE ATT&CK framework

D. The CVSS standard

63. Ted needs to preserve a server for forensic purposes. Which of the following should he not do?

A. Turn the system off to ensure that data does not change.

B. Remove the drive while the system is running to ensure that data does not change.

C. Leave the machine connected to the network so that users can continue to use it.

D. All of the above.

64. Jessica wants to review the network traffic that her Windows system has sent to determine if a file containing sensitive data was uploaded from the system. What Windows log file can she use to find this information?

A. The application log

B. The network log

C. The security log

D. None of the above

65. What term is used to describe the documentation trail for control, analysis, transfer, and final disposition of evidence for digital forensic work?

A. Evidence log

B. Paper trail

C. Chain of custody

D. Digital footprint

66. Nathan needs to know how many times an event occurred and wants to check a log file for that event. Which of the following `grep` commands will tell him how many times the event happened if each occurrence is logged independently in the `logfile.txt` log file, and uses a unique event ID, `event101`?

A. `grep logfile.txt -n 'event101'`

B. `grep -c 'event101' logfile.txt`

C. `grep logfile.txt -c 'event101'`

D. `grep -c event101 -i logfile.txt`

67. Eric wants to determine how much bandwidth was used during a compromise and where the traffic was directed to. What technology can he implement before the event to help him see this detail and allow him to have an effective bandwidth monitoring solution?

   A. A firewall

   B. NetFlow

   C. Packetflow

   D. A DLP

68. Naomi has acquired an image of a drive as part of a forensic process. She wants to ensure that the drive image matches the original. What should she create and record to validate this?

   A. A third image to compare to the original and new image

   B. A directory listing to show that the directories match

   C. A photographic image of the two drives to show that they match

   D. A hash of the drives to show that their hashes match

69. Ryan has been asked to run Nessus on his network. What type of tool has he been asked to run?

   A. A fuzzer

   B. A vulnerability scanner

   C. A WAF

   D. A protocol analyzer

70. Michelle wants to check for authentication failures on a RedHat Linux–based system. Where should she look for these event logs?

   A. /var/log/auth.log

   B. /var/log/fail

   C. /var/log/events

   D. /var/log/secure

71. Nelson has discovered malware on one of the systems he is responsible for and wants to test it in a safe environment. Which of the following tools is best suited to that testing?

   A. strings

   B. scanless

   C. Cuckoo

   D. Sn1per

72. Lucca wants to review metadata related to a JPEG file. What will he need to do to review it?

   A. Change the JPEG to a GIF to see the metadata.

   B. Download the metadata file from the original author.

   C. Use a metadata viewer.

   D. Analyze the hash of the file.

73. Jason is conducting a forensic investigation and has retrieved artifacts in addition to drives and files. What should he do to document the artifacts he has acquired?

  A. Image them using dd and ensure that a valid MD5sum is generated.

  B. Take a picture of them, label them, and add them to the chain-of-custody documentation.

  C. Contact law enforcement to properly handle the artifacts.

  D. Engage legal counsel to advise him how to handle artifacts in an investigation.

74. Joseph is writing a forensic report and wants to be sure he includes appropriate detail. Which of the following would not typically be included while discussing analysis of a system?

  A. Validation of the system clock's time settings

  B. The operating system in use

  C. The methods used to create the image

  D. A picture of the person from whom the system was taken

75. Elaine wants to determine what websites a user has recently visited using the contents of a forensically acquired hard drive. Which of the following locations would not be useful for her investigation?

  A. The browser cache

  B. The browser history

  C. The browser's bookmarks

  D. Session data

76. Susan has discovered evidence of a compromise that occurred approximately five months ago. She wants to conduct an incident investigation but is concerned about whether the data will exist. What policy guides how long logs and other data are kept in most organizations?

  A. The organization's data classification policy

  B. The organization's backup policy

  C. The organization's retention policy

  D. The organization's legal hold policy

77. Alaina sets her antimalware solution to move infected files to a safe storage location without removing them from the system. What type of setting has she enabled?

  A. Purge

  B. Deep-freeze

  C. Quarantine

  D. Retention

78. A senior vice president in the organization that Chuck works in recently lost a phone that contained sensitive business plans and information about suppliers, designs, and other important materials. After interviewing the vice president, Chuck finds out that the phone did not have a passcode set and was not encrypted, and that it could not be remotely wiped.

What type of control should Chuck recommend for his company to help prevent future issues like this?

A. Use containment techniques on the impacted phones.

B. Deploy a DLP system.

C. Deploy an MDM system.

D. Isolate the impacted phones.

79. Charles wants to ensure that the forensic work that he is doing cannot be repudiated. How can he validate his attestations and documentation to ensure nonrepudiation?

A. Encrypt all forensic output.

B. Digitally sign the records.

C. Create a MD5 checksum of all images.

D. All of the above.

80. Megan needs to conduct a forensic investigation of a virtual machine (VM) hosted in a VMware environment as part of an incident response effort. What is the best way for her to collect the VM?

A. As a snapshot using the VMware built-in tools

B. By using dd to copy the VM to an external drive

C. By using dd to copy the VM to an internal drive

D. By using a forensic imaging device after removing the server's drives

81. Which of the following groups is not typically part of an incident response team?

A. Law enforcement

B. Security analysts

C. Management

D. Communications staff

82. Bob needs to block Secure Shell (SSH) traffic between two security zones. Which of the following Linux `iptables` firewall rules will block that traffic from the 10.0.10.0/24 network to the system the rule is running on?

A. `iptables -A INPUT -p tcp --dport 22 -i eth0 -s 10.0.10.0/24 -j DROP`

B. `iptables -D OUTPUT -p udp -dport 21 -i eth0 -s 10.0.10.255 -j DROP`

C. `iptables -A OUTPUT -p udp --dport 22 -i eth0 -s 10.0.10.255 -j BLOCK`

D. `iptables -D INPUT -p udp --dport 21 -I eth0 -s 10.0.10.0/24 -j DROP`

83. A Windows system that Maria is responsible for has been experiencing service outages. The outages correspond to processes run on another system in the datacenter, and Maria believes that unexpected traffic may be sent to the Windows system. Which of the following data sources should Maria use to best understand what is happening?

    A. Perform a packet capture.

    B. Enable a network firewall.

    C. Use SIEM logs.

    D. Perform a forensic drive copy.

84. Amanda's organization does not currently have an incident response plan. Which of the following reasons is not one she should present to management in support of creating one?

    A. It will prevent incidents from occurring.

    B. It will help responders react appropriately under stress.

    C. It will prepare the organization for incidents.

    D. It may be required for legal or compliance reasons.

85. Which of the following scenarios is least likely to result in data recovery being possible?

    A. A file is deleted from a disk.

    B. A file is overwritten by a smaller file.

    C. A hard drive is quick-formatted.

    D. A disk is degaussed.

86. Henry records a video of the removal of a drive from a system as he is preparing for a forensic investigation. What is the most likely reason for Henry to record the video?

    A. To meet the order of volatility

    B. To establish guilt beyond a reasonable doubt

    C. To ensure data preservation

    D. To document the chain of custody and provenance of the drive

87. Charlene wants to set up a tool that can allow her to see all the systems a given IP address connects to and how much data is sent to that IP by port and protocol. Which of the following tools is not suited to meet that need?

    A. IPFIX

    B. IPSec

    C. sFlow

    D. NetFlow

88. Tools like PRTG and Cacti that monitor SNMP information are used to provide what type of information for an incident investigation?

    A. Authentication logs

    B. Bandwidth monitoring

    C. System log information

    D. Email metadata

89. The company Charles works for has recently had a stolen company cell phone result in a data breach. Charles wants to prevent future incidents of a similar nature. Which of the following mitigation techniques would be the most effective?

A. Enable FDE via MDM.

B. A firewall change.

C. A DLP rule.

D. A new URL filter rule.

90. What incident response step is missing from point X in the following image?

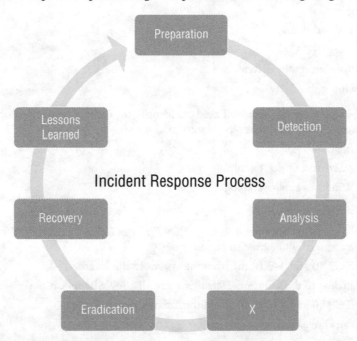

A. Business continuity

B. Containment

C. Response

D. Discovery

91. Jill has been asked to perform data recovery due to her forensic skills. What should she tell the person asking to perform data recovery to give her the best chance of restoring lost files that were accidentally deleted?

A. Immediately reboot using the reset switch to create a lost file memory dump.

B. Turn off Secure Delete so that the files can be more easily recovered.

C. Do not save any files or make any changes to the system.

D. All of the above.

92. Veronica has completed the recovery phase of her organization's incident response plan. What phase should she move into next?

   A. Preparation

   B. Lessons learned

   C. Recovery

   D. Documentation

93. Michelle has been asked to sanitize a number of drives to ensure that sensitive data is not exposed when systems are removed from service. Which of the following is not a valid means of sanitizing hard drives?

   A. Physical destruction

   B. Degaussing

   C. Quick-formatting the drives

   D. Zero-wiping the drives

94. Bart is investigating an incident, and needs to identify the creator of a Microsoft Office document. Where would he find that type of information?

   A. In the filename

   B. In the Microsoft Office log files

   C. In the Windows application log

   D. In the file metadata

95. Nathaniel wants to allow Chrome through the Windows Defender firewall. What type of firewall rule change will he need to permit this?

   A. Allow TCP 80 and 443 traffic from the system to the Internet.

   B. Add Chrome to the Windows Defender Firewall allowed applications.

   C. Allow TCP 80 and 443 traffic from the Internet to the system.

   D. All of the above.

96. What key forensic tool used to generate reports about what happened relies on correctly set system clocks to work properly?

   A. Disk hashing

   B. Timelining

   C. Forensic disk acquisition

   D. File metadata analysis

97. Valerie is writing her organization's forensic playbooks and knows that the state that she operates in has a data breach notification law. Which of the following key items is most likely to be influenced by that law?

   A. Whether Valerie calls the police for forensic investigation help

   B. The maximum amount of time until she has to notify customers of sensitive data breaches

   C. The certification types and levels that her staff have to maintain

   D. The maximum number of residents that she can notify about a breach

98. As part of a breach response, Naomi discovers that Social Security numbers (SSNs) were sent in a spreadsheet via email by an attacker who gained control of a workstation at her company's headquarters. Naomi wants to ensure that more SSNs are not sent from her environment. What type of mitigation technique is most likely to prevent this while allowing operations to continue in as normal a manner as possible?

    A. Antimalware installed at the email gateway

    B. A firewall that blocks all outbound email

    C. A DLP rule blocking SSNs in email

    D. An IDS rule blocking SSNs in email

99. Troy wants to review metadata about an email he has received to determine what system or server the email was sent from. Where can he find this information?

    A. In the email message's footer

    B. In the to: field

    C. In the email message's headers

    D. In the from: field

100. Isabelle wants to gather information about what systems a host is connecting to, how much traffic is sent, and similar details. Which of the following options would not allow her to perform that task?

    A. IPFIX

    B. NetFlow

    C. NXLog

    D. sFlow

101. Valerie wants to check to see if a SQL injection attack occurred against her web application on a Linux system. Which log file should she check for this type of information?

    A. The security log

    B. The DNS log

    C. The auth log

    D. The web server log

102. Jean's company is preparing for litigation with another company that they believe has caused harm to Jean's organization. What type of legal action should Jean's lawyer take to ensure that the company preserves files and information related to the legal case?

    A. A chain-of-custody demand letter

    B. An e-discovery notice

    C. A legal hold notice

    D. An order of volatility

103. What type of mitigation places a malicious file or application in a safe location for future review or study?

A. Containment

B. Quarantine

C. Isolation

D. Deletion

104. What phase of the incident response process often involves adding firewall rules and patching systems to address the incident?

A. Preparation

B. Detection

C. Recovery

D. Analysis

105. Tim wants to check the status of malware infections in his organization using the organization's security information and event management (SIEM) device. What SIEM dashboard will tell him about whether there are more malware infections in the past few days than normal?

A. The alerts dashboard

B. The sensors dashboard

C. The trends dashboard

D. The bandwidth dashboard

106. Michelle has been asked to use the CIS benchmark for Windows as part of her system security process. What information will she be using?

A. Information on how secure Windows is in its default state

B. A set of recommended security configurations to secure Windows

C. Performance benchmark tools for Windows systems, including network speed and firewall throughput

D. Vulnerability scan data for Windows systems provided by various manufacturers

107. All of your organization's traffic flows through a single connection to the Internet. Which of the following terms best describes this scenario?

A. Cloud computing

B. Load balancing

C. Single point of failure

D. Virtualization

108. Nina is tasked with putting radio frequency identification (RFID) tags on every new piece of equipment that enters her datacenter that costs more than $500. What type of organizational policy is most likely to include this type of requirement?

A. A change management policy

B. An incident response policy

C. An asset management policy

D. An acceptable use policy

109. Megan is reviewing her organization's datacenter network diagram as shown in the following image. What should she note for point A on the diagram?

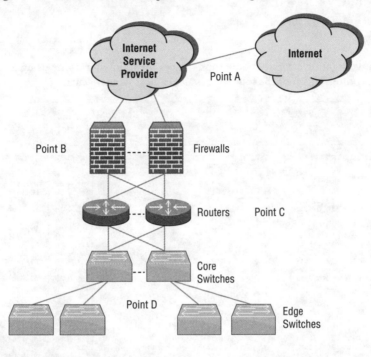

A. A wireless link

B. A redundant connection

C. A wired link

D. A single point of failure

110. Juan's team is in charge of responding to potential phishing attacks and advertises an infosec@example.com email address to his organization to send examples of potential phishing attacks to. Which of the following is not a benefit Juan's team would get from automating the creation of tickets in their support tool based on these emails?

A. The ability to track whether they've been resolved

B. Automated phishing prevention

C. The ability to correlate multiple emails into a single event

D. The ability to trigger additional actions

111. Valerie wants to implement an email security framework that will help to ensure that only authorized systems send email on behalf of her domains. Which of the following should she implement?

    A. DKIM

    B. DMARC

    C. STP

    D. SPF

112. Jake is investigating a service outage and notices the following traffic using a Wireshark packet capture. Which of the following issues is most likely occurring?

No.	Time	Source	Destination	Protocol	Length	Info
3	0.000268222	10.0.2.11	10.0.2.15	TCP	60	1784 → 80 [SYN] Seq=0 Win=512 Len=0
7	41.935569169	10.0.2.11	10.0.2.15	TCP	60	1304 → 80 [SYN] Seq=0 Win=512 Len=0
11	75.483849323	10.0.2.11	10.0.2.15	TCP	60	1309 → 80 [SYN] Seq=0 Win=512 Len=0
13	75.483919052	10.0.2.11	10.0.2.15	TCP	60	1310 → 80 [SYN] Seq=0 Win=512 Len=0
15	75.483935503	10.0.2.11	10.0.2.15	TCP	60	1311 → 80 [SYN] Seq=0 Win=512 Len=0
17	75.483997037	10.0.2.11	10.0.2.15	TCP	60	1312 → 80 [SYN] Seq=0 Win=512 Len=0
19	75.484021710	10.0.2.11	10.0.2.15	TCP	60	1313 → 80 [SYN] Seq=0 Win=512 Len=0
21	75.484106918	10.0.2.11	10.0.2.15	TCP	60	1314 → 80 [SYN] Seq=0 Win=512 Len=0
23	75.484148795	10.0.2.11	10.0.2.15	TCP	60	1315 → 80 [SYN] Seq=0 Win=512 Len=0
25	75.484166768	10.0.2.11	10.0.2.15	TCP	60	1316 → 80 [SYN] Seq=0 Win=512 Len=0
27	75.484362785	10.0.2.11	10.0.2.15	TCP	60	1317 → 80 [SYN] Seq=0 Win=512 Len=0
29	75.484404374	10.0.2.11	10.0.2.15	TCP	60	1318 → 80 [SYN] Seq=0 Win=512 Len=0
31	75.484420886	10.0.2.11	10.0.2.15	TCP	60	1319 → 80 [SYN] Seq=0 Win=512 Len=0
33	75.484475319	10.0.2.11	10.0.2.15	TCP	60	1320 → 80 [SYN] Seq=0 Win=512 Len=0
35	75.484556713	10.0.2.11	10.0.2.15	TCP	60	1321 → 80 [SYN] Seq=0 Win=512 Len=0
37	75.484580255	10.0.2.11	10.0.2.15	TCP	60	1322 → 80 [SYN] Seq=0 Win=512 Len=0
39	75.484636314	10.0.2.11	10.0.2.15	TCP	60	1323 → 80 [SYN] Seq=0 Win=512 Len=0
41	75.484677632	10.0.2.11	10.0.2.15	TCP	60	1324 → 80 [SYN] Seq=0 Win=512 Len=0
43	75.484729142	10.0.2.11	10.0.2.15	TCP	60	1325 → 80 [SYN] Seq=0 Win=512 Len=0
45	75.484752320	10.0.2.11	10.0.2.15	TCP	60	1326 → 80 [SYN] Seq=0 Win=512 Len=0
47	75.484804015	10.0.2.11	10.0.2.15	TCP	60	1327 → 80 [SYN] Seq=0 Win=512 Len=0
49	75.484832250	10.0.2.11	10.0.2.15	TCP	60	1328 → 80 [SYN] Seq=0 Win=512 Len=0
51	75.484898465	10.0.2.11	10.0.2.15	TCP	60	1329 → 80 [SYN] Seq=0 Win=512 Len=0
53	75.484927363	10.0.2.11	10.0.2.15	TCP	60	1330 → 80 [SYN] Seq=0 Win=512 Len=0
55	75.484942900	10.0.2.11	10.0.2.15	TCP	60	1331 → 80 [SYN] Seq=0 Win=512 Len=0
57	75.485004562	10.0.2.11	10.0.2.15	TCP	60	1332 → 80 [SYN] Seq=0 Win=512 Len=0
59	75.485023999	10.0.2.11	10.0.2.15	TCP	60	1333 → 80 [SYN] Seq=0 Win=512 Len=0
61	75.485041155	10.0.2.11	10.0.2.15	TCP	60	1334 → 80 [SYN] Seq=0 Win=512 Len=0
63	75.485058339	10.0.2.11	10.0.2.15	TCP	60	1335 → 80 [SYN] Seq=0 Win=512 Len=0
65	75.485124928	10.0.2.11	10.0.2.15	TCP	60	1336 → 80 [SYN] Seq=0 Win=512 Len=0
67	75.485149472	10.0.2.11	10.0.2.15	TCP	60	1337 → 80 [SYN] Seq=0 Win=512 Len=0
69	75.485166197	10.0.2.11	10.0.2.15	TCP	60	1338 → 80 [SYN] Seq=0 Win=512 Len=0
71	75.485222925	10.0.2.11	10.0.2.15	TCP	60	1339 → 80 [SYN] Seq=0 Win=512 Len=0
73	75.485248954	10.0.2.11	10.0.2.15	TCP	60	1340 → 80 [SYN] Seq=0 Win=512 Len=0
75	75.485313609	10.0.2.11	10.0.2.15	TCP	60	1341 → 80 [SYN] Seq=0 Win=512 Len=0
77	75.485342005	10.0.2.11	10.0.2.15	TCP	60	1342 → 80 [SYN] Seq=0 Win=512 Len=0
79	75.485357867	10.0.2.11	10.0.2.15	TCP	60	1343 → 80 [SYN] Seq=0 Win=512 Len=0
81	75.485374225	10.0.2.11	10.0.2.15	TCP	60	1344 → 80 [SYN] Seq=0 Win=512 Len=0
83	75.485468683	10.0.2.11	10.0.2.15	TCP	60	1345 → 80 [SYN] Seq=0 Win=512 Len=0
85	75.485493736	10.0.2.11	10.0.2.15	TCP	60	1346 → 80 [SYN] Seq=0 Win=512 Len=0

    A. An email phishing campaign

    B. A SQL injection attack

    C. A dropped network connection

    D. A denial-of-service attack

113. Gary wants to deploy a tool that will allow him to identify and effectively respond to ransomware that might target systems that his company owns. He knows that he is likely to need to identify threats based on behavior rather than just using signatures, and he wants to have a dashboard-style view of his data. What tool should Gary select to meet this need?

A. IPS

B. NAC

C. DLP

D. EDR

114. Carl wants to test his organization's incident response process. He conducts a tabletop exercise for his security team. Which of the following best describes this type of exercise?

A. A scenario is introduced and each member of the team takes actions that they would use to respond to the scenario.

B. Third-party penetration testers work with the security team to address issues they discovered during their penetration test.

C. The security team meets to talk through what they would do in a given scenario and takes notes on what works and what doesn't.

D. The organization's datacenter is manually forced to fail over to an alternate site to test the scenario's objectives.

115. Michelle wants to determine why attackers were able to take her organization's web server cluster offline after an incident occurred. What process should she and her team follow to determine this?

A. Threat hunting

B. Root cause analysis

C. A lessons learned analysis

D. Recovery

116. Randy wants to harden mobile devices used by his organization. Which of the following is not a typical mobile device hardening step?

A. Disable Bluetooth.

B. Use strong screen lock passwords.

C. Install software updates.

D. Jailbreak the device.

117. Lucca wants to ensure that his organization's mobile device connections are secure. Which of the following connectivity options is the most secure choice?

A. WPA2 Personal

B. WPA3 Personal

C. WPA3 Enterprise

D. WPA4 Enterprise

118. The percentage of the value of an asset that is lost due to an incident or loss event is known as what?

    A. Asset depreciation

    B. Exposure factor

    C. Annual loss event

    D. Asset valuation adjustment

119. Derek's organization has recently set up a notification process that sends a text message to system administrators when security exception log events occur on the systems they arc responsible for. Unfortunately, Derek and his team have received dozens of alerts at all times of the day due to the log event happening for failed logins when users type their passwords incorrectly. What should Derek and his team do next to help with this?

    A. Set alert thresholds.

    B. Engage in alert tuning.

    C. Disable the alerts.

    D. Move the alerts to email.

120. Jill wants to configure her IPS to detect a SQL injection attack that has become increasingly common against an open source web application that her organization runs. What information would she need to create a signature for the attack?

    A. The source IP address

    B. The SQL code

    C. The hash of the attack

    D. The source port

121. Ben's organization has hired a new HR supervisor, Jack. When Jack was hired, Ben was asked to provide Jack with the same rights and permissions as the other HR supervisor, Erin. What is the most important issue Ben should identify with this process if the organization wants to follow identity and access management best practices?

    A. Jack's account should be provisioned based on his role, not on Erin's rights.

    B. Jack may not be senior enough to have access to the same systems as Erin does.

    C. Erin may work with a different staff than Jack does.

    D. Jack should not have access to Erin's files.

122. Ian wants to deploy multifactor tokens to his organization. Which of the following provides the greatest security?

    A. Hardware tokens

    B. Application-based tokens

    C. SMS multifactor

    D. Extended password length

123. Gurvinder wants to explain the advantages of investing in automating security workflows to his organization's leadership. Recent audit findings have shown that systems are not all fully patched and that settings may vary between systems using the same operating system. Which common benefit of automation should he emphasize with leadership?

    A. Enforcing baselines

    B. Scaling in a secure manner

    C. Improving reaction time

    D. Automation's role as a workforce multiplier

124. Jake wants to understand the root cause of a security incident. He knows a number of the events that occurred, but he wants to engage other staff members to define the root cause. What common root cause analysis (RCA) technique should he use?

    A. The Five W's

    B. A fishbone diagram

    C. The Five Why's

    D. A recursion analysis

125. Amanda is testing her company's incident response process and has her staff perform actual recovery actions without impacting production to validate how long it would take to accomplish them. What type of event has she conducted?

    A. A fail over test

    B. A simulation

    C. A plan review

    D. A tabletop exercise

126. Liam's company has been notified of impending legal action and has been told to place a legal hold on related items. What must Liam's company do?

    A. Continue their normal operations, including data life-cycle–related activities.

    B. Identify data covered by the hold and preserve it, regardless of normal data life cycles or activities.

    C. Engage a law firm to preserve the data required by the legal hold.

    D. Contact law enforcement to allow them to gather the data required by the legal hold.

127. Paul wants to integrate his organization's web application with common cloud identity providers like Google and Microsoft. What authentication standard should he select if he wants to maximize interoperability?

    A. OAuth

    B. Kerberos

    C. LDAP

    D. Active Directory

128. Jim wants to ensure that users who are located in his organization's London office have access to the building. What type of access control scheme should he select to best fit this specific need?

    A. Rule BAC

    B. ABAC

    C. Role BAC

    D. MAC

129. Dane wants to implement passwordless authentication for his organization. What type of device should he issue to his users to support this type of authentication?

    A. A password manager

    B. An RFID card

    C. A security key

    D. A biometric token

130. Ensuring that inetd services like echo, time, rsh, and telnet are not enabled are all examples of what type of action?

    A. Preventing SQL injection

    B. Hardening a Linux system

    C. Hardening a Windows system

    D. Patching insecure services

131. What mobile device deployment model provides the least control for the organization and leaves the end user with the greatest choice?

    A. BYOD

    B. COPE

    C. CYOD

    D. COBO

132. Akio has set the `Secure Cookie` attribute as part of her web application's process for sending new cookies to users. What does this attribute do?

    A. It encrypts the cookie's content when it is stored.

    B. It stores the cookie on the server instead of on the remove device.

    C. It removes the cookie after it has been used.

    D. It requires that the cookie be sent only via HTTPS.

133. Helen wants to sign her code. What will the output of code signing be?

    A. An encrypted copy of the code using her private key

    B. A signed hash of the software using her private key

    C. A signed hash of the software using her public key

    D. An encrypted copy of the code using her public key

134. Naomi's organization has recently acquired another company. Naomi is concerned about asset tracking and inventory because the acquired company does not have an inventory of their systems and devices. What major security concern should she express about this from a hardware asset management perspective?

A. There may not be an appropriate hardware life-cycle process.

B. Manufacturer support may not be possible without an inventory.

C. There is no way to know if systems are missing.

D. Vulnerability scans may not be accurate without an inventory.

135. As part of his CI/CD pipeline process, Felix reviews source code manually to identify any flaws or security concerns. What type of process is Felix following?

A. Dynamic analysis

B. Agile code development

C. Static analysis

D. Internal review

136. As part of his research, Pedro uses a TOR browser to access threat actors' sites. He is able to see information about recent breaches and can download data dumps provided by the threat actors. What information source is Pedro using?

A. The dark web

B. An information-sharing organization

C. Proprietary information

D. A threat feed

137. Alaina has completed the eradication and recovery steps of the incident response process. What step commonly comes after these two phases?

A. A lessons learned session

B. Detection

C. Training

D. A tabletop exercise

138. Lucca knows that the CVSS environmental score is made up of three components, including an impact metric. What three components does he need to consider as part of the impact metric score?

A. Confidentiality, integrity, and availability

B. Network, disk, and memory

C. Severity, likelihood, and impact

D. Probability, impact, and cost

139. What tool is commonly used to allow for measurement and monitoring of security settings to align with NIST 800-53 controls?

A. SAML

B. CVE

C. CVSS

D. SCAP

140. Adam has implemented a WPA3 Enterprise network. What type of encryption will be used to protect data sent across the Wi-Fi connection?

A. AES

B. 3DES

C. SHA-1

D. SHA-256

141. Tom wants to set up an authentication service for network devices. Which of the following is commonly used for authentication to enterprise network devices?

A. Kerberos

B. SAML

C. TKIP

D. OpenID

142. Ian wants to test embedded device web servers for potential security issues with the version of the web server software. What tool should he select to do this most effectively across his large organization's network of IoT devices?

A. A WAF

B. Pentesting

C. A vulnerability scanner

D. A port scanner

143. Tom wants his email servers to reject email that is not authenticated in a way to prevent spoofing. Which of the following should he implement?

A. SPF

B. DMARC

C. DKIM

D. TLS

144. Wayne has identified a vulnerable server that is part of his organization's critical infrastructure but that is no longer supported by the vendor and for which no additional patches exist. Every time Wayne scans the server using his vulnerability scanner, the services on the device crash. What should Wayne do?

A. Report the server as vulnerable and suggest that it be replaced immediately.

B. Disable the network connection on the device and isolate the server to protect it.

    C. Identify a third-party insurance provider who will insure the organization against potential issues with the server.

    D. Document an exemption, remove the server from automated scans, and implement compensating controls.

145. Valentine's organization wants to ensure that users who sign up for their web services are who they claim to be. As part of the process they ask for information like birth date, Social Security number, and previous addresses. What type of activity is Valentine's organization engaging in?

    A. Provisioning user accounts

    B. Identity proofing

    C. Deprovisioning user accounts

    D. Social identity

146. Sam has completed patching of a critical vulnerability. What step is often performed next to ensure that the patching occurred properly?

    A. Noting false positives

    B. Rebooting the system

    C. Rescanning the system

    D. Performing an audit

147. Joan's organization has recently remediated issues in their credit card processing environment. If Joan wants to be able to attest to the security of the environment, what action might she need to take to prove the security of the environment to customers?

    A. Have third-party auditors validate the remediation.

    B. Rescan the systems and document the differences between the scans.

    C. Rescan the systems and provide updated reports to customers.

    D. Allow customers to scan the systems to validate the changes.

148. Alan wants to configure his firewall to allow Microsoft SQL traffic through to the database server from web application servers in a screened subnet design. What is the minimum set of ports that he should port to allow this?

    A. TCP 3389 and 1433

    B. TCP 1433

    C. TCP 8080

    D. TCP 139 and 445

149. Which of the following terms refers to the process of establishing a standard for security?

    A. Baselining

    B. Security evaluation

    C. Hardening

    D. Normalization

150. Zhen's new organization has informed him that they used a COPE model for their mobile devices. What does this tell Zhen about what he can do with the device?

    A. He can choose what device he uses, but the organization will own it.

    B. He will be provided with a device but can use it for reasonable personal use.

    C. He will be provided with a device and can only use it for business purposes.

    D. He will have to bring his own device but can use it for personal and business use.

151. The Windows Task Manager can be used to identify malware through what technique?

    A. Dynamic analysis

    B. Process auditing

    C. CVSS matching

    D. Vulnerability scanning

152. Ujama wants to deploy a network device that will allow him to use policy-based controls for email as well as active defenses against phishing attacks before email is delivered to his users. Which of the following devices is best suited to this purpose?

    A. A web application firewall

    B. An email security gateway

    C. A DKIM appliance

    D. A DMARC appliance

153. Allison wants to aggregate her logs and have them automatically correlated and reported on. What sort of tool should she acquire for her organization?

    A. MDM

    B. A jump server

    C. SDN

    D. SIEM

154. Natasha's staff have been complaining about repetitive tasks that must be manually accomplished to secure endpoint devices, then they are deployed. What could Natasha ask her team to do to address this?

    A. Leverage automation and scripting.

    B. Deploy fewer devices.

    C. Leverage baselines.

    D. Move devices to the cloud.

155. Which of the following methods typically provides the greatest insight into vulnerabilities that exist on systems owned by a company?

    A. Penetration tests

    B. Authenticated scans

    C. Unauthenticated scans

    D. Port scans

156. Quarantine and isolation are both common options in what phase of the incident response process?

   A. Detection

   B. Analysis

   C. Containment

   D. Eradication

157. Rick is reviewing Linux system permissions and finds a directory that is set to:

```
-rwxr--r--
```

Who will have access to the directory to read the file?

   A. The user

   B. The user and their group

   C. All users

   D. No users except root

158. Beena is granted access to her organization's customer information because she is a data steward; her access occurs between 8 a.m. and 5 p.m., and it is occurring from a known workstation that has passed security checks. What type of access control scheme is in use?

   A. Rule-based access control

   B. Role-based access control

   C. Mandatory access control

   D. Attribute-based access control

159. Juan wants to use his IDS to detect anomalous behavior. What type of detection technique would most effectively help him identify unknown new attacks?

   A. Trend analysis

   B. Signature-based detection

   C. IP-based detection

   D. Port-based detection

160. Geenah wants to identify where Wi-Fi signals are weakest in her building. What should she create to visually display signal coverage and strength throughout her building?

   A. A war walk

   B. A spectrum analysis

   C. An SSID plot

   D. A heatmap

161. What term describes the concept that individuals should be given the minimum permissions necessary to accomplish their role or tasks?

   A. Zero trust

   B. Provisioning

   C. Least privilege

   D. Deprovisioning

162. Joanna wants to explain the advantages of automation for user and resource provisioning. Which of the following is not an advantage of automation over manual processes for provisioning?

    A. Automation ensures consistency in the provisioning process.

    B. Automation provides faster provisioning.

    C. Automation decreases mistakes in provisioning.

    D. Automation provides auditability of provisioning.

163. Bug bounty programs are an example of what type of program?

    A. Contracted penetration testing

    B. Responsible disclosure

    C. Third-party bounty

    D. Trusted threat

164. Jack is hardening a Cisco switch based on the CIS IOS benchmark. As part of the configuration process, he configures settings including `ntp authenticate` and `ntp trusted-key`. Why would Jack configure this on his network switches?

    A. To ensure that the switch has Network Terminal Protocol enabled

    B. To prevent attackers from modifying logs

    C. To prevent attackers from capturing network time traffic

    D. To ensure that network time is from a trusted source

165. Tony wants to use a cellular connection to transfer data to his organization. What should he do to ensure that his data is as secure as possible?

    A. Make sure he is connected to his cellular provider's towers.

    B. Fully patch the phone.

    C. Use a VPN.

    D. Deploy a security baseline to the phone.

166. The hospital that Isabella works for leverages threat information from the Health-ISAC as part of their security team's work. What type of threat information provider is the Health-ISAC?

    A. An OSINT provider

    B. A dark web source

    C. An information-sharing organization

    D. A proprietary threat data source

167. Mark presents his driver's license as part of the creation of his user account for a secure online service. What process requires this type of information to validate ownership of an identity?

    A. Attestation

    B. Provisioning

    C. SSO

    D. De-provisioning

168. Hector is concerned about Bluetooth security. Which of the following is a legitimate security concern about Bluetooth?

A. It is not encrypted.

B. Bluetooth is only useful at short range.

C. Bluejacking may occur.

D. Bluetooth devices can be fingerprinted.

169. Privileged access management (PAM) tools provide functions for enterprise access management. Which of the following is not a common PAM component?

A. Just-in-time permissions

B. Password vaulting

C. Ephemeral credentials

D. Password persistence

170. What role do port scans play in asset tracking?

A. Enumeration of assets.

B. They provide OSINT.

C. Version tracking for assets.

D. They do not play a role in asset tracking.

171. A fingerprint is an example of what type of authentication factor?

A. Something you know

B. Something you have

C. Something you are

D. Somewhere you are

172. Dana wants to ensure that her software acquisition process for open source software is as secure as possible. What should she to do validate the security of the open source software?

A. Ensure that the software source code is escrowed.

B. Review the source code for the software.

C. Check dependencies for known vulnerabilities.

D. Purchase the software from a software vendor.

173. Sharon wants to implement WPA3 Enterprise. What technology will she need to use for authorization after wireless devices associate with access points?

A. LDAP

B. 802.1X

C. Kerberos

D. SAML

174. What purpose do the password history and password minimum age settings have in Windows?

  A. To prevent attackers from resetting passwords

  B. To prevent brute-force attacks

  C. To prevent password reuse

  D. To ensure proper password expiration

175. A CVSS score is based on what three metric groups of data?

  A. Scope, Impact, Environmental

  B. Base, Temporal, and Environmental

  C. Risk, Threat, Impact

  D. Time, Risk, Scope

176. Quentin wants to decommission solid-state drives (SSDs). What process should he follow if he wants to be absolutely certain that the data cannot be recovered?

  A. Zero wiping

  B. Destruction

  C. Sanitation

  D. Reformatting

177. What challenge is commonly encountered when organizations want to harden IoT devices?

  A. The devices have limited security options.

  B. The devices cannot run current operating systems.

  C. Industry benchmarks for security are not up-to-date.

  D. Central management tools only support new devices.

178. Guillermo wants to establish his organization's security baseline for Linux systems. After selecting the CIS benchmark that best matches his organization's commonly used Linux distribution, what should he do next?

  A. Deploy the benchmark to a test system to see how it performs in normal use.

  B. Install SELinux to allow for the baseline to be implemented fully.

  C. Review the baseline to determine any settings that are not a good fit for the organization's usage.

  D. Identify the deployment method for the baseline to the Linux systems.

179. Renee has implemented WPA3 Enterprise, and she wants to use an EAP protocol for secure authentication. What EAP version should she implement?

  A. LEAP

  B. EAP-TLS

  C. EAP-PSK

  D. EAP-PWD

180. The organization that Chris works for has recently acquired another company. As part of the acquisition, Chris is preparing to address the data that the newly acquired company used, including setting up rules to handle it in his data loss prevention (DLP) system. What step is commonly required prior to data being protected by a DLP system?

A. Hashing the data and creating signatures

B. Encrypting the data

C. Classifying and tagging the data

D. Applying a mandatory access control scheme to the data

181. Mark wants to have a way to determine if attackers have modified files on a critical web application server. What type of tool should he deploy if he wants to be able to check for changes of this nature?

A. Drive encryption

B. File availability monitoring

C. File encryption

D. File integrity monitoring

182. Katie's organization uses an IoC feed that helps her to identify new threats. A recent feed update includes the following hash for Emotet malware:

cecc5bba6193d744837e689e68bc25c43eda7235

Where is Katie most likely going to be able to use this hash to identify potential attacks?

A. Via her EDR tools

B. Via her firewall

C. Via her system logs

D. All of the above

183. Which of the following tools is best suited to deploying and maintaining a secure baseline for Windows systems for an entire enterprise?

A. PowerShell

B. Group Policy

C. Manual configuration

D. Script-based deployments

184. Perry wants to ensure that an unsecure protocol is secured when in transit through his local network. What solution could he adopt to ensure that this traffic is protected?

A. Use SD-WAN.

B. Wrap the protocol using TLS.

C. Encrypt all files that are sent using AES.

D. Encrypt all files that are sent using SHA-1.

185. Annie wants to implement a passwordless authentication system. Which of the following would not meet her needs?

A. Windows Hello

B. A PIN-based factor

C. A cell-phone authenticator application

D. A FIDO2 security key

186. Laura wants to harden an ICS and SCADA devices her organization uses to manage critical infrastructure. The devices are old and unsupported, without recent updates. What hardening techniques are most likely to be available to her to help deal with these devices?

   A. Isolation

   B. Segmentation

   C. Adding host-based firewalls

   D. Configuring host-based IPS

187. Bob uses an IoC feed to allow his SIEM to identify and correlate common malicious activity. What phase of the incident response process best describes this?

   A. Preparation

   B. Detection

   C. Containment

   D. Eradication

188. Yael's organization has received a very convincing phishing email that has resulted in staff clicking on a malicious link. If Yael can't remove the email from inboxes, which of the following options will allow her to quickly prevent users from being compromised?

   A. Set up DNS filtering using the URL from the email.

   B. Disable the organization's Internet connection.

   C. Block inbound traffic from the phishing email's source IP.

   D. Enable reputation services for the email.

189. Nick is reviewing his system configurations and notes that logon event auditing settings on the system are set as shown in the example figure. What concern should he express about the setting?

A. Log files may fill up quickly.

B. Successful authentication will not be logged.

C. Failed authentication will not be logged.

D. Policy may not be enforced properly.

190. Brian is reviewing vulnerabilities discovered as part of a vulnerability scan. He sees a score for a vulnerability of 3.0. What does he know about this vulnerability based on its score?

A. It is a high-severity vulnerability and should be addressed quickly.

B. It is a low-severity vulnerability and may not need to be addressed.

C. It is a medium-severity vulnerability and should be reviewed before being addressed.

D. It is a critical vulnerability and should be addressed immediately.

191. Nick wants to allow email servers to validate that email from his servers is actually from them. What email security framework should he adopt to allow this?

A. DKIM

B. DMARC

C. SPF

D. SMTP

192. Jack wants to configure a Linux system to use mandatory access controls. What tool should he select that is commonly used to provide this functionality?

A. Group Policy

B. CIS benchmarks

C. SELinux

D. Containerization

193. What process is commonly used with open source tools to ensure that dependencies are secure?

A. Static analysis

B. Package monitoring

C. Fagan testing

D. Port scanning

194. Yarif wants to harden his SaaS cloud infrastructure. Which of the following hardening techniques is he most likely to be able to implement in an SaaS environment?

A. Host-based firewalls

B. Least privilege

C. Operating system security configuration

D. Physical security for systems

195. Which of the following is not a technical control used to address a vulnerability?

   A. Insurance

   B. Patching

   C. Segmentation

   D. Firewalling

196. Kelsey's organization has established an asset and inventory management process for servers. Which of the following is not a common part of asset tracking?

   A. Data classification

   B. Identifying owners

   C. Documenting acquisition dates

   D. Sanitization

197. Kirk needs to allow system administrators to access root passwords in emergencies. What type of solution could he implement to allow them to check out passwords when needed while also tracking those checkouts and requiring the passwords to be changed after use?

   A. EAP

   B. Multifactor authentication

   C. An enterprise password manager

   D. Passwordless

198. Selah wants to prevent staff in her organization from visiting malicious websites while they're in the office. If she wants to use the most up-to-date threat data, what web filter capability should she take advantage of?

   A. Agent-based web filtering

   B. Reputation tools

   C. A centralized web filtering proxy

   D. URL scanning

199. Joe has configured ACLs on a Cisco network device. The ACL he has configured is as follows:

```
interface ethernet0
 ip access-group 111 in
!
access-list 111 deny tcp any any eq http
access-list 111 permit ip any any
access-list 111 deny tcp any any eq https
```

What does this ACL do?

   A. Blocks HTTP traffic

   B. Blocks both HTTP and HTTPS traffic

   C. Prevents web application attacks

   D. Allows for inspection of web traffic

200. The use of machine learning and algorithms to analyze user behavior in order to identify anomalous behavior is a feature of what specialized type of tool?

A. UEBA

B. SIEM

C. EDR

D. DMARC

201. What password best practice is supported by the ability to set password history in Windows?

A. Password length

B. Password complexity

C. Password reuse

D. Password age

202. Donna is reviewing a script that was found on a Windows system. What does the following script do?

```
$ip = "10.1.1.101"
$svc_name = "WinDefend"
get-service -ComputerName $ip | Where-Object {$_.Name -eq $svc_name} |
Stop-Service | Set-Service -StartupType Disabled
```

A. Stops the Windows Defender service

B. Starts the Windows Defender service

C. Stops and disables the Windows Defender service

D. Enables the Windows Defender service

203. Batu has been asked to build scripts that will allow automated ticket creation through a new help desk tool for his organization. As he considers the lifespan of the scripts, which of the following concerns should he address to ensure that the scripts do not become an issue over time?

A. Their initial creation cost

B. Their ongoing supportability

C. Existing technical debt

D. Whether they're a single point of failure

204. Alex is responsible for his organization's vulnerability management program. A recent vulnerability scan shows that IoT devices that are used for building automation are vulnerable to a known issue with their built-in web server. After reviewing the manufacturer's website, Alex is unable to find an updated operating system or software update. He chooses to move the IoT devices to a protected VLAN and require a jump server to access them. What vulnerability remediation option has he used?

A. A compensating control

B. Patching

C. Insurance

D. An exemption

205. Wiping a drive and reinstalling from known good media is an example of what incident response option?

   A. Recovery

   B. Containment

   C. Eradication

   D. Root cause elimination

206. Melissa's company wants to contract with a third-party organization to oversee their hardware decommissioning and disposal process. What should she ask the company to do to prove that the disposal process was done properly?

   A. Certification.

   B. Follow a data retention policy.

   C. Provide photographic evidence.

   D. Keep a log of devices.

207. Sally wants to identify a way to prioritize vulnerabilities discovered by her vulnerability scanner. Which of the following options will allow her to prioritize vulnerabilities effectively while taking her own organization's needs into account?

   A. Use CVSS base and temporal metrics.

   B. Use a qualitative risk assessment process.

   C. Use CVSS scores that include environmental metrics.

   D. Use a quantitative risk assessment process.

208. Henry wants to prevent password reuse outside of his organization from impacting the accounts his staff use. Which of the following password settings can have the largest impact if passwords are reused outside of his organization and they are breached due to a security issue at the third-party site or service?

   A. Password expiration policies

   B. Password length policies

   C. Password complexity policies

   D. Password minimum age policies

209. Fuzzing is an example of what type of code analysis?

   A. Static analysis

   B. Code review

   C. Pentesting

   D. Dynamic analysis

210. Steve's organization is concerned about the potential for devices they are purchasing to be modified before they reach the organization. Which of the following solutions will help the most in preventing this potential issue?

   A. Buying from a value-added reseller

   B. Buying directly from the OEM

    C. Buying from a gray market seller

    D. Buying from a local reseller

211. What password setting has the greatest impact when attempting to prevent brute-force password cracking?

    A. Password history settings

    B. Password length increases

    C. Password expiration settings

    D. Password length decreases

212. Jill wants to identify a potential network-based distributed denial-of-service (DDoS) attack. Which of the following log sources is most likely to provide information that will allow her to identify the attack?

    A. OS-specific security logs

    B. Endpoint logs

    C. IDS/IPS logs

    D. Authentication logs

213. Jake has configured WPA3 Personal for his network. What feature makes WPA3 more secure than WPA2's PSK mode?

    A. SAE

    B. PKI

    C. TLS

    D. EAP

214. Molly wants to harden embedded systems in her environment. Which of the following options is most likely to be available?

    A. Hardening benchmarks.

    B. Central management tools.

    C. Add-on security software.

    D. None; embedded systems have very limited hardening options.

215. Jean wants to use an identity proofing process as part of her user account creation process. Which of the following is most likely to be useful for identity proofing?

    A. A Google email account

    B. A state or nationally issued ID

    C. A Facebook account

    D. A credit card

Chapter

5

Domain 5.0: Security Program Management and Oversight

THE COMPTIA SECURITY+ EXAM SY0-701 TOPICS COVERED IN THIS CHAPTER INCLUDE THE FOLLOWING:

✓ **5.1 Summarize elements of effective security governance**

- Guidelines
- Policies
    - Acceptable use policy (AUP)
    - Information security policies
    - Business continuity
    - Disaster recovery
    - Incident response
    - Software development lifecycle (SDLC)
    - Change management
- Standards
    - Password
    - Access control
    - Physical security
    - Encryption
- Procedures
    - Change management
    - Onboarding/offboarding
    - Playbooks

- External considerations
  - Regulatory
  - Legal
  - Industry
  - Local/regional
  - National
  - Global
- Monitoring and revision
- Types of governance structures
  - Boards
  - Committees
  - Government entities
  - Centralized/decentralized
- Roles and responsibilities for systems and data
  - Owners
  - Controllers
  - Processors
  - Custodians/stewards

✓ **5.2 Explain elements of the risk management process**

- Risk identification
- Risk assessment
  - Ad hoc
  - Recurring
  - One-time
  - Continuous
- Risk analysis
  - Qualitative
  - Quantitative
  - Single loss expectancy (SLE)

- Annualized loss expectancy (ALE)
- Annualized rate of occurrence (ARO)
- Probability
- Likelihood
- Exposure factor
- Impact
- Risk register
  - Key risk indicators
  - Risk owners
  - Risk threshold
- Risk tolerance
- Risk appetite
  - Expansionary
  - Conservative
  - Neutral
- Risk management strategies
  - Transfer
  - Accept
    - Exemption
    - Exception
  - Avoid
  - Mitigate
- Risk reporting
- Business impact analysis
  - Recovery time objective (RTO)
  - Recovery point objective (RPO)
  - Mean time to repair (MTTR)
- Mean time between failures (MTBF)

✓ **5.3 Explain the processes associated with third-party risk assessment and management**

- Vendor assessment
    - Penetration testing
    - Right-to-audit clause
    - Evidence of internal audits
    - Independent assessments
    - Supply chain analysis
- Vendor selection
    - Due diligence
    - Conflict of interest
- Agreement types
    - Service-level agreement (SLA)
    - Memorandum of agreement (MOA)
    - Memorandum of understanding (MOU)
    - Master service agreement (MSA)
    - Work order (WO)/statement of work (SOW)
    - Non-disclosure agreement (NDA)
    - Business partners agreement (BPA)
- Vendor monitoring
- Questionnaires
- Rules of engagement

✓ **5.4 Summarize elements of effective security compliance**

- Compliance reporting
    - Internal
    - External
- Consequences of non-compliance
    - Fines
    - Sanctions
    - Reputational damage

- Loss of license
- Contractual impacts
- Compliance monitoring
  - Due diligence/care
  - Attestation and acknowledgement
  - Internal and external
  - Automation
- Privacy
  - Legal implications
    - Local/regional
    - National
    - Global
  - Data subject
  - Controller vs. processor
  - Ownership
  - Data inventory and retention
  - Right to be forgotten

✓ **5.5 Explain types and purposes of audits and assessments**

- Attestation
- Internal
  - Compliance
  - Audit committee
  - Self-assessments
- External
  - Regulatory
  - Examinations
  - Assessment
  - Independent third-party audit
- Penetration testing
  - Physical

- Offensive
- Defensive
- Integrated
- Known environment
- Partially known environment
- Unknown environment
- Reconnaissance
  - Passive
  - Active

✓ **5.6 Given a scenario, implement security awareness practices**

- Phishing
  - Campaigns
  - Recognizing a phishing attempt
  - Responding to reported suspicious messages
- Anomalous behavior recognition
  - Risky
  - Unexpected
  - Unintentional
- User guidance training
  - Policy/handbooks
  - Situational awareness
  - Insider threat
  - Password management
  - Removable media and cables
  - Social engineering
  - Operational security
  - Hybrid/remote work environments

- Reporting and monitoring
  - Initial
  - Recuring
- Development
- Education

1. The company that Scott works for has experienced a data breach, and the personal information of thousands of customers has been exposed. Which of the following impact categories is not a concern as described in this scenario?

    A. Reputation

    B. Financial

    C. Availability loss

    D. Data loss

2. Sameer wants to assess whether the key risk indicators (KRIs) his team have suggested are appropriate for his organization. Which of the following is not a common characteristic of a useful KRI?

    A. Actionable

    B. Measurable

    C. Relevant

    D. Inexpensive

3. Jill's organization wants to ensure that services and systems are back online and functioning normally within 4 hours of an event or incident. What term best describes this goal?

    A. An RTO

    B. An MTTR

    C. An RPO

    D. An MTBF

4. Eric's organization has created a policy document that describes how users can and cannot use the organization's network, systems, and services. What type of policy has he created?

    A. Business continuity policy.

    B. An acceptable use policy.

    C. An incident response policy.

    D. This is a standard, not a policy.

5. Angie is performing a penetration test and has gathered information using the Shodan search engine about her target. What type of reconnaissance has she performed?

    A. Active

    B. Commercial

    C. Scanner-based

    D. Passive

6. What role do data processors have in an organization?

    A. They determine how data is processed.

    B. They own the data.

    C. They process data on behalf of a controller.

    D. They contract with third parties to use the data.

7. Ginger's personal data is used by an organization, including identifiable information like her name, address, and Social Security number. What term best describes Ginger?

    A. Data owner

    B. Data controller

    C. Data processor

    D. Data subject

8. Hong's company conducts regular risk assessments. As part of their assessment process, they gather a team of experts who assess risks on a scale from low to high based on their knowledge and experience. What type of risk assessment is Hong's company conducting?

    A. Ad hoc

    B. Quantitative

    C. Qualitative

    D. Continuous

9. How is likelihood measured in qualitative risk assessments?

    A. A scale like high, medium, low

    B. A numeric scale from 0 to 1

    C. By calculating loss events per year

    D. A numeric scale from 1 to 100

10. Grace wants to establish a governance structure that will leverage third-party experts who are paid by her organization. What governance structure should she select?

    A. Board-based

    B. Committee-based

    C. Government-based

    D. Market-based

11. Carmen's organization wants to purchase cybersecurity insurance to offset the cost of potential breaches. What risk management strategy has her organization adopted?

    A. Transfer

    B. Accept

    C. Avoid

    D. Mitigate

12. Marissa has been recruited to a group that provides oversight for an organization but that doesn't engage in the day-to-day operations of the organization. The group focuses on strategy and direction for the organization and meets a few times a year. What type of governance group is Marissa part of?

    A. An activist investor's group

    B. A committee

    C. A board

    D. A regulator

13. Governance at Selah's organization is delegated to business units. This allows the units to determine how to balance their operational needs against their governance processes. What type of governance is this?

    A. Centralized

    B. Board-based

    C. Decentralized

    D. Committee-based

14. Sharon's organization wants to understand the risks that it will experience due to acquiring a new subsidiary, but it needs to conduct the assessment quickly while leveraging their industry expertise. Which of the following risk assessment options should Sharon recommend to address this need?

    A. Conduct an ad hoc risk assessment.

    B. Conduct a one-time risk assessment.

    C. Conduct a third-party risk assessment.

    D. Build a continuous risk assessment process.

15. What term describes a third party that takes actions on behalf of a data controller?

    A. Data subject

    B. Data owner

    C. Data processor

    D. Data administrator

16. Which of the following will provide a customer the opportunity to engage a third party to deliver an SOC 2, Type 1 report created by third-party assessors?

    A. A penetration testing agreement

    B. A risk assessment agreement

    C. A vulnerability scan clause

    D. A right-to-audit clause

17. Isaac has been asked to be his organization's data owner for customer data. Which of the following is not a typical part of that role?

    A. Processing the data

    B. Classifying data

    C. Protecting data

    D. Ensuring the quality of the data

18. Pedro's organization uses industrial machinery, which runs an RTOS that is no longer supported. His organization's policies require systems to be removed from service if they cannot be patched for security issues, and the RTOS has a known vulnerability. The machines are

very expensive and are a core part of the organization's industrial processes. What risk process would Pedro follow if he wanted to retain the devices, despite the risk?

A. Transfer the risk.

B. Seek an exception.

C. Document the risk.

D. Mitigate the risk.

19. Jake's team has begun handling new data related to customers, including their personally identifiable information. Jake takes on a new role that has responsibilities including classifying each data element gathered about customers. What is Jake's role in the data handling process?

A. Controller

B. Custodian

C. Owner

D. Processor

20. Which of the following measures is not commonly used as part of a business impact analysis?

A. RTO

B. MTTR

C. ARO

D. MTBF

21. As part of her organization's marketing efforts, Julie's team gathers information about customers and others who visit their website. Julie has engaged an analytics company that uses the data gathered to identify trends and potential new market opportunities. What data role does this third-party company play?

A. Data owner

B. Data processor

C. Data controller

D. Data custodian

22. Neil's organization has signed a contract that includes guarantees of 99.9 percent uptime. What type of agreement has Neil's organization created?

A. An MSA

B. An NDA

C. A MTBF

D. An SLA

23. Which of the following best describes a data controller?

A. Manages the flow of data between custodians

B. Creates and formats data when it is collected or created

C. Any system that handles data

D. Determines the purpose and methods of processing data

24. As part of his role, Augie is responsible for implementation of business rules related to data, as well as for storage, and use of data and datasets. What data-related role does Augie hold?

    A. Data owner

    B. Data custodian

    C. Data processor

    D. Data subject

25. Which of the following penalties is most typically imposed on a country rather than on a company?

    A. Fines

    B. Loss of license

    C. Sanctions

    D. Mandatory reporting

26. Which of the following is not a commonly used term to describe risk appetite?

    A. Intentional

    B. Neutral

    C. Expansionary

    D. Conservative

27. What does a data steward do?

    A. Create data.

    B. Carry out data use and security policies.

    C. Explain compliance requirements for data.

    D. Oversee data throughout its life cycle.

28. Marcus determines what organizationally owned data is used for a given purpose and how it is processed. What data role does he have in his organization?

    A. He is a data controller.

    B. He is a supervisory authority.

    C. He is a data protection officer.

    D. He is a data processor.

29. Colleen's organization has deployed web application firewalls (WAFs) to protect their web services from being impacted by a known SQL injection attack. What risk management strategy has the organization adopted?

    A. Transfer

    B. Accept

    C. Avoid

    D. Mitigate

30. Requiring all web traffic to be sent via HTTPS is an example of what type of standard?

A. Access control

B. Encryption

C. Password

D. Physical security

31. Why are cloud IaaS vendors unlikely to agree to including a right-to-audit clause in their contracts?

A. The risk to their other customers is too great.

B. The cost of the assessment is too high.

C. They may not pass the audit.

D. They have competing regulatory requirements.

32. Chuck's organization requires that user accounts only be able to log in during the staff member's working hours. What type of standard would drive a setting like this?

A. Access control

B. Encryption

C. Password

D. Physical security

33. Frankie wants to establish her organization's encryption standard. Which of the following should she recommend for a default encryption algorithm for general use if cryptographic strength is a critical feature?

A. AES-128

B. SHA-1

C. AES-256

D. SHA-2

34. Jill's organization has selected Agile with a CI/CD process for their organization. What type of policy would document this selection?

A. Business continuity

B. Disaster recovery

C. Incident response

D. Software development life cycle

35. Megan's organization wants to create a change management policy. Which of the following is not a typical change type found in a change policy?

A. Preauthorized changes

B. Emergency changes

C. Legislated changes

D. Standard changes

36. Liz wants to assess the critical functions of her business and ensure that the systems that are part of those functions are assessed to determine how often they are likely to fail, how long it would take to restore them, and what recovery objectives will be. What process should she engage in?

    A. A quantitative risk assessment

    B. A business impact analysis

    C. A qualitative risk assessment

    D. A penetration test

37. What describes the key difference between policies and standards?

    A. Policies are defined by third parties; standards are defined by organizations.

    B. Policies are defined by organizations; standards are defined by third parties.

    C. Policies are a statement of intent; standards define how rules help enforce policy.

    D. Policies are legally enforceable; standards are optional.

38. Sophie wants to ensure that her vendor meets their SLA. What does Sophie need to do?

    A. Ensure performance targets are defined in the contract with appropriate penalties.

    B. Establish key performance indicators (KPIs) for her team and assess them regularly.

    C. Ensure that security levels are not reduced when performing maintenance.

    D. Determine if supply chain levels are met in order to meet demand.

39. Tuan is assessing risk and knows that he needs to be able to explain risk to his management. What two factors are combined to describe risk?

    A. Impact and acceptance

    B. Likelihood and ALE

    C. Probability and impact

    D. Probability and SLE

40. Marco wants to conduct active reconnaissance of a target for a penetration test. Which of the following is an appropriate action based on this desire?

    A. Looking up information in Shodan

    B. Conducting a nmap scan

    C. Querying local DNS for the organization

    D. Using public records to gather information

41. Beth is a data owner in her company. Which of the following is not a typical part of the role of data owner?

    A. They categorize data.

    B. They are responsible for processing data.

    C. They are responsible for protecting data.

    D. They are responsible for data quality.

42. NIST SP 800-63B, Digital Identity Guidelines, provides advice on passwords and password standards. Why does the guide recommend that knowledge-based authentication like "What was your mother's maiden name?" not be used for processes like password reset and recovery?

A. Users may not remember the answer.

B. Knowledge-based authentication information is often easily discovered through searches and social media.

C. Knowledge-based authentication information is not a valid factor for MFA.

D. Attackers can easily recover knowledge-based information from compromised authentication stores.

43. The company that Leon works for has experienced a significant malware infection and has segmented their network to prevent further spread. What risk mitigation strategy have they chosen?

A. Avoid

B. Transfer

C. Accept

D. Mitigate

44. Not using hints, preventing password expiration, storing passwords only in a hashed and salted form, and using minimum password length settings are all examples of what?

A. Password standards

B. Multifactor authentication

C. Establishing knowledge-based passwords

D. Biometrics

45. Anastasia works for a government entity that requires very strong risk controls and that has significant regulatory requirements it must meet. What risk appetite model should she expect her organization to adopt?

A. Expansionary

B. Conservative

C. Authoritarian

D. Legislative

46. Jack recently joined his organization's security team. A system was identified as likely being impacted by ransomware, and Jack was given a document that described the organization's ransomware handling practices. What common security document has he been given?

A. The IR policy

B. A ransomware cookbook

C. A ransomware playbook

D. A disaster recovery handbook

47. Connie wants to explain the consequences of noncompliance with data regulations to her organization's management. Which of the following is the most common statutory consequence of noncompliance with regulations?

A. Data breaches

B. Reputational damage

C. Contractual impacts

D. Fines

48. Hank wants to create a playbook for his incident response process. What will he create?

A. A detailed process for incident response

B. A legal document describing incident response

C. A high-level statement of purpose for incident response

D. A document describing the general incident response (IR) process

49. What type of agreement is used by organizations that want to protect their proprietary data while working with third parties or individuals who will have access to the data?

A. SLAs

B. NDAs

C. MSAs

D. BPAs

50. Oliver has joined an organization and has completed employee orientation, has received his username and password, and has reviewed the new employee security training. What process has he participated in?

A. Identity proofing

B. Mandatory access control

C. Onboarding

D. Biometric enrollment

51. What GDPR provision allows individuals to ask organization to delete their personal data?

A. The right to be forgotten

B. The right to deletion

C. The right to privacy

D. The right to ownership

52. Damian has provided a comprehensive risk register to his management, including a risk of employees violating policy by taking pictures of sensitive information displayed on their screens using their cell phones. Damian's recommendation was to ban employees from carrying personal cell phones inside the office, but management has overruled that recommendation and will allow phones. What risk management strategy has his organization's leadership chosen?

A. Transfer

B. Accept

C. Avoid

D. Mitigate

53. Which of the following is not a typical part of an offboarding process?

    A. Returning company equipment

    B. Copying files to a USB drive for the departing employee

    C. Disabling or removing accounts

    D. Changing passwords on shared accounts

54. Daryl wants to ensure that his organization balances risks and its goals. What risk appetite model should he suggest the organization adopts?

    A. Conservative

    B. Expansionary

    C. Reactionary

    D. Neutral

55. Charlene is preparing to conduct a penetration test and has been provided with access to all of her organization's information about the systems, services, and configurations involved. What type of penetration test is she conducting?

    A. A partially known environment test

    B. An unknown environment test

    C. A known environment test

    D. A third-party test

56. The company that Omar works for wants to co-develop a mobile application with a third-party company. What type of agreement should they both sign as part of this?

    A. An SLA

    B. An NDA

    C. An MSA

    D. A BPA

57. Alex wants to hire a penetration tester who will simulate an attacker's potential attacks against his environment. What type of test best fits this model?

    A. A partially known environment test

    B. An unknown environment test

    C. A known environment test

    D. A third-party test

58. What term describes the possibility of a risk occurring?

    A. Impact

    B. Likelihood

    C. Potential

    D. Rate of occurrence

59. Killian's organization wants to perform a penetration test that will provide the maximum amount of information about his organization and that will optimize penetration testers' time. What type of test should he have conducted?

    A. A partially known environment test

    B. An unknown environment test

    C. A known environment test

    D. A third-party test

60. Justin's organization has recently undergone a third-party audit that determined that their data-handling processes don't comply with the GDPR. Changes to become compliant will take almost a year due to existing systems and software. What risk management strategy is Justin's organization choosing if they continue to operate knowing they are noncompliant?

    A. Transfer

    B. Exception

    C. Avoidance

    D. Mitigate

61. Risk assessments required for regulatory compliance are most frequently conducted in which of the following modes?

    A. As ad hoc risk assessments

    B. As one-time risk assessments

    C. As recurring risk assessments

    D. As continuous risk assessments

62. Jack's organization has engaged penetration testers for their annual penetration test. As part of the contract, the testers are provided with a list of target systems, operating systems, and software that they will be testing. What type of penetration test is Jack's organization conducting?

    A. A partially known environment test

    B. An unknown environment test

    C. A known environment test

    D. A third-party test

63. The company that Jim works for is willing to accept significant risk in order to expand. How should Jim describe the organization's risk appetite?

    A. Conservative

    B. Expansionary

    C. Limited

    D. Neutral

64. As part of the early stages of a penetration test, Hui has researched her target organization's domain names and IP addresses, and has conducted a port scan. What type of activity is Hui engaging in?

    A. Reconnaissance

    B. An unknown environment test

    C. A known environment test

    D. OSINT gathering

65. What role does a person who has exercised the GDPR's right to be forgotten hold?

    A. Data subject

    B. Data controller

    C. Data processor

    D. Data owner

66. How is exposure factor (EF) expressed for risk calculations?

    A. As a calculation of the ALE multiplied by the ARO

    B. As the likelihood of loss

    C. As a potential percentage of loss

    D. As a calculation of the SLE multiplied by the ARO

67. As part of his penetration testing process Nick intends to follow an employee of his target company into a secured area. What type of penetration testing is Nick engaged in?

    A. Defensive

    B. Offensive

    C. Physical

    D. Integrated

68. Valerie's organization wants to ensure that their access control vestibule, ID card system, and guards are effective in stopping unwanted entrance. What type of penetration test should she use to validate this?

    A. Physical

    B. Offensive

    C. Defensive

    D. Integrated

69. Jason's organization has engaged a penetration testing firm that specializes in using techniques commonly employed by nation-state actors, including using social engineering techniques, advanced tools, and methods that will provide significant footholds within his infrastructure. What type of penetration test best describes this?

    A. Physical

    B. Offensive

    C. Defensive

    D. Integrated

70. Joshua's organization is required to comply with the EU's GDPR. As part of their annual assessments, they conduct a GDPR compliance review and receive a report from their auditors. What type of assessment is this?

    A. A penetration test

    B. A regulatory assessment

    C. An internal audit

    D. An attestation-based assessment

71. Alexandria wants to mitigate the risk of ransomware during its initial infection stages. Which of the following strategies should she employ?

    A. Deploy an EDR tool.

    B. Purchase cybersecurity insurance.

    C. Use secure, ransomware-resistant backups.

    D. Continue to operate as usual.

72. Shane's organization has determined that they can accept up to $10,000,000 a year in risk-related loss in support of their strategic plans. What term best describes this?

    A. Risk acceptance

    B. Risk appetite

    C. Ad hoc risk

    D. A conservative risk tolerance

73. Eric manages his organization's internal security team and wants to leverage a penetration test as part of his team's testing that allows them to respond to simulated attacks. What type of model best describes this?

    A. Physical

    B. Offensive

    C. Defensive

    D. Integrated

74. Henry's organization leverages penetration testing as part of its ongoing security practices, using attacker techniques as well as blue teaming to improve security constantly. What type of penetration testing methodology is Henry's organization using?

    A. Physical

    B. Offensive

    C. Defensive

    D. Integrated

75. Jackie is an auditor and has completed an SOC 2, Type 2 audit. Her firm then provides a statement about the organization's audit results and posture. What is this process known as?

    A. Penetration testing

    B. Audit sign-off

    C. Regulatory defense

    D. Attestation

76. Joe is an auditor who is on the staff of an organization that employs him to audit their own practices. What type of audit does Joe perform?

    A. Internal

    B. Regulatory

    C. External

    D. Compliance

77. Irene's organization needs to follow PCI DSS standards. If she engages a third party to assess this, what type of audit is she having performed?

    A. An internal regulatory audit

    B. An external regulatory audit

    C. An internal compliance audit

    D. An external compliance audit

78. Anton's organization processes credit cards but is a small organization. As part of their annual requirements related to PCI DSS, Anton fills out a form about their PCI DSS compliance and submits it to their acquiring bank. What type of assessment has his organization conducted?

    A. An internal regulatory audit

    B. A self-assessment

    C. An independent, third-party audit

    D. An external compliance audit

79. What organization typically includes an audit committee for a company?

    A. The security office

    B. The shareholders

    C. The board of directors

    D. The third-party assessors

80. What type of risk assessment process is most commonly associated with a CI/CD pipeline model?

    A. Ad hoc risk assessments

    B. One-time risk assessments

    C. Third-party risk assessments

    D. Continuous risk assessments

81. Cristobal wants to ensure that a vendor his company is considering hiring has conducted an SOC 2, Type 2 audit that is reliable and that will reveal any critical issues. What should he ensure was done?

    A. An internal audit with attestation by the CEO

    B. An independent, third-party audit

    C. A self-assessment

    D. A third-party penetration test with attestation

82. Kim's organization has assessed the risk of floods that may impact their datacenter and has determined that the likely rate of occurrence and its cost if it does occur are not acceptable. Given this, the organization has opted to move their datacenter in the next year. What has occurred?

    A. The risk dropped below their risk threshold.

    B. The risk assessment failed.

    C. A control failure occurred.

    D. The risk passed their risk threshold.

83. Vanessa's organization is a US-based health-care organization that is required to be compliant with HIPAA. What type of external assessment should they conduct?

    A. Regulatory

    B. Offensive

    C. Known environment

    D. Physical

84. Jaime wants to establish her organization's change management policy. What should the policy include?

    A. High-level descriptions of how the organization will review, approve, and implement proposed changes

    B. A detailed process for review and approval of changes

    C. Descriptions of how a change request should be created, formatted, reviewed, and approved

    D. An outline of the regulatory requirements for changes

85. Marek's organization has a system that needs to receive a deviation from a defined security process. What best practice should he follow to ensure that this is done correctly?

    A. He should conduct a risk assessment and document the results.

    B. He should remove the system from the network segment to protect it.

    C. He should ensure the deviation is approved through change management processes.

    D. All of the above.

86. What is the key difference between a business continuity plan and a business continuity policy?

    A. The plan describes how an organization will respond, whereas the policy outlines the high-level intent of the organization's business continuity efforts.

    B. The plan includes detailed steps for each part of the response, including how to restore systems and investigate issues, whereas the policy outlines the high-level intent of the organization's business continuity efforts.

    C. The plan describes the high-level intent of the organization's business continuity efforts, whereas the incident response policy describes how the organization will respond.

    D. They are the same; the terms are interchangeable.

87. Christina has prepared a document that includes high-level statements about how her organization will handle major incidents and what its overall stance on incidents is. What has she created?

    A. An incident response process

    B. A runbook

    C. An incident response policy

    D. An incident response standard

88. Terry wants to have all of his account data removed from organizations he has interacted with. What GDPR right can he leverage if he is an EU citizen?

    A. Data stewardship

    B. Personal data ownership

    C. The right to be forgotten

    D. His HIPAA rights

89. Probability and impact are used to rate what key security item?

    A. Cost

    B. Risk

    C. Vulnerability

    D. Audit findings

90. Gary wants to determine the probability of a risk occurring. What should he base his assessment on if he is performing a qualitative risk assessment?

    A. A calculated rate of occurrence using industry statistical data

    B. A rating from an experienced team of staff

    C. The number of times it has happened to their competitors in a year

    D. Actuarial tables provided by his insurance broker

91. Which of the following is not a common element for a penetration test's rules of engagement?

    A. Handling of sensitive and pentest-related data

    B. A list of passwords

    C. A list of in-scope IPs or domains

    D. A list of emergency contacts

92. Maeve is preparing to sign a penetration testing contract with a third-party security service provider. The security service provider provides a questionnaire that asks the scope of systems that can and cannot be tested, the schedule and times that penetration testing can and cannot occur, and what to do if a preexisting compromise is discovered. What document is the third-party service provider assembling?

    A. A right-to-audit clause

    B. A service-level agreement

    C. A memorandum of understanding

    D. Rules of engagement

93. Alaina wants to describe the level of impact and probability where her organization will either accept or attempt to mitigate or otherwise handle a risk at. What term describes this?

    A. Risk threshold

    B. Ad hoc risk level

    C. Third-party risk level

    D. Risk appetite

94. Alaina has been asked to create an AUP for her organization. Which of the following should she include?

    A. An access and usage policy that lists times and roles allowed to access specific resources

    B. A document that describes how the organization intends to approach change and related functions

    C. An antivirus (AV) update policy that describes when and how AV updates are deployed

    D. A description of acceptable use by organizational users

95. Kyle's organization is a very well-known, multinational organization. A recent data breach has exposed data for millions of customers, including all of their account information. As part of the breach, Kyle's company was discovered to have not followed common security practices, and in fact was operating in intentionally careless ways. Which of the following consequences should he highlight as most critical to the organization's ongoing operations when he considers their customer base?

    A. Fines

    B. Due diligence

    C. Reputational damage

    D. Contractual impacts

96. What type of agreement do organizations create after signing an MSA that describes the specific tasks or deliverables that will be created or performed?

    A. A MOU

    B. A SOW

    C. A punch list

    D. A BPA

97. Jack's organization recently received a shipment of SSDs and has begun to deploy them. What information would best help Jack assess the useful life of the devices?

    A. An RTO

    B. An MTTR

    C. An RPO

    D. An MTBF

98. The hard drives that Jason's organization recently purchased have an MTBF of 300,000 hours. When can Jason expect the first drive to fail?

A. At 150,000 hours

B. At 300,000 hours

C. At 450,000 hours

D. None of the above

99. Melissa's organization wants to establish a metric that defines how much data could be lost if an issue occurs. What should they set?

A. An RTO

B. An MTTR

C. An RPO

D. An MTBF

100. What common terms are used to categorize anomalous behavior?

A. Risky, unexpected, and unintentional

B. Recurring, occasional, and unique

C. Unintentional, insider, and accidental

D. Active, passive, and integrated

101. Greg is reviewing a server and notices that it is both running outdated software and that the organization heavily relies on the services that it provides. He pulls together a team to determine what the risk of operating the server is and what issues would occur if it were removed from service that day. What type of assessment has he conducted?

A. An ad hoc risk assessment

B. A one-time risk assessment

C. A third-party risk assessment

D. A continuous risk assessment

102. Olivia's organization operates servers in a datacenter that support customers across the country. As Olivia is determining her service level agreements, what information is most important in determining how quickly a server can be restored to operation if its motherboard fails?

A. An RTO

B. An MTTR

C. An RPO

D. An MTBF

103. Irina's organization wants to work with one of their vendors and wishes to establish an ongoing relationship with them. What type of agreement should they create between the organizations so that they can create SOWs as they determine what services they need from their service provider's organization?

A. An MOU

B. An SLA

C. An MSA

D. A BPA

104. Dani's organization relies on journaling to help protect transactions that occur through its database. Which of the following does journaling impact the most?

A. An RTO

B. An MTTR

C. An RPO

D. An MTBF

105. Henry's organization has set their RTO to 12 hours. What does this mean?

A. Outages must be less than 6 hours long.

B. Recovery from outages should take less than 12 hours.

C. Outages longer than 12 hours will require fail over to a warm site.

D. SLAs for third-party services should specify a 12 hour MTBF.

106. Valerie knows that her organization's datacenter power infrastructure has an MTTR of 24 hours. What should she do if there is a critical component failure in her power infrastructure, and the organization has a warm site with an activation of 12 hours and needs to be back online as soon as possible?

A. Wait to see if the recovery can be done in less than 24 hours.

B. Immediately begin a move to the warm site.

C. Wait to see if the recovery can be done in less than12 hours.

D. Wait for 12 hours, then begin the move to the warm site.

107. Peter's risk assessment process includes calculations of single loss expectancy, the annualized rate of occurrence of risks, and the annualized loss expectancy. What type of risk assessment is Peter conducting?

A. Quantitative

B. Calculated

C. Qualitative

D. Registered

108. What organizational document is used to enumerate and rate an organization's risks?

A. A risk appetite plan

B. A risk register

C. A quantitative register

D. A qualitative assessment report

109. Amanda's organization wants to conduct a risk assessment and needs to prioritize a timely completion of the process over rigorous detail. What type of assessment should she advise her organization to select?

A. Internal

B. External

C. Qualitative

D. Quantitative

110. Chuck wants to conduct a quantitative risk assessment. Which of the following will he need to be able to determine the single loss expectancy for a server?

A. Its purchase date

B. Which department manages the server

C. The operating system the server uses

D. The cost of the server

111. Shawna's organization has undertaken reasonable steps to meet their compliance requirements for data handling. What is this process or effort called?

A. Data stewardship

B. Due diligence

C. Attestation

D. Data sanctioning

112. Jeremy knows that his customer data is worth $500,000, and that the value of the data would be reduced by 25 percent if it was exposed. What is the SLE for this data?

A. $25,000

B. $125,000

C. $250,000

D. $375,000

113. Ian wants to calculate the annualized loss expectancy for an asset. What two values does he need to know?

A. SLE and ARO

B. ARO and MTBF

C. SLE and RPO

D. MTBF and RTO

114. Waylon is charged with ensuring that risks related to customer data used as part of his organization's primary application are managed appropriately. What is his role?

A. Board member

B. Data processor

C. Auditor

D. Risk owner

115. Nathaniel's organization is reviewing potential issues that may result from noncompliance with regulations that apply to his company. Which of the following would create the most significant operational harm?

    A. Reputational damage

    B. Loss of license

    C. Fines

    D. Contractual impacts

116. Susan wants to calculate the annualized loss expectancy for an asset that has a value of $50,000, an exposure factor of 50 percent, and an annual rate of occurrence of 2. What is the annualized loss expectancy for the asset?

    A. $5,000

    B. $25,000

    C. $50,000

    D. $100,000

117. Tim's organization knows that a major breach occurs once every four years, resulting in a loss of $250,000 for his organization. What is the annual rate of occurrence that Tim should use in his risk calculations?

    A. .25

    B. $75,000

    C. .75

    D. $50,000

118. Charlene wants to calculate the annualized loss expectancy for a risk event. What two factors does she need to know to calculate the ALE for a risk?

    A. ARO and TCO

    B. SLE and RPO

    C. TCO and RPO

    D. ARO and SLE

119. John is conducting a penetration test of a client's network. He is currently gathering information from sources such as archive.org, netcraft.com, social media, and information websites. What best describes this stage?

    A. Active reconnaissance

    B. Passive reconnaissance

    C. Initial exploitation

    D. Pivot

120. Juan is responsible for incident response at a large financial institution. He discovers that the company Wi-Fi has been breached. The attacker used the same login credentials that ship with the wireless access point (WAP). The attacker was able to use those credentials

to access the WAP administrative console and make changes. Which of the following best describes the lack of standards or procedures that caused this vulnerability to exist?

A. Improperly configured accounts

B. Untrained users

C. Using default settings

D. Failure to patch systems

121. What is the primary difference between active and passive reconnaissance?

A. Active will be done manually, passive with tools.

B. Active is done with unknown environment tests and passive with known environment tests.

C. Active is usually done by attackers and passive by testers.

D. Active will actually connect to the network and could be detected; passive won't.

122. The type and scope of testing, client contact details, how sensitive data will be handled, and the type and frequency of status meetings and reports are all common elements of what artifact of a penetration test?

A. The unknown environment (black-box) outline

B. The rules of engagement

C. The known environment (white-box) outline

D. The close-out report

123. Charlene has been asked to write a business continuity (BC) plan for her organization. Which of the following will a BC plan best handle?

A. How to respond during a person-made disaster

B. How to keep the organization running during a system outage

C. How to respond during a natural disaster

D. All of the above

124. Alaina's company is considering signing a contract with a cloud service provider and wants to determine how secure their services are. Which of the following is a method she is likely to be able to use to assess it?

A. Ask for permission to vulnerability scan the vendor's production service.

B. Conduct an audit of the organization.

C. Review an existing SOC audit.

D. Hire a third party to audit the organization.

125. Gurvinder's corporate datacenter is located in an area that FEMA has identified as being part of a 100-year flood plain. He knows that there is a chance in any given year that his datacenter could be completely flooded and underwater, and he wants to ensure that his organization knows what to do if that happens. What type of plan should he write?

A. A continuity of operations plan

B. A business continuity plan

C. A flood insurance plan

D. A disaster recovery plan

126. Which of the following environments is least likely to allow a right-to-audit clause in a contract?

    A. A datacenter co-location facility in your state

    B. A rented facility for a corporate headquarters

    C. A cloud server provider

    D. A datacenter co-location facility in the same country but not the same state

127. Ben writes down the checklist of steps that his organization will perform in the event of a cryptographic malware infection. What type of response document has he created?

    A. A playbook

    B. A DR plan

    C. A BC plan

    D. A runbook

128. Caroline has been asked to find an international standard to guide her company's choices in implementing information security management systems. Which of the following would be the best choice for her?

    A. ISO 27002

    B. ISO 27701

    C. NIST 800-12

    D. NIST 800-53

129. Which of the following principles stipulates that multiple changes to a computer system should not be made at the same time?

    A. Due diligence

    B. Acceptable use

    C. Change management

    D. Due care

130. You are a security engineer and discovered an employee using the company's computer systems to operate their small business. The employee installed their personal software on the company's computer and is using the computer hardware, such as the USB port. What policy would you recommend the company implement to prevent any risk of the company's data and network being compromised?

    A. Acceptable use policy

    B. Clean desk policy

    C. Mandatory vacation policy

    D. Job rotation policy

131. What standard is used for credit card security?

    A. GDPR

    B. COPPA

    C. PCI DSS

    D. CIS

132. Which of the following techniques attempts to predict the likelihood a threat will occur and assigns monetary values should a loss occur?

A. Change management

B. Vulnerability assessment

C. Qualitative risk assessment

D. Quantitative risk assessment

133. Which of the following agreements is less formal than a traditional contract but still has a certain level of importance to all parties involved?

A. SLA

B. BPA

C. ISA

D. MOU

134. You have an asset that is valued at $16,000, the exposure factor of a risk affecting that asset is 35 percent, and the annualized rate of occurrence is 75 percent. What is the SLE?

A. $5,600

B. $5,000

C. $4,200

D. $3,000

135. You are a security administrator for your company and you identify a security risk. You decide to continue with the current security plan. However, you develop a contingency plan in case the security risk occurs. Which of the following type of risk response technique are you demonstrating?

A. Accept

B. Transfer

C. Avoid

D. Mitigate

136. Which of the following is not a common security policy type?

A. Acceptable use policy

B. Business continuity

C. Incident response

D. Parking policy

137. Your security manager wants to decide which risks to mitigate based on cost. What is this an example of?

A. Quantitative risk assessment

B. Qualitative risk assessment

C. Business impact analysis

D. Threat assessment

138. Your company has outsourced its proprietary processes to Acme Corporation. Due to technical issues, Acme wants to include a third-party vendor to help resolve the technical issues. Which of the following must Acme consider before sending data to the third party?

   A. This data should be encrypted before it is sent to the third-party vendor.

   B. This may constitute unauthorized data sharing.

   C. This may violate the privileged user role-based awareness training.

   D. This may violate a nondisclosure agreement.

139. Which of the following is typically included in a BPA?

   A. Clear statements detailing the expectation between a customer and a service provider

   B. The agreement that a specific function or service will be delivered at the agreed-on level of performance

   C. Sharing of profits and losses and the addition or removal of a partner

   D. Security requirements associated with interconnecting IT systems

140. A security administrator is reviewing the company's continuity plan, and it specifies an RTO of four hours and an RPO of one day. Which of the following is the plan describing?

   A. Systems should be restored within one day and should remain operational for at least four hours.

   B. Systems should be restored within four hours and no later than one day after the incident.

   C. Systems should be restored within one day and lose, at most, four hours' worth of data.

   D. Systems should be restored within four hours with a loss of one day's worth of data at most.

141. Which of the following statements is true regarding a data retention policy?

   A. Regulations require financial transactions to be stored for seven years.

   B. Employees must remove and lock up all sensitive and confidential documents when not in use.

   C. It describes a formal process of managing configuration changes made to a network.

   D. It is a legal document that describes a mutual agreement between parties.

142. How do you calculate the annual loss expectancy (ALE) that may occur due to a threat?

   A. Exposure factor (EF) / single loss expectancy (SLE)

   B. Single loss expectancy (SLE) × annual rate of occurrence (ARO)

   C. Asset value (AV) × exposure factor (EF)

   D. Single loss expectancy (SLE) / exposure factor (EF)

143. You are a security administrator for your company and you identify a security risk that you do not have in-house skills to address. You decide to acquire contract resources.

The contractor will be responsible for handling and managing this security risk. Which of the following type of risk response techniques are you demonstrating?

A. Accept

B. Mitigate

C. Transfer

D. Avoid

144. You are a server administrator for your company's private cloud. To provide service to employees, you are instructed to use reliable hard disks in the server to host a virtual environment. Which of the following best describes the reliability of hard drives?

A. MTTR

B. RPO

C. MTBF

D. ALE

145. Which of the following best describes a key challenge of quantitative risk analysis compared to qualitative risk analysis?

A. Quantitative risk analysis requires detailed financial data.

B. Quantitative risk analysis is sometimes subjective.

C. Quantitative risk analysis requires expertise on systems and infrastructure.

D. Quantitative risk provides clear answers to risk-based questions.

146. Categorizing residual risk is most important to which of the following risk response techniques?

A. Risk mitigation

B. Risk acceptance

C. Risk avoidance

D. Risk transfer

147. You are the IT manager and one of your employees asks who assigns data labels. Which of the following assigns data labels?

A. Owner

B. Custodian

C. Privacy officer

D. System administrator

148. A security analyst is analyzing the cost the company could incur if the customer database was breached. The database contains 2,500 records with personally identifiable information (PII). Studies show the cost per record would be $300. The likelihood that the database would be breached in the next year is only 5 percent. Which of the following would be the ALE for a security breach?

A. $15,000

B. $37,500

C. $150,000

D. $750,000

149. Which of the following concepts defines a company goal for system restoration and acceptable data loss?

   A. MTBF

   B. MTTR

   C. RPO

   D. ARO

150. You are a network administrator and have been given the duty of creating user accounts for new employees the company has hired. These employees are added to the identity and access management (IAM) system and assigned mobile devices. What process are you performing?

   A. Offboarding

   B. System owner

   C. Onboarding

   D. Executive user

151. Visa's published documentation for "What to Do if Compromised" includes requirements to notify Visa within 3 days of an incident, to provide notice to other relevant parties, and to conduct forensic investigations while preserving evidence. What type of document is this?

   A. A policy

   B. A playbook

   C. A checklist

   D. A procedure

152. An organization's information security policy framework typically contains what four types of documents?

   A. A risk register, an audit report, a vulnerability scan, and a pentest report

   B. Policies, standards, procedures, and guidelines

   C. Laws, policies, standards, and practices

   D. Policies, practices, procedures, and playbooks

153. Which of the following terms is used to measure how maintainable a system or device is?

   A. MTBF

   B. MTTF

   C. MTTR

   D. MITM

154. Helen's organization provides telephone support for their entire customer base as a critical business function. She has created a plan that will ensure that her organization's Voice over IP (VoIP) phones will be restored in the event of a tornado. What type of plan has she created?

   A. A disaster recovery plan

   B. An RPO plan

   C. An incident response plan

   D. An MTBF plan

155. Greg has data that is classified as health information that his organization uses as part of their company's HR data. Which of the following statements is true for his company's security policy?

   A. The health information must be encrypted.

   B. Greg should review relevant law to ensure the health information is handled properly.

   C. Companies are prohibited from storing health information and must outsource to third parties.

   D. All of the above.

156. What type of impact is an individual most likely to experience if a data breach that includes PII occurs?

   A. IP theft

   B. Reputation damage

   C. Fines

   D. Identity theft

157. Isaac has been asked to write his organization's access control standards. What policy is commonly put in place for service accounts?

   A. They must be issued only to system administrators.

   B. They must use multifactor authentication.

   C. They cannot use interactive logins.

   D. All of the above.

158. Emma is reviewing third-party risks to her organization, and Nate, her organization's procurement officer, notes that purchases of some laptops from the company's hardware vendor have been delayed due to lack of availability of SSDs (solid-state drives) and specific CPUs (central processing units) for specific configurations. What type of risk should Emma describe this as?

   A. Financial risk

   B. A lack of vendor support

   C. System integration

   D. Supply chain

159. Patching systems immediately after patches are released is an example of what risk management strategy?

   A. Acceptance

   B. Avoidance

   C. Mitigation

   D. Transference

160. What key element of regulations, like the European Union's GDPR, drive organizations to include them in their overall assessment of risk posture?

    A. Potential fines

    B. Their annual loss expectancy (ALE)

    C. Their recovery time objective (RTO)

    D. The likelihood of occurrence

161. What phases of handling a disaster are covered by a disaster recovery plan?

    A. What to do before the disaster

    B. What to do during the disaster

    C. What to do after the disaster

    D. All of the above

162. Naomi's organization has recently experienced a breach of credit card information. After investigation, it is discovered that her organization was inadvertently not fully compliant with PCI DSS and is not currently fully compliant. Which of the following penalties is her organization most likely to incur?

    A. Criminal charges

    B. Fines

    C. Termination of the credit card processing agreement

    D. All of the above

163. What law or regulation requires a DPO in organizations?

    A. FISMA

    B. COPPA

    C. PCI DSS

    D. GDPR

164. Your company is considering moving its mail server to a hosting company. This will help reduce hardware and server administrator costs at the local site. Which of the following documents would formally state the reliability and recourse if the reliability is not met?

    A. MOU

    B. SLA

    C. ISA

    D. BPA

165. Risk severity is calculated using the equation shown here. What information should be substituted for X?

Risk severity = X * Impact

    A. Inherent risk

    B. MTTR (mean time to repair)

    C. Likelihood of occurrence

    D. RTO (recovery time objective)

166. How is asset value determined?

    A. The original cost of the item

    B. The depreciated cost of the item

    C. The cost to replace the item

    D. Any of the above based on organizational preference

167. What process is used to help identify critical systems?

    A. A BIA

    B. An MTBF

    C. An RTO

    D. An ICD

168. Zarmeena wants to transfer the risk for breaches to another organization. Which of the following options should she use to transfer the risk?

    A. Explain to her management that breaches will occur.

    B. Blame future breaches on competitors.

    C. Sell her organization's data to another organization.

    D. Purchase cybersecurity insurance.

169. The financial cost of a breach is an example of what component of risk calculations?

    A. Probability

    B. Risk severity

    C. Impact

    D. All of the above

170. Joanna's penetration test target is an unknown environment that is isolated from the Internet and requires VPN access. What type of testing will she need to do to gather vulnerability information from systems?

    A. Passive reconnaissance

    B. OSINT reconnaissance

    C. Active reconnaissance

    D. Known environment reconnaissance

171. Olivia's cloud service provider claims to provide zero data loss from storage, and Olivia's company wants to take advantage of that service because loss of data would be extremely costly for the business. What business agreement can Oliva put in place to help ensure that the reliability that the vendor advertises is maintained?

    A. An MOU

    B. An SLA

    C. An MSA

    D. A BPA

172. How is SLE calculated?

  A. AV * EF

  B. RTO * AV

  C. MTTR * EF

  D. AV * ARO

173. Wayne has estimated the ARO for a risk in his organization to be 3. How often does Wayne think the event will happen?

  A. Once every 3 months

  B. Three times a year

  C. Once every three years

  D. Once a year for three years

174. Elle works for a credit card company that handles credit card transactions for businesses around the world. What data privacy role does her company play?

  A. A data controller

  B. A data steward

  C. A data custodian

  D. A data processor

175. Nicole determines how her organization processes data that it collects about its customers and also decides how and why personal information should be processed. What role does Nicole play in her organization?

  A. Data steward

  B. Data custodian

  C. Data controller

  D. Data consumer

176. Kirk's organization has been experiencing large-scale denial-of-service (DoS) attacks against their primary website. Kirk contracts with his Internet service provider to increase the organization's bandwidth and expands the server pool for the website to handle significantly more traffic than any of the previous DoS attacks. What type of risk management strategy has he employed?

  A. Acceptance

  B. Avoidance

  C. Transfer

  D. Mitigation

177. After Angela left her last organization, she discovered that she still had access to her shared drives and could log in to her email account. What critical process was likely forgotten when she left?

  A. An exit interview

  B. Job rotation

  C. Offboarding

  D. Governance

178. Kelly's organization has created an incident response policy that outlines the high-level goals of the IR process. Next, she wants to create detailed documents that describe the steps to handle specific incident types like denial-of-service attacks. What document should she create?

   A. Standards

   B. Playbooks

   C. Regulations

   D. Guidelines

179. Mohammed wants to show his organization's senior leadership the impact of their risk management process over time. What risk reporting method effectively conveys this in an easily digestible visual format for senior leadership?

   A. Ad hoc reports

   B. Risk registers

   C. Risk trend analysis

   D. Risk event reports

180. Presenting certification that a third-party organization has validated a vendor's practices against ISO 27001 is an example of what practice?

   A. Internal audit

   B. Vendor assessment

   C. Vulnerability scanning

   D. Data inventory

181. What common limitation do IaaS vendors place on penetration testing by their customers?

   A. It can only be done by third parties.

   B. It must be prescheduled.

   C. It can only be done by the customers themselves.

   D. Notification must be sent immediately after it occurs.

182. Chandra is providing guidance on recognizing phishing campaigns. Which of these is not a common way to recognize phishing emails?

   A. It creates a false sense of urgency.

   B. The IP address of the recipient.

   C. The attachment is encrypted and password protected.

   D. The email claims that there is a problem with your password.

183. Juan's company trains users to be cautious about revealing information about security controls, practices, configurations, and even the tools and software the company deploys. What is this practice known as?

   A. Awareness training

   B. Social engineering

   C. An insider threat

   D. Operational security

184. Mark's organization operates in the EU and sells products in multiple countries. It wants to determine its compliance requirements based on regulations that will impact it. Which of the following regions should it focus its review of legal implication on?

  A. Local

  B. National

  C. Global

  D. All of the above

185. What occurs when a vendor has a competing interest that could influence their behavior in a way that is not aligned with the best interests of one of their customers?

  A. An insider threat

  B. A MOU violation

  C. A conflict of interest

  D. A SOW violation

186. Selma's organization allows individual business units to manage their cybersecurity needs and practices as they see fit. What type of governance structure have they adopted?

  A. Centralized

  B. Board-based

  C. Committee-based

  D. Decentralized

187. The US Treasury Department regulates banks and their behaviors, including security-related regulations. What term best describes this type of governance structure?

  A. Government entity–based

  B. Shareholder driven

  C. Board-based

  D. Centralized

188. The company that Sandra wants to work with does not provide third-party audit statements. If Sandra wants to engage with them, what should she request as part of her vendor assessment process prior to signing a contract in order to have the most useful data available?

  A. A right-to-audit clause

  B. A supply chain analysis

  C. Evidence of internal audits

  D. A due diligence statement

189. Leigh wants to provide new users with information about her organization's security goals and high-level practices. What do organizations typically provide to accomplish this?

  A. Audit reports

  B. Policy handbooks

  C. Runbooks

  D. User awareness training

190. Jodi wants to prepare her staff to defend against social engineering. What should she invest in to help her staff address this threat?

    A. EDR tools

    B. Awareness training

    C. A NGFW

    D. Security policies

191. How do audits and examinations differ?

    A. An examination is simpler and less costly.

    B. Audits are external and examinations are internal.

    C. Audits are internal and examinations are external.

    D. An audit is simpler and less costly.

192. Evangeline wants to develop a security training program. What should she do first?

    A. Determine how the training will be presented.

    B. Establish a budget.

    C. Review regulatory requirements for training.

    D. Assess the threats and risks the organization faces.

193. Angelo is designing his organization's security governance groups and has created a committee. Which of the following is not a typical member of internal security governance committees?

    A. Subject matter experts

    B. Regulators

    C. Management

    D. Internal legal counsel

194. Dana wants to assess regulatory impacts on her organization's security policy. Which of the following is not a typical regulatory impact she will need to assess?

    A. Global

    B. National

    C. Local

    D. Corporate

195. Marty wants to ensure that his security policies are up-to-date and effective. Which of the following data sources is least likely to be useful as he reviews his organization's security policies?

    A. Security system logs and reports

    B. Staff feedback

    C. NDAs

    D. Review of regulations

196. What term describes a formal document that outlines the terms and details of an agreement between two organizations, including the roles and responsibilities each will have?

A. A statement of work

B. A business partners agreement

C. A memorandum of agreement

D. A service level agreement

197. Victoria wants to understand a potential vendor's security practices. Which of the following is the simplest way for her to gather that information from multiple potential vendors?

A. Third-party audits

B. Questionnaires

C. Penetration testing

D. OSINT

198. What two things most frequently drive external compliance reporting?

A. Regulatory bodies and contractual obligations

B. Internal and external audit

C. Contractual requirements and board reporting

D. Regulatory bodies and KPIs

199. Blaine wants to ensure that his organization consistently meets PCI DSS requirements. What should he implement to meet this goal?

A. Annual PCI DSS internal audits

B. Automated compliance monitoring

C. Annual PCI DSS external audits

D. Compliance KPIs

200. Ujama is reviewing logs and notices that one of his users has repeatedly failed their login process. After calling the user, he discovers that the user had mistyped their password multiple times. What type of anomalous behavior should he classify this as?

A. Insider

B. Risky

C. Unintentional

D. Unexpected

201. Common password management practices include which of the following?

A. Disabling MFA

B. Reusing passwords across multiple sites

C. Enabling password hints

D. Changing passwords only when necessary

202. Mark is responsible for the execution of his organization's security awareness program. Why might he deploy multiple training methods like workshops, online training, and simulations as part of the training?

   A. To meet compliance requirements

   B. To address learning preferences

   C. To decrease costs for training

   D. To meet KPIs

203. Natasha wants to establish a vendor monitoring practice for her organization. What should she establish to ensure that her vendor is performing as expected?

   A. A MOU

   B. Ongoing compliance audits

   C. Regulatory requirements

   D. KPIs

204. Mikayla is working remotely in a public space and has been trained to make sure that others cannot see her screen or keyboard. What term is used to describe this?

   A. Insider threats

   B. Situational awareness

   C. Social engineering

   D. Unintentional risky behavior

205. What data role is typically the most senior in an organization?

   A. Data processor

   B. Data controller

   C. Data owner

   D. Data steward

206. Which of the following is not a common hybrid work environment security practice?

   A. Use of VPNs

   B. Use of secure Wi-Fi networks

   C. Ensuring physical security

   D. Deploying security cameras

207. Which of the following is not a common driver of external compliance reporting?

   A. Contracts

   B. Regulation

   C. Reputation

   D. Licensing

208. Justin wants to have work done by a contractor with whom his organization has a master services agreement. What should he prepare to fully document the required work?

   A. A work order

   B. A service level agreement

   C. A memorandum of understanding

   D. A memorandum of agreement

209. What measure is used to describe the average functional lifespan of a device in use?

   A. An RTO

   B. An MTTR

   C. An RPO

   D. An MTBF

210. Jackie wants to use an ISO standard to help her select and implement information security controls and to develop information security management guidelines. Which ISO standard should she use?

   A. ISO 27001

   B. ISO 27701

   C. ISO 27002

   D. ISO 31000

211. Establishing requirements like the height of fences is part of what standard for most organizations?

   A. Physical security

   B. Access control

   C. Business continuity

   D. Onboarding

212. What organization typically elects an organization's board of directors in a public company?

   A. The employees

   B. The CEO

   C. Shareholders

   D. All relevant stakeholders

213. Greg wants to classify anomalous behavior he has observed. The behavior involves a user's workstation sending large volumes of data to an off-site web server. How should he classify this behavior?

   A. Risky

   B. Unexpected

   C. Unintentional

   D. An insider threat

214. Amber is responsible for compliance with PCI DSS in her organization and wants to ensure that she meets ongoing compliance monitoring requirements. Which of the following options will best help her achieve ongoing compliance?

A. Conduct quarterly audits.

B. Use compliance monitoring capabilities in scanning and management tools.

C. Conduct regular training on compliance requirements.

D. Require an auditor's attestation of compliance.

215. The third-party auditors that Dion hired for his organization have completed their audit. What action does the audit firm take after management acknowledgment is received from Dion's company?

A. Compliance reports are sent to third parties.

B. Regulatory statements are sent to customers.

C. Attestation is provided by the auditor.

D. Follow-up vulnerability scans will validate findings.

216. Latisha is conducting a security review and notices that one of her users consistently uses her organization's VPN from Chile while the employee is based in the United States. After reviewing logs, she notes that the user is sometimes logged in from both the US and the remote location in Chile, and believes that the user may be allowing a third party to access their VPN account to perform some or all of their job tasks. What type of threat most accurately describes this?

A. Anomalous

B. Insider

C. Social engineering

D. Nation-state

217. Marzita wants to respond to a phishing campaign that is sending links to malware to organizations. What effective tactic can she use to react to these campaigns quickly?

A. Deploy a WAF to block suspicious links.

B. Subscribe to a threat feed and automatically block phishing campaign URLs.

C. Manually block phishing URLs as they are reported by users.

D. Implement user awareness training.

218. Amanda discovers that a member of her organization's staff has installed a remote access Trojan on their accounting software server and has been accessing it remotely. What type of threat has she discovered?

A. Zero-day

B. Insider threat

C. Misconfiguration

D. Weak encryption

219. Phil recently received an email claiming to be from HR with a link to a list of every employee's compensation attached. Phil clicks on it without checking the URL because he is curious about the pay that others in his department receive. How would this behavior be classified?

    A. Risky

    B. Irresponsible

    C. Unexpected

    D. Unintentional

220. What should Ben do if he wants to assess the initial state of his information security awareness?

    A. Implement security awareness based on a standard like ISO 27001.

    B. Conduct a baseline analysis to determine his starting state.

    C. Implement security awareness based on NIST standards.

    D. Conduct a penetration test to determine how staff respond to security issues.

221. During an incident investigation, Naomi notices that a second keyboard was plugged into a system in a public area of her company's building. Shortly after that event, the system was infected with malware, resulting in a data breach. What should Naomi look for in her in-person investigation?

    A. A Trojan horse download

    B. A malicious USB cable or drive

    C. A worm

    D. None of the above

222. Jill wants to train her users to appropriately respond to suspicious email messages. Which of the following will provide her organization with the most useful input from users?

    A. Ask users to report the email to the email provider using a reporting button.

    B. Ask users to report the email to an internal security team.

    C. Ask users to delete the email to avoid further issues.

    D. Ask users to click on the message and links to explore the potential security issue.

223. Marcia wants to assess the effectiveness of her security awareness program. What should she do?

    A. Establish and monitor awareness KPIs.

    B. Require a third-party awareness audit.

    C. Conduct regular surveys about security awareness.

    D. Track incident rates versus training participation.

224. Myles wants to describe the impact of noncompliance with regulations on his organization's business. If his organization is not compliant, what impact is most likely to occur related to his customers?

    A. Fines

    B. Contractual impacts

    C. Loss of license

    D. Sanctions

225. Sabrina wants to train her users on password management best practices. Which of the following options will have the largest impact on her organization's password security?

   A. Implementing biometrics authentication factors

   B. Conducting annual training on password best practices

   C. Adopting NIST password length and complexity standards

   D. Requiring staff to use an enterprise password manager

226. Jill wants to explain her organization's risks to senior management, but she knows that the risk register is lengthy and detailed. What type of document is commonly used to convey the most important high-level information found in a risk register to senior leaders?

   A. A risk matrix

   B. An SLE report

   C. An ALE report

   D. A risk KPI list

227. Which of the following best describes guidelines?

   A. They outline the principles and rules that guide the execution of security efforts throughout the enterprise.

   B. They provide advice to organizations seeking to comply with the policies and standards.

   C. They provide mandatory requirements describing how an organization will carry out its information security policies.

   D. They are detailed, step-by-step processes that individuals and organizations must follow in specific circumstances.

Appendix

Answers to Review Questions

Chapter 1: Domain 1.0: General Security Concepts

1. B. File encryption meets all of the needs described. Full-disk encryption is easier to deploy and manage but does not protect individual files in motion and does not effectively support multiuser scenarios. Partition-level encryption has the same challenges, albeit at a partition rather than full-disk level. Record-level encryption is typically used in databases to protect individual records or entries.

2. D. Wildcard certificates are used to handle multiple subdomains with a single certificate. A self-signed certificate will not be recognized by browsers and other services, creating confusion for customers. Root of trust certificates and CRL certificates are not types of certificates.

3. A. Gap analysis considers control objectives and the controls that are intended to meet the objectives.

4. D. In most production environments downtime is the primary concern when considering an application restart. Many application architectures are designed to allow restarts of individual systems or services without creating an outage or downtime. Configuration changes should not be created by a restart, patches generally apply properly, and security controls should be in place throughout the process.

5. C. Organizations frequently use tools like `git` to build repositories that support their need for version control. Backout plans might note that you need to return to the prior version but will need to include how to do so. Stakeholder analysis and SOPs are not specifically supported by or improved by using `git`.

6. B. Key stretching makes potentially weak keys more resistant to brute-forcing and often involves using a hash or block cipher repeatedly to make the original value harder to crack. Key rotation is the process of changing keys on a periodic basis to limit the impact of potential exposure. Master keying and passphrase armoring are not commonly used concepts for information security, although master keys are used for physical locks.

7. C. Operational controls like log monitoring, change management processes, and vulnerability management are all put in place to support managing and using technology in a secure manner.

8. D. Retaining the actual password is not a best practice, and thus encrypting password plain text is not a common technique to make passwords harder to crack. Since the application would need the cryptographic key to read the passwords, anybody who had access to that key could decrypt the passwords. Using a salt, a pepper, and a cryptographic hashing algorithm designed for passwords are all common best practices to prevent offline brute-force attacks.

9. C. Both Diffie–Hellman and RSA are key exchange algorithms designed to securely allow key exchange between users or systems that have not previously communicated.

10. B. Backout plans document what to do to return to a state prior to the change being made and are designed to be implemented if the change fails. They may involve undoing changes,

restoring from backups, or taking other steps and they must contain an appropriate level of detail to ensure that the change can be undone. An impact analysis looks at the potential impact of a change, regression testing ensures that old issues are not introduced in new updates, and maintenance windows are scheduled to allow for downtime or other maintenance activities with appropriate communications, staffing, and other needed elements.

11. D. The CIA triad is confidentiality, availability, and integrity. Theresa's extended outage window will impact the availability of her applications and services.

12. C. Bollards are used to protect infrastructure and structures, and they are usually concrete or steel posts, planters, or similar structures that are intended to prevent a vehicle from impacting what they protect. Speed bumps won't prevent an impact, although they might slow it. Access control vestibules are used to ensure only authorized personnel access a space, and chain-link fences are not typically sufficient for this type of control.

13. D. This is a preventive control that is intended to prevent sensitive data from being sent outside the organization. Managerial controls are procedural mechanisms, corrective controls remediate security issues that have already occurred, and detective controls identify security events that have already occurred.

14. A. Policies and procedures are examples of directive control that inform employees and others of what they should do to achieve security objectives. Corrective controls remediate already existing security issues, detective controls identify security events that have already happened, and preventive controls attempt to stop a security issue before it occurs.

15. D. This solution monitors for changes and is therefore a detective control. It does not prevent changes, and intruders and malicious actors are unlikely to know about it, making it a poor deterrent. Since it is not a policy or practice, it is not a directive control.

16. C. Zero trust designs implement continuous verification, which is an effective control used to limit the threat scope of compromised credentials. While multifactor authentication can be a useful control in this circumstance, a fully implemented zero-trust design will provide greater control than just MFA alone. Single sign-on and federation are both likely to increase threat scope in a compromised credential scenario.

17. A. Tokens replace data with a value that is linked specifically to the data, allowing it to be referenced and used without the field being exposed. Encryption is not used for this purpose, data masking hides elements of a data field like digits from a credit card number, and data randomization is not an obfuscation method.

18. A. The sender uses the receiver's public key to encrypt the message, then the receiver uses their private key to decrypt the message. This ensures that the receiver is the only person who can decrypt a message sent using public key encryption.

19. C. If a certificate may have been breached, organizations should immediately revoke the certificates and place them on a certificate revocation list (CRL). They will then need to replace the certificates with new certificates, but changing hostnames is not required as the certificates themselves will be new. The other options are not typical practices.

20. A. Attackers are unlikely to be able to compromise a system or service while it is offline. They may, however, be able to take advantage of the restart or shutdown process if critical security processes are not online for some portion of the process. Unexpected downtime and dependencies between systems must also be considered when planning patching and system updates.

21. B. Version control is important to ensure that the current and correct version of an application or component is deployed. Dependency mapping can be important to ensure that changed versions don't cause other issues, but it isn't specifically needed to ensure that the current version is what you're deploying. Impact analysis and allow/deny lists are not directly relevant to this requirement.

22. C. Version control systems track versions but don't do testing themselves. Atomic operations ensure that actions like commits don't overwrite other commits in progress. File locking allows a developer to check out a file while it is being worked on, and tagging and labeling helps developers track files and versions.

23. B. Security guards are expensive but offer the most flexibility when organizations need intelligence and reasoning to be applied to security events and unexpected needs. Christina knows that guards can often identify issues that a fixed sensor or control cannot.

24. B. Full-disk encryption provides the most security in situations like this if the device is locked or off. Volume- and partition-level encryption may leave some drive information or even entire volumes or partitions unencrypted, and file-level encryption is typically selective instead of covering every file on a drive.

25. C. In most organizations attempting to use an allow list for websites will take up a lot of time. Mahmoud knows that allow lists can be set up for websites, often at a central network security device–level like a firewall. Bypassing allow lists may be possible, but this can largely be prevented if desired. Allow lists are not overly permissive unless they are configured that way.

26. B. Administrators and system owners typically build backout plans. Stakeholders are involved in impact analysis as they help technical staff understand what the impact of changes will be on business areas. They engage in the change approval process, and they help to determine the maintenance window to ensure that impact on the business is minimized.

27. C. A TPM, or trusted platform module, is a hardware-based, cryptographic processor that is used to generate, store, and manage cryptographic keys. It is also used to help ensure platform integrity by allowing boot validation processes to occur in a secure manner. A CPU is the main processor for a system, NSA is the National Security Agency, and a CCA is a chosen ciphertext attack, a type of attack against cryptographic systems where the attacker can cause a cryptographic system to encrypt known text for analysis.

28. D. The Online Certificate Status Protocol (OCSP) is used to validate certificate status, including checking to see if the certificate is on a certificate revocation list (CRL). TLS is Transport Layer Security, a protocol used to encrypt data in transit between systems that relies on cryptographic certificates, but it is not used to validate the status of certificates on a CRL. Despite SSL itself being outmoded, the term SSL is commonly used to refer to TLS— but here, neither TLS nor SSL is the right option. OCRS was made up for this question.

29. B. A root of trust–based secure boot process validates each signed component as it starts and ensures that the trusted components are all loaded as part of the boot process. Changes to the components are reported as exceptions, meaning that the boot process cannot be properly verified or trusted. Secure initiation manager, boot hash, cryptographic boot manager were made up for this question.

30. B. Alice has deployed a compensating control since she cannot apply controls like patching, configuration, or updates. Directive controls provide formal directions to staff, detective controls detect issues rather than preventing them directly, and procedural controls are not a type of control type used on the Security+ exam.

31. C. Apple devices use a specialized, separate coprocessor that uses encrypted memory and storage as well as dedicated cryptographic functions called a secure enclave. This is distinct from a TPM or HSM, and a screened subnet is a networking concept for a space that will be exposed to the less secure zones while needing to remain secure.

32. A. Standard operating procedures (SOPs) are an organization's normal processes that it uses. SOPs are helpful to ensure that organizations have consistent practices that are in use on an ongoing basis. A change plan is specific to a change, and a backout plan is used to undo a change if problems arise. Fixed operating procedures is not a common term used in change management.

33. A. Transparent data encryption, field-level, and column-level encryption are all common types of database encryption. Sensitivity-based encryption is not and was made up for this question.

34. C. Gap analysis focuses on reviewing a security program against common best practices to identify where gaps between practices exist. Ujamaa will select an information security standard like NIST 800-53, ISO 27001, or another relevant standard and will validate his organization's controls implementation against it. This may include things like which services are not configured properly, whether patches are installed, and if legal requirements are being met, but any of those answers is not a complete answer in this context.

35. C. Video surveillance is a detective control and is useful for detecting security events after they have happened. Fencing, bollards, and lighting are typically considered preventive controls.

36. B. Honeypots are designed to appear to be vulnerable. They are heavily instrumented to capture attacker techniques and tools, allowing for analysis by defenders. Tarpits slow down attackers, beehives are not a term used in this context, and intrusion detection systems (IDSs) are designed to identify and alert about attacks but are not designed to appear to be vulnerable.

37. B. Calculating a cryptographic hash allows the log's hash to be compared against copies to validate that they match. Digitally signing the hash ensures that it can be verified to be the original. Encrypting the log does not allow it to be verified against an original. Without a digital signature, a hash does not meet Renee's requirement for nonrepudiation.

38. A. Infrared sensors are commonly used in open spaces. They are well suited to detecting individuals and are less likely to be overly sensitive. They can cover broader fields than a pressure sensor, and ultrasonic sensors are not commonly deployed as facility-level security sensors.

39. C. Certificates are commonly used to identify both individuals and systems. Tokens, smartcards, and usernames are primarily used by individuals.

40. D. Database and network connectivity, authentication system access, and network time availability are all common dependencies that must be considered when making changes. Applications and services may fail to start properly if these dependencies are not available when they attempt to start.

41. B. Policy engines decide whether to grant access to resources based on policies created by administrators and based on data provided by tools like endpoint detection and response tools, threat intelligence feeds, and security information and event management tools. It does not create or suggest administrative policies, and it does not directly enforce policies—that occurs at a policy enforcement point, typically through a zero-trust agent on the client and at the resource or service side.

42. D. Contracts tend to be updated as part of a contract renewal process, not as part of a change management process related to technical change.

43. B. Change windows rely on the documented change being able to be made. Patching and other technical changes may lead to unexpected interactions or dependency changes that are not accounted for in the original change window. Scaling a clustered system up or down does not change the systems and should not be restricted during a change management window.

44. D. Blockchain ledgers are immutable—they cannot be changed after they are recorded, and they are shared, which means that each participant in the blockchain has access to the entire ledger. Transactions are recorded only once and cannot be tampered with—in fact, if an error is made and recorded, a new record has to be created including the fix, and both records will be accessible to show the history of what occurred.

45. A. Damian has created a certificate signing request, which he can submit to a certificate authority (CA).

46. B. Preplanned times when maintenance is done and outages may occur is known as a maintenance window. An unscheduled outage is just that—unscheduled and unplanned, often due to a failure or other issue. Allocated downtime and allowed outages are not common terms for this.

47. B. An estimate of the downtime expected as part of the change will help Megan to assess the impact of the change on her organization's business operations. A backout plan is useful if something goes wrong and can help estimate impact if that happens, but it does not identify impact under normal circumstances. A list of stakeholders can help when communicating with stakeholders to notify them of what will occur, but without the estimate of downtime, Megan will not be able to ask them what the impact would be. Finally, a list of dependencies is helpful to ensure that the change does not have unexpected issues and can help with the impact assessment to determine if other systems may be impacted, but the downtime expected remains the most important item.

48. C. Organizations often perform changes in a test environment to allow accurate time estimates and to determine if there are issues with the change like undocumented dependencies or problems with patches. Average downtime is a poor indicator of what a specific change may require, a fixed maintenance window does not ensure the change will take that amount of time, and vendors rarely have a full understanding of the environment an organization is operating in.

49. C. Symmetric encryption uses the same key for all participants in an exchange. Asymmetric encryption uses public and private keys where public keys are shared and private keys are retained. Shared hashing and universal encryption are not terms commonly used to describe encryption.

50. D. Asymmetric encryption makes key exchange possible because public keys are just that: public. They can be shared without causing a loss of cryptographic security or repudiation. They do not help with collision resistance, key length, or evil twins (which are malicious wireless access points).

51. A. A TPM is used to validate secure boot processes. A hardware security module (HSM) is used for key generation, storage, and management as well as for encrypting and decrypting data and creating and validating digital signatures.

52. A. Steganography is the art of hiding additional data in images. Michelle can use steganography detection tools to attempt to find the data, but attackers may use custom tools that could avoid detection as well. The other options were made up for this question.

53. C. SAML is the Security Assertion Markup Language, used to exchange authentication and authorization data between identity providers and service providers. TLS, IPSec, and SSH are all common transport encryption protocols.

54. B. Record-level encryption is commonly associated with databases, where it is used to encrypt each record with a unique encryption key, allowing it to be more secure than database-level encryption.

55. C. Yasmine's company has implemented a key escrow process where encryption keys are retained by the organization in case the files on the drive need to be accessed by someone with proper authority. A hardware security module (HSM) is a hardware device used to create and store encryption keys, among other encryption-related functions. Perfect forward secrecy (PFS) is a term used in encryption systems that change keys frequently to ensure that even if a key is hacked, the attacker's access to data will exist in a limited window. Private keys are part of asymmetric encryption schemes and do not reflect the full solution Yasmine's organization is using.

56. B. Certificates are commonly used for system authentication in AAA systems. While asymmetric and symmetric are forms of encryption, they are not authentication schemes, and PIN-based authentication is not commonly used for system authentication.

57. C. Honeyfiles are files that are intentionally made to look attractive while being configured for detection by data loss prevention and intrusion prevention/detection systems. A honeypot is an intentionally vulnerable system that is used to monitor attacker behavior and techniques for analysis. Honeynets are networks that are configured to be intentionally vulnerable and that operate much like honeypots at a network level. Honeytokens are credentials that are not actually used but that are monitored for use in case an attacker is able to capture them.

58. B. Lighting is a deterrent control type and would typically be categorized as a physical control.

59. C. Any control that requires constant human presence like security guards is likely to have a higher ongoing cost than controls that can be put in place and operate without human intervention or presence.

60. C. SHA-256 is the current, secure hashing standard. While it is unlikely that a malicious actor would exploit known flaws in MD5 and SHA-1, in most normal operations SHA-256 remains the preferred option when it is available. The Advanced Encryption Standard (AES) is used for encryption, not hashing.

61. B. Policies are examples of directive controls. This could also be considered a corrective control, but that is not one of the options listed. Detective controls identify security events that have already occurred, and this does not detect the compromised account—it directs what must happen afterward. A compensating control mitigates risks due to exceptions in the security policy like a violation of policy due to an inability to implement a specific technical control like patching. A preventive control attempts to stop a security issue before it occurs. Here, the issue has already occurred. The policy of directive control tells staff what do to, and the action of locking the account is a corrective control.

62. C. RADIUS is commonly used for AAA for network devices. OpenID and SAML are more commonly associated with federated services, and TANGENT is not an AAA protocol or server.

63. C. Physical security sensors are not typically part of a zero-trust policy engine feed. Zero-trust environments primarily focus on network and systems access rather than physical security and access.

64. A. Valerie is interacting with a policy enforcement point, the agent and resource-side elements that validate trust by requiring authentication and authorization before allowing access to a resource. The policy enforcement point will validate her access through the policy engine, which will be configured by the policy administrator. Trust managers are not a typical component of the zero-trust model.

65. B. Identity, devices, networks, applications and workloads, and data are all assessed as part of the NIST Zero Trust Maturity Model. The model does not assess an organization's business model or practices.

66. A. OpenID is an open standard for decentralized authentication that is used by many cloud service providers. Kerberos, LDAP, and TACACS+ are all most commonly associated with on-site usage.

67. A. Corrective controls attempt to remediate security issues that have already occurred. Patching the flaw that allowed an attack to succeed is an example of a corrective control. Deploying full-disk encryption or an EDR tool are both examples of preventive controls, and logging and log monitoring are examples of detective controls. It is important to note that in many cases, controls could be identified as multiple potential control types. In cases where controls might fit multiple control types, you should look for the control that is most obviously the correct control type.

68. C. Symmetric encryption does not support nonrepudiation because both parties have the same key. Both asymmetric and symmetric encryption can provide confidentiality, integrity, and authentication.

69. C. A KMS, or key management system, is a solution that allows you to safely store and manage secrets like keys and certificates. Centralizing a KMS allows organizations to effectively manage their secrets, including tracking their life cycle and rotation. A TPM is used for hardware security on physical systems, a CA is a certificate authority used to create and sign certificates, and a CSR is a certificate signing request.

70. B. Data masking conceals elements of a data field or entry, preventing all of it from being seen but leaving it accessible through the database when masking is not used. Tokenization replaces values with a reference value—often a hash that can be used to refer to the value without using the actual entry. Hashing is a one-way function that produces an input of arbitrary length. Field encryption is not a common term.

71. A. In a decentralized blockchain, no individual or group controls the blockchain. Blockchains can store many types of data, including but not limited to transactions. Blockchain transactions are permanent once written, and a new transaction or update would need to be recorded rather than revising an existing transaction. Blockchain transactions are stored on the blockchain maintained by participants, not on central servers chosen by election.

72. B. Subordinate CAs avoid the cost of maintaining a root CA while providing control over certificates that are issued and allowing specialized support for different types of certificates like SSL and S/MIME. Subordinate CAs can issue certificates for any allowed domain or subdomain, are not required to ensure auditability, and can sign certificates themselves.

73. B. Pressure sensors can be deployed to detect footsteps in a secured area. Infrared and microwave sensors are more commonly used to detect motion, and ultrasonic sensors are rarely used for security purposes.

74. D. Firewalls are a technical control, not a managerial control that focuses on the mechanics of the risk management process.

75. C. Third-party certificates allow customers to have full control over the certificate, including the private key and certificate signing request. By bringing your own certificate, encrypted traffic cannot be decrypted by the cloud provider. Using provider-provided or -created certificates leads to a potential risk if the provider is malicious or compromised and private keys managed by the provider are compromised. Bringing your own certificate does not necessarily reduce costs. Providers typically allow certificate signing requests for customer domains and subdomains as needed and supported by the service.

76. C. Disk encryption is commonly used to ensure confidentiality of data. UPS, load balancers, and redundant Internet connectivity all support availability.

77. B. Honeynets are collections of decoy systems and devices that are instrumented and monitored, providing organizations and individuals with information about how threat actors attack targeted systems. Honeyfarm and honeycluster are not industry terms, and darknets are segments of unused network space that should not receive traffic. Darknets are monitored to help identify scanning and other attacks since traffic should not flow to them.

78. A. Fencing is considered a deterrent because it will discourage potential intruders from accessing facilities. Generators are used to ensure availability and are a preventive control. Access badges are a technical and preventive control in most cases. A camera system is a detective, technical control.

79. C. The root certificate, or top certificate for a certificate chain, is the root of trust of the chain, and it must be kept secure so the entire certificate and CA hierarchy can be trusted. Hardened hardware devices may be used to store it, but they are not the actual root itself. A TPM is used to store system-specific security data, and wildcard certificates cover more than one subdomain for an organization.

80. B. By definition, open public ledgers are open and public—anyone can join at any time. No vote is required, and creators do not control the ledger once it is made public.

81. A. Some software may attempt to validate the certificates in use and could fail. This may also lead to unexpected differences between production certificates and test certificates, which is undesirable in a test environment intended to mirror production. Both internal users and external users can still successfully use self-signed certificates for SSL, but they will receive warnings in modern browsers. Browsers can typically be told to bypass warnings, or self-signed certificates can be added to system certificate chains as needed, although this requires additional work from system administration teams and may not be desirable.

82. C. The most effective way to ensure that all dependencies have been satisfied is to perform the change in a matching test environment to ensure that all issues have been identified and resolved. Updating policies and procedures as well as diagrams is typically done after major changes that result in a need for updates. Legacy applications that may create dependencies are not the only potential source of dependency issues.

83. B. Kerberos uses authentication tickets and ticket-granting tickets to grant session keys for services that clients present to services to access them. TACACS+, MS-CHAP, and EAP do not use this ticket-based approach.

84. A. AES-256 is the only currently recommended encryption solution on the list. SHA-1 is a hashing algorithm. DES and Blowfish both have vulnerabilities and have been replaced in modern usage.

85. D. Lighting, fences, bollards, and access control vestibules are all examples of physical controls.

86. B. Jack should digitally sign the file and provide his public key to the other organization. This will allow them to validate his signature, as well as the integrity of the signed file.

Encrypting the file does not ensure its integrity but does protect its confidentiality. Sending a hash does not ensure that the email was not modified, and emailing file size and name does not ensure the file was not changed.

87. D. Certificates expire, but expiration does not place them on a CRL. That avoids extremely long CRLs in most cases, and the expired certificate contains sufficient information to know that the certificate is expired without being on a CRL. Reasons to add a certificate to a CLR include the CA being compromised, the certificate's private key being compromised, a mis-issued certificate, certificate detail changes that require a reissued certificate, or certificates that were fraudulently signed, typically by a subordinate CA that was exploited or had poor practices.

88. D. SHA-256 is the only hashing algorithm listed that is considered current and secure as of the publication of this book. MD5 and SHA-1 both have known security issues, and AES-256 is an encryption algorithm.

89. C. To verify whether a message was signed by a sender, the recipient needs the sender's public key.

90. B. Creating a complete backout plan and implementing it if something goes wrong that cannot be remediated during a change window is the accepted best practice in this scenario. That may involve restoring from backups or uninstalling the patch, but neither of these options is necessarily the correct answer in all circumstances. Similarly, declaring an outage may be necessary, but following the backout plan and communicating effectively is the best option.

91. A. This is a corrective control because it remediates a security issue after the event has occurred. A compensating control would attempt to mitigate a risk associated with exceptions made to a security policy. Deterrent controls attempt to prevent an attacker from violating security policies, and detective controls identify security events that have already happened.

92. D. A zero-trust system should validate its level of confidence in a request that it receives once the basic criteria have been met. This may involve checking the access against known patterns of access by the user, validating current threat feed information, or checking other details that will help ensure the security and authenticity of the request.

93. A. While many honeyfiles use canary tokens, simply monitoring for known files exiting systems that should not be accessed under normal circumstances is also a valid means to construct a honeypot and honeyfile-based detection system. Charles can use the file and the isolated system to detect attackers who attempt to exfiltrate the file. The other answers were made up for this question.

94. B. Salting uses a unique, randomly generated string that is added to each password before it is hashed. That means that even matching passwords will not have the same hash. This prevents rainbow tables from being effectively used against password hashes due to the added computational load it creates for precomputing hashes.

95. B. Secure enclaves are used by Apple devices to securely store security information like cryptographic keys.

96. C. Implementing key stretching techniques can help short—and thus weak—passwords resist brute-force hash cracking techniques. They won't help against brute-force password guessing attacks, so Isaac will need to implement other controls against that type of attack. Pass-the-hash attacks reuse hashes, and thus aren't a technique used to prevent brute-force attacks against hashed passwords. Collision resistance is a requirement for an effective hashing algorithm and should be part of any password hash storage implementation. Encrypting passwords is not a recommended practice because it leaves passwords in the hands of the organization rather than hashes and requires the organization to decrypt passwords to check them when they are used, creating frequent opportunities for exposure.

97. B. RFID badges are the most commonly implemented wireless identification badges. Wi-Fi and Bluetooth both require additional power for devices and thus are not a good fit for a badge, and NFC-enabled badges have not come into common use at this time, although they are increasingly available for mobile device–enabled badges.

98. B. A compensating control helps to mitigate a risk due to an exception to a security policy. Here, the devices cannot be patched or fixed but are important to the operations of the organization. Moving them to a protected network will help compensate for the lack of patching. Since no security issues have occurred, this is not a corrective control. Confidentiality and coordinated controls are not control types for the Security+ exam.

99. B. Adaptive authentication looks at the context of a login, including where they're logging in from—both geographically, and from a network trust perspective, what device they're logging in from, and if the device is configured correctly. In modern, multidevice usage, whether the user has logged in recently from another device isn't as likely to be considered, but if the devices were in different countries it would likely raise a flag!

100. A. One of the basic tenets of zero-trust architecture is that all communication is secured, regardless of the security zone or trust zone that it occurs in. Additional security should not be required, nor should communications receive less security in higher trust zones. All zero-trust networks are considered potential risk areas—thus the zero in zero trust!

101. C. Microwave sensors work in temperature ranges that infrared sensors do not, and they can penetrate walls and some small spaces allowing more complete coverage. Microwave sensors cannot detect heat signatures, are not cheaper than infrared sensors, and can interfere with some types of sensitive equipment.

102. C. Access control vestibules are intended to make it obvious that someone is following you through secured doors and may only be large enough for a single person to come through at once. Larger vestibules rely on staff noticing that the person following them through is not providing credentials and ensuring that doors close between access attempts.

103. B. Data masking reveals only part of a field and is often used with details like credit card numbers or Social Security numbers where only the last four digits will be revealed for validation purposes.

104. B. While version control has many useful impacts on security, tracking workload is not a security-related issue for version control.

105. D. While auditors may request application version information during audits, they are not typically notified during normal application updates and patching cycles. Application administrators, service owners, and system administrators are all commonly notified about functional validation test results so that they can take further action or know that the service update is complete.

106. B. Each individual has their own keypair in asymmetric encryption systems; thus, for four individuals to communicate securely using asymmetric encryption four keypairs are needed.

107. D. A dedicated, hardware-based, cloud-hosted hardware security module (HSM) is an appropriate solution for Michelle's needs. Cloud providers often provide shared HSMs as a service, which can increase perceived risk due to the shared underlying hardware. Dedicated hardware is typically available at a higher cost. Trusted platform modules (TPMs) are used to provide secure boot and related services, not to store secrets for an organization.

108. B. To sign a file, Murali needs to use his own private key. The recipient can then use their public key to validate the signature.

109. C. OCSP requests must include the certificate's serial number to allow the OCSP responder to check the CA database for the certificate and its status. It does not require the domain name or requestor's name. Open public ledgers are part of blockchains, not OCSP.

110. C. Wildcard certificates have a * in them, denoting that they can be used for any subdomain. For example, in this question, the wildcard would match any *.example.com subdomain like test.example.com and sales.example.com. Self-signed certificates will not link to a root or intermediate CA, and thus cannot be verified with CAs.

111. A. Policies and procedures are examples of directive controls. Deterrent controls attempt to dissuade attackers from taking action. Preventive controls attempt to stop security issues from occurring. Proactive controls are not a control category used on the Security+ exam.

112. A. Allow lists can be difficult to manage over time, particularly as manufacturers and vendors add additional download and update sites and subdomains. This creates additional work for administrators and can cause errors or issues with updates and patching if not carefully monitored. Allow lists do prevent sites from being visited if they are not on the list, they can be configured with wildcards to allow entire domains or subdomains if desired, and they only allow sites that are added, meaning any problems with unwanted sites are the responsibility of the allow list administrator.

113. A. EAP is commonly used for authentication to wireless networks. MS-CHAP is used with PPTP-based VPNs, Kerberos is used for organizationwide authentication, and LDAP is used as part of authentication in Microsoft Active Directory domains, among other uses.

114. A. Validation testing should follow application restarts to ensure the application is working as expected after the restart. Documentation and updating version information can be done after the validation because if validation fails the change may need to be reversed. Vulnerability scanning should have been done prior to implementation in a test environment if needed, and then should be done as part of ongoing security operations.

115. A. Microwave sensors are commonly used to detect motion and have advantages over infrared sensors because they can work in a greater temperature range as well as traveling through some obstacles that would not allow infrared to penetrate them. They do not capture audio and are therefore not used for glass-break sensors, they do not capture thermal data like infrared sensors, and they are not pressure sensors.

116. C. In order for a drive to be used, it must be accessible to the operating system, meaning that when the system is logged in and in use data can be accessed. When full-disk encryption systems are booting and not logged in or when they are being shut down, they are typically not in a greater risk state, and they are most secure when shut down.

117. A. Full-disk encryption primarily supports confidentiality by preventing unwanted access to the drive if it is stolen or otherwise exposed. The three objectives are confidentiality, integrity, and availability, which means authenticity is not a possible answer. Encryption does not increase availability, and integrity ensures that data has not been changed inadvertently or maliciously. Thus, encryption can help, but it is not as strong of an answer as confidentiality.

118. B. A gap analysis is used to determine whether controls meet control objectives for a service, an organization, or a system. Penetration tests simulate an attacker trying to gain access or breach systems and other controls. Boolean analysis is not a security term, and risk analysis is done as part of risk assessment.

119. C. Access control lists are best described as technical controls. Managerial controls are procedural mechanisms; physical controls are controls that impact the physical world, like locks or fences; and operational controls are processes used to manage technology in a secure manner, like the change management process Frank will likely follow to make changes to the access control list.

120. B. Video surveillance system storage can drive additional costs based on decisions like how long video is retained, sensitivity levels, video resolution, and how heavily trafficked camera covered areas are. Licensing may grow if additional cameras are added, but there is no information in the question indicating changes in the size of the implementation. Since this is an unmonitored system, no guards are involved, and camera maintenance is not a typical issue for a newly deployed system.

121. D. Restoring from backups helps to remediate a security issue, making this a corrective control. Preventive controls for Henry's situation might include endpoint detection and response (EDR) tools, directive controls would include policies and procedures for ransomware events, and compensating controls would be used if exceptions to the security policies needed to be made.

122. B. Tokenization commonly uses randomly generated values that are assigned to replace existing known values. The token is stored in a lookup table, allowing the token to be checked against the table if needed. Hashing relies on a hash function, which is not mentioned here; randomization is not a data obfuscation technique; and masking replaces some or all of a sensitive field with a replacement character to ensure the data is unreadable when displayed.

123. C. Key exchange algorithms focus on how to securely exchange keys so that others cannot obtain a copy of the key. Asymmetric encryption is used instead of symmetric encryption to resolve the issue of large numbers of symmetric keys; keys are either public or private in asymmetric systems and determining if they are public is not considered a problem; and keys are not returned to their owner, as only public keys should be exchanged.

124. D. Legal counsel is not typically part of change management processes. Stakeholders, service owners, and system administrators are commonly involved in impact analysis sessions.

125. D. Certificate requests include the common name (CN); organization (O); organization unit in the organization (OU); city or locality (L); the state, county, or region (S); country (C); and organizational contact email address.

126. C. Tony is salting his password, which involves adding a string of characters to the password before it is hashed. This creates a unique hash, even if the password itself is an easily guessed or common password.

127. A. While cryptocurrency is a common use of blockchain technology, it isn't the only use. Values of blocks are not determined as part of transactions—in fact, even in cryptocurrency uses, values are determined by prices set on exchanges as sellers and buyers exchange cryptocurrencies.

128. B. TLS, or Transport Layer Security, is a cryptographic protocol used to secure network traffic in transit. S/MIME, or Secure MIME, is used for digital signatures and encryption for email. MPLS is multiprotocol label switching, a network routing technique. SSH is Secure Shell and is used for encrypted command-line access as well as to tunnel other protocols in some cases.

129. C. Legacy applications are often unsupported, don't receive new patches or updates, and have a shrinking or nonexistent base of consultants and experts. Licensing for legal applications is often not available; this making ongoing licensing costs a less frequent concern.

130. A. Change management processes typically focus on documenting dependencies and ensuring they are met. That may involve ensuring that the appropriate version is installed or that applications are restarted in a specific order, or that a service is available that is needed for a system to successfully function. Removing dependencies is unlikely, patching may or may not be required, and updating diagrams is less important than ensuring the dependencies are understood and met.

131. A. Record-level encryption relies on a unique key for each record, keeping records private to a user or account in typical usage.

132. A. Justin's laptop is a subject. Subjects like users, applications, or devices are not trusted by default. Justin's system is also likely a policy enforcement point, not a policy application point, and will run a zero-trust client application that will interface with the zero-trust framework to determine if the system is secure as part of authentication and authorization processes. Policy engines evaluate policies and use threat information and other data to determine if access should be given in the context of the time, place, and system the request is made from. Service providers are concepts used in federation, rather than in zero-trust environments.

133. C. Policy-driven access control focuses on using rules to determine who can access a service based on security state and other information. Adaptive authorization adjusts authorization levels based on factors like device status, user behavior, and location. Threat scope reduction is a key concept in zero trust that focuses on ensuring that threats have less of a target to attack if they enter the secure environment. Secured zones are no longer a critical concept for zero trust, as continuous verification means all interactions are secured and validated.

134. B. OCSP, or the Online Certificate Status Protocol, provides a way to check on the status of a certificate, including whether it has been revoked.

135. D. Key rotation should occur when a user leaves, even if the key is escrowed. Regulatory compliance as well as providing access for administrative or emergency access to organizational data are common reasons to implement key escrow.

136. C. Once a private key has been exposed, it should not be considered secure, even in an organization of trusted users. Since Yariv exposed his private key via email, he cannot ensure that it is not available in another user's email archives, and he must immediately create a new keypair and advise individuals that he works with of his new public key.

137. B. Since blockchains are not changed after transactions are recorded, a new transaction must be recorded and both transactions remain in the record as part of the ledger.

138. B. Patches and updates are less likely to result in a need to update policies and procedures. New applications, lessons learned exercises, and regulatory changes are all likely to result in changes to policies and procedures.

139. C. Access badges are an example of something you have, and PINs are an example of something you know. Combining the two is a common requirement to help prevent a lost badge from providing access to a secure facility. A security desk with a guard is more costly but can be more effective if the guards are well trained and diligent, but the needs of Hrant's organization are met properly by the access badge and PIN.

140. C. Microwave sensors are not commonly used to detect intruders. Infrared and ultrasonic sensors are commonly used, and pressure sensors may be used in special circumstances.

141. C. Secure cryptographic hash systems should not generate the same output for two different inputs. They should, however, be one-way functions and generate fixed length output, and they are commonly used to verify the integrity of files.

142. C. Access control vestibules are designed to stop tailgating attacks, which occur when someone follows an authorized user into a space. Access badges do not prevent this, as tailgating relies on passing through a door someone with access has opened. Video surveillance may allow you to see the attack but won't stop it, and bollards are used to prevent vehicles from passing through a space.

143. B. Requiring a PIN is the best option unless guards are in place to validate that the person using the badge matches the badge. Even then a PIN may be better than a picture if the badge does not have other elements like holographic seals that will prevent it from being modified. Barcode and RFID badges can still be cloned and are not as effective as requiring a knowledge-based identifier as well as a possession-based identifier.

144. B. A feature of digital signatures is nonrepudiation. A signed file or message can be proven to be from the signer, proving that it is legitimate. Key stretching describes techniques used to make it harder to crack weak keys. Authentication is the process of validating that a person is who they say they are but is not specific to digital signatures. Ledger-based validation was made up for this question.

145. B. Public keys can simply be sent to another user if so desired. It is common to provide public keys via key servers or even in email signatures, although addition verification that the key belongs to an individual may be desirable, if not required.

146. C. Generating a unique salt for each hashed entry is the most secure option among those listed. Storing a fixed salt in a database or in code reduces the complexity of the salted information, making it possible for an attacker to acquire the single salt and then attack the stored hashes. Generating a unique salt every time a value is used is impractical due to the rate of change.

147. B. Risk assessments are an example of a managerial control, which includes procedural mechanisms related to the risk management process. Technical controls enforce confidentiality, integrity, and availability using technical means. Physical controls like locks and fences impact the physical world. Operational controls include processes put in place to manage technology in a secure manner.

148. B. Removing malicious software is an example of a corrective control, which seeks to remediate security issues that have already occurred. Preventive controls are intended to stop security issues from occurring. Compensating controls are designed to mitigate risks associated with exemptions to the security policy, like moving systems to a secure network segment because they cannot be patched. Deterrent controls attempt to prevent a malicious actor from violating security policies.

149. B. Root certificates are at the root of trust in a CA hierarchy and allow signing keys to be created and used to sign certificates. They are not used to authorize new CA users or to remove certificates from a CRL. Key stretching is used to make weak keys stronger, not as part of cryptographic certificates.

150. D. Authentication requires that users provide (claim) an identity and then provide one or more authentication factors like a password, biometric factor, or multifactor code. Authorization relies on matching users and roles to allow users to perform tasks once they are authenticated. Biometric enrollments and identity proofing may be desirable but are not necessarily required for any given authentication system.

Chapter 2: Domain 2.0: Threats, Vulnerabilities, and Mitigations

1. C. Nation-state actors are typically advanced persistent threats (APTs) and their motivations commonly include espionage, data exfiltration, disruption/chaos, and war. Financial gain is more commonly associated with organized crime, blackmail with insider threats, and ethical with hacktivists.

2. C. Spear phishing is targeted to a specific group, in this case insurance professionals. Although this is a form of phishing, the more specific answer is the one you will need to choose on questions like this. Phishing uses social engineering techniques to succeed but is once again a broader answer than spear phishing and thus is not the correct choice. Finally, a Trojan horse pretends to be a legitimate or desirable program or file, which this scenario doesn't describe.

3. B. A logic bomb is malware that performs its malicious activity when some condition is met. A worm is malware that self-propagates. A Trojan horse is malware attached to a legitimate program, and a rootkit is malware that gets root or administrative privileges.

4. C. Using appropriate contractual terms is usually the best available option for handling third-party vendor risk. The terms can include things like security practices, such as pentesting, incident response exercises, and vulnerability scanning, and can also have sufficient penalties to ensure ongoing compliance from responsible companies.

5. B. This is an example of a virtual machine (VM) escape vulnerability. Jailbreaking and side-loading are terms used to describe mobile device–related means of violating security, and resource reuse is a VM concern if data is not properly removed before a resource is given to another VM.

6. B. Endpoint protection software like an endpoint detection and response (EDR) or extended detection and response (XDR) tool will provide the greatest protection against ransomware. Firewalls and intrusion prevention systems (IPSs) are less likely to prevent ransomware from being installed, and removing unnecessary software may reduce the attack surface but most ransomware is installed via attacks that leverage users.

7. B. Wi-Fi Protected Access 3 (WPA-3) is the most modern, most secure option from the list. WPA-4 does not currently exist as of this writing. WPA-2 Enterprise requires an authentication server and is less secure than WPA-3, while WPA-2 Personal allows for a single, set password.

8. C. Cross-site scripting (XSS) involves entering a script into text areas that other users will view. SQL injection (SQLi) is not about entering scripts but rather SQL commands. Clickjacking is about tricking users into clicking on the wrong thing. Bluejacking is a Bluetooth attack.

9. C. There are many indicators of compromise (IoCs), including unusual outbound network traffic, geographical irregularities like logins from a country where the person normally does not work, or increases in database read volumes beyond normal traffic patterns. Predictive analysis is analysis work done using datasets to attempt to determine trends and likely attack vectors so that analysts can focus their efforts where they will be most needed and effective. OSINT is open source intelligence, and threat maps are often real-time or near-real-time visualizations of where threats are coming from and where they are headed.

10. B. On-path attacks that route traffic through a system or device that the attacker controls allow the attacker to both receive and modify traffic, making replay attacks more likely to succeed. SQL injection attacks are associated with web applications and databases. Brute-force and distributed denial-of-service (DDoS) attacks are not typically associated with replay attacks.

11. A. Since Valerie is investigating an incident, she should immediately consider the potential that the logs were wiped. That likely means that the intruder has gained privileged access to the system, which should worry her even more! Reboots do not wipe `audit.log`, and Valerie should have permissions appropriate to perform her function. System errors could explain an empty `audit.log`, but are unlikely, and an empty log found during an investigation is a cause for concern.

12. B. Jack has attempted a watering hole attack that leverages a frequently visited site to target a specific group of people. In this case, he is targeting his penetration testing target's users. Misinformation and disinformation are used to change opinions or to provide false information, and while business email compromise attacks are part of the Security+ exam outline, business website compromise attacks are not.

13. C. While malware, modified firmware, and lack of availability are common concerns with the hardware supply chain, hardware modifications remain relatively uncommon.

14. B. On-path attacks are used to capture, then replay valid credentials for attackers to use. Session tokens are used to counter this type of attack in some cases. Phishing email and brute-force password attacks can help obtain credentials but do not involve credential replay. Injection attacks are typically conducted against database servers.

15. B. Common motivations for internal threat actors include blackmail, financial gain, and ethical reasons. Nation-state threats are more likely to be interested in espionage and war, and hacktivists in political beliefs.

16. B. These are all common examples of bloatware, unwanted but typically not harmful software installed by manufacturers and as part of the installation processes for desired applications. MSPs are managed service providers, ransomware is malware that attempts to hold files for ransom, and rootware was made up for this question.

17. C. Impossible travel describes scenarios where logins or other actions occur from separate physical locations that are too far apart to travel between before the action occurs. Here it is impossible to travel from China to the UK in an hour, and Ilya may need to check in with the employee since no VPN usage was described. It is possible the employee's account is compromised or some other questionable activity is occurring.

18. D. Radio frequency identification (RFID) badges can be cloned, but adding an additional factor like a PIN means the badge alone is not sufficient to gain access. Piggybacking involves following an authorized user through a security door or gate. On-path attacks inject an attacker into the middle of a transaction or network connection, allowing them to view and potentially modify traffic. Concurrent session usage or access is an indicator of compromise (IoC) that focuses on multiple systems or users using the same credentials.

19. B. Business email compromise (BEC) scams appear to come from legitimate sources and make requests that may seem reasonable like a payment change to a different wire transfer method. Vishing is done via voice, smishing via SMS, and pretexting uses excuses or reasons that the requested action must be taken.

20. B. The primary concern for security professionals around legacy hardware is their lack of patches and updates, meaning that security fixes and updates will not exist. While the hardware could fail, that would typically lead to replacement with more modern, supportable options and is a concern for the system administrators and owners. Lack of vendor support and inability to support modern protocols are primarily concerns for owners and system administrators.

21. A. From the description it appears that they are not connecting to the real web server but rather a fake server. That indicates typo squatting: having a URL that is named very similarly to a real site so that when users mistype the real site's URL they will go to the fake site.

22. C. Domain hijacking, or domain theft, occurs when the registration or other information for the domain is changed without the original registrant's permission. This may occur because of a compromised account or due to a breach of the domain registrar's security. A common issue is a lapsed domain being purchased by a third party, and this can look like a hijacked domain, but it is a legitimate occurrence if the domain is not renewed! DNS hijacking inserts false information into a DNS server, on-path (man-in-the-middle) attacks capture or modify traffic by causing the traffic to pass through a compromised midpoint, and zero-day attacks are unknown to product vendors and, therefore, no patches are available to correct them.

23. C. Open source software dependencies are a primary challenge when considering open source supply chain concerns. In this case, Lucia is using a third-party vendor who can provide support, open source code is auditable, and updates are likely to occur with a vendor involved.

24. A. Server-side request forgery (SSRF) attempts typically attempt to get HTTP data passed through and will not include SQL injection. Blocking sensitive hostnames, IP addresses, and URLs are all valid ways to prevent SSRF, as is the use of allow list–based input filters.

25. D. A host-based intrusion prevention system (HIPS) can monitor, identify, and stop network traffic that displays network traffic to identify attacks, suspicious behavior, and known bad patterns using signatures. A firewall stops traffic based on rules; antimalware tools are specifically designed to stop malware, not attacks and suspicious network behavior; and a host-based intrusion detection system (HIDS) can only detect, not stop, these behaviors.

26. D. Unskilled attackers, often called script kiddies, tend to use premade tools in unsophisticated ways. Hacktivists take action based on political motivation, insiders operate from inside of an organization, and nation-state actors are typically highly capable and well resourced.

27. B. Phishing is intended to acquire data, most often credentials or other information that will be useful to the attacker. Spam is a broader term for unwanted email, although the term is often generally used to describe unwanted communications. Spear phishing targets specific individuals, whereas whaling targets higher-ups such as CEOs in an organization. Smishing is sent via SMS (text message). Malware can be sent in any of these instances, but there is not a specific related term that means "spam with malware in it."

28. B. Systems and software that no longer have vendor support can be a significant security risk, and ensuring that a vendor will continue to exist and provide support is an important part of many procurement processes. Selah's questions are intended to assess the longevity and viability of the company and whether buying from them will result in her organization having a usable product for the long term.

29. B. His machines are part of a distributed denial-of-service (DDoS) attack. This scenario describes a generic DDoS, not a specific one like SYN flood, which would involve many SYN packets being sent without a full three-way TCP handshake. These machines could be part of a botnet or they may just have a trigger that causes them to launch the attack at a specific time. The real key in this scenario is the DDoS attack. Finally, a backdoor gives an attacker access to the target system.

30. B. A Trojan attaches a malicious program to a legitimate program. When the user downloads and installs the legitimate program, they get the malware. A logic bomb is malware that does its misdeeds when some condition is met. A rootkit is malware that gets administrative, or root, access. A macro virus is a virus that is embedded in a document as a macro.

31. A. Hacktivists are defined by their political motivation. Organized crime is most frequently associated with financial gain as a motivation. While unskilled attackers and insider threats may have political motivations, hacktivists remain the most likely of this list.

32. D. Organized crime may produce, sell, and support malware tools, or may deploy them themselves. Crypto malware and other packages are examples of tools often created and used by criminal syndicates. State actors are more likely to be associated with advanced persistent threats (APTs) aimed at accomplishing goals of the nation-state that supports them. Hacktivists typically have political motivations, whereas unskilled attackers (script kiddies) may simply be in it for recognition or fun.

33. A. Bluejacking involves sending unsolicited messages to Bluetooth devices when they are in range. Bluesnarfing involves getting data from the Bluetooth device. An evil twin attack uses a rogue access point whose name is similar or identical to that of a legitimate access point.

34. A. An on-path attack redirects all traffic through an attacker's system that would normally pass through a network gateway. Dennis will be able to see all traffic bound for remote systems, but some of it may be encrypted.

35. B. When malicious actors claim to represent a company or organization to accomplish their goals, it is an example of a brand impersonation attack. Here, this is a combination of a vishing attack and a brand impersonation attack. Smishing occurs via SMS, watering hole attacks target sites that their intended victims commonly visit, and business email compromise attempts to gain access to or leverages email accounts.

36. A. Cryptographic downgrade attacks like POODLE, FREAK, and Logjam all rely on flaws that cause software to use weaker encryption options. This could allow attackers to capture traffic encrypted with weaker encryption, potentially allowing them to decrypt the traffic and read it. They do not allow hashing changes to recover passwords, reversion to old versions of software, or encryption to be entirely turned off.

37. D. Segmentation can be used to separate systems and applications of different sensitivity levels. A breach of one segmented group should not automatically mean that the other groupings are in immediate danger. Application allow lists control what applications can be installed but do not introduce separation between systems and applications. Monitoring would allow visibility but does not meet the goal Rick has. Least privilege is an effective practice to ensure only the rights required are in place, but again this does not meet the goal.

38. B. This is vishing, or using voice calls for phishing. Spear phishing is targeting a small, specific group. War dialing is dialing numbers hoping a computer modem answers. Robocalling is used to place unsolicited telemarketing calls.

39. C. This is an example of a least privilege implementation where only the privileges required are issued. The checkout process is a modern addition to least privilege environments where even privileges needed are only issued temporarily, making least privilege even more secure. Segmentation and isolation are used to separate systems or environments, and configuration enforcement is used to ensure that configurations continue to be set as expected.

40. A. An insecure, unencrypted, unprotected wireless network will have all of its traffic exposed. If the network is not using WPA-2 or WPA-3, it is trivial to observe network traffic even if an old protocol like WEP was in use.

41. B. Zero-day exploits are new, and they are not in the virus definitions for the antivirus (AV) programs. This makes them difficult to detect, except by their behavior. Remote-access Trojans (RATs), worms, and rootkits are more likely to be detected by AV programs.

42. C. Brute force tries every possible combination with small changes each time. Dictionary attacks use a list of words that are believed to be likely passwords. A rainbow table is a precomputed table of hashes. Session hijacking is when the attacker takes over an authenticated session.

43. C. A nation-state advanced persistent threat (APT) involves sophisticated (i.e., advanced) attacks over a period of time (i.e., persistent). A distributed denial-of-service (DDoS) could be a part of an APT, but in and of itself is unlikely to be an APT. Brute force attempts every possible random combination to get the password or encryption key. In a disassociation attack, the attacker attempts to force the victim into disassociating from a resource.

44. B. Phishing is not commonly used to acquire email addresses. Phishing emails target personal information and sensitive information like passwords and credit card numbers in most cases.

45. B. A keylogger is a software or hardware tool used to capture keystrokes. Keyloggers are often used by attackers to capture credentials and other sensitive information. A rootkit is used to obtain and maintain administrative rights on a system, and a worm is a self-spreading form of malware that frequently targets vulnerable services on a network to spread.

46. D. Acquisition via the gray market can lead to lack of vendor support, lack of warranty coverage, and the inability to validate where the devices came from. Nick should express concerns about the supply chain, and if his devices need to be from a trusted source or supplier with real support he may need to change his organization's acquisition practices.

47. B. A host-based firewall is an excellent first line of defense for systems that will be deployed to untrusted networks. EDR and XDR are useful for preventing malicious software installs like ransomware, but they do not directly protect against network-based attacks, and disk encryption is a confidentiality control, not a useful tool to prevent network-based attacks.

48. C. The marketing team has created a shadow IT solution—a solution put in place without central or formal IT support, typically done without IT's assistance or awareness. This creates a risk to the organization due to lack of support and may bring additional risks like licensing and compliance risks. The team did not intend to create an issue and is not actively working against the organization, meaning that they are not unskilled attackers, insider threats, or hacktivists.

49. A. Resource inaccessibility is a common symptom of a denial-of-service attack. Impossible travel is typically found in log events through correlation. Missing logs are frequently indicators of compromised accounts deleting logs, and blocked content is most likely due to reputation service usage.

50. B. Since the drives stored sensitive data and no mention of encryption was made, the drives should be physically destroyed to ensure that no data leakage can occur. It is not necessary to destroy the entire system to ensure this. Reformatting drives does not wipe data, and simply removing the system from inventory is typically part of the process but does not protect organizational data.

51. B. A security information and event management tool (SIEM) is designed to ingest and analyze large volumes of logs and then alert on issues and events. Centralized logging is useful but needs additional tools to alert on issues. An IPS is used to detect and potentially respond to network-based attacks, not to gather and analyze logs, and EDR tools are useful for monitoring endpoints, not for large-scale log ingestion and analysis.

52. C. Patrick knows that the first thing he should do is change the administrator password. Any further security changes, including updating firmware and disabling unnecessary services, can be made once the administrative account has been properly secured. Changing the default IP address does not necessarily improve security for the device.

53. B. Paul knows that SSH typically uses port 22, HTTP uses port 80, and HTTPS uses port 443. HTTP is the only unencrypted protocol from that list, and thus he should disable port 80.

54. C. An on-path attack redirects traffic to allow an attacker to see and potentially modify the traffic as shown in the graphic. SQL injection is accomplished by inserting SQL into web queries or application traffic, denial-of-service will target a service and no indication of that is shown, and a directory traversal attack will typically show directory manipulation like ../../.

55. B. While dated, NTLM was historically one of the most common targets of credential relay attacks. RDP, SQL, and TLS are less commonly associated with credential relay attacks. Modern protocols implement encryption, session, IDs, and one-time passwords to prevent this type of attack.

56. A. Encryption is the appropriate solution to prevent data loss if a system is stolen. A HIPS, disabling ports and protocols, and changing default passwords will not prevent data acquisition from a drive.

57. D. Derek knows that attacking a digital signature requires that hashes match for both an original document and a malicious document. He will modify the malicious document until he finds a way to convey the changes he needs while retaining the matching hash. This type of attack is why hashing algorithms needs to be resistant to birthday attacks.

58. A. Ashley's organization was the target of a reflected (and amplified) DDoS where attackers took advantage of DNS queries to make small amounts of spoofed traffic into very large amounts of data sent to her servers. DNS floods, mirrored DDoSs, and supersized query attacks were made up for this question.

59. B. Collisions occur when two files have the same hash. Secure hashing solutions are collision resistant, meaning that collision-based hash attacks should be unlikely unless an insecure or outdated hash algorithm like MD5 is selected. Birthday attacks leverage the likelihood of collisions in a random set of attacks rather than by progressing linearly through the solution set. Bingo attacks and match-the-hash are both made up for this question.

60. C. Firmware is typically not encrypted, but it is commonly digitally signed. Using input validation and code review both help to keep firmware secure.

61. D. Annie's company is facing a disinformation campaign. If users were simply getting facts wrong, this would be misinformation, but since bots are intentionally misstating information, it is disinformation. Pretexting would attempt to exploit human behaviors to explain why something needed to occur or why an attacker was asking for something. Impersonation occurs when an attacker pretends to be someone they are not.

62. B. In many cases, the best option to limit the attack surface of messaging applications is to use a trusted, internally managed organizational instance rather than public tools or instances. EDR, firewalls, and IPS are not as effective with messaging-based attacks.

63. C. End-of-life announcements typically mean that the equipment is no longer being produced or sold. The equipment will typically have a longer supported life, so Ana can continue to use it but should plan for what to do when end-of-support occurs. At that time, replacing it, isolating it, or purchasing third-party support are all possible solutions depending on Ana's needs.

64. A. Removable devices like USB thumb drives, digital picture frames, and even keyboards and mice with onboard storage rely on `autorun.inf` files to automatically run software they provide. While that functionality typically focuses on printing, opening folders, or running media players, it can also be leveraged to automatically run malware. For this reason, many organizations ban removable drives or prohibit autorun from working. Open service ports are commonly associated with applications and services, and autorun doesn't set up or run these, nor does it impact Wi-Fi. Watering hole attacks require attackers to compromise or gain access to a site that targets commonly visit so that they deliver malware to their targets.

65. C. Raj knows that removing unnecessary software reduces a system's attack surface and also means that he won't have to patch and maintain the software he removes. Encrypting a drive, installing EDR, and changing default passwords won't reduce patch management, but EDR and changing default passwords could help with remote exploit prevention.

66. C. A race condition can occur when multiple threads in an application are using the same variable and the situation is not properly handled. A buffer overflow is attempting to put more data in a buffer than it is designed to hold. A logic bomb is malware that performs its misdeed when some logical condition is met. As the name suggests, improper error handling is the lack of adequate or appropriate error handling mechanisms within software.

67. A. A monitored camera system will detect the broadest range of attacks. Guards will only detect brute-force attacks when they are in the area, and cameras can cover more spaces at once. Inspections may miss attacks where camera recordings and monitoring can show failed and successful attacks. An alarm system won't detect attacks by insiders, who may access spaces they have access to in order to perform malicious actions.

68. C. Images are not a common threat vector via SMS. Malicious links, phishing via text, and multifactor authentication (MFA) exploits, including sending MFA notices until the recipient approves an MFA request, are all common SMS-related threat vectors.

69. B. Jennifer should note this as out-of-cycle logging. It could simply indicate a flaw in the script or another innocuous issue, or it could indicate an attacker exploring scripts to identify what information can be obtained. Concurrent session use occurs when a session is in use from multiple browsers or systems, missing logs are when logs are entirely missing or empty rather than occurring with more frequency than expected, and impossible travel occurs when events or logins occur from different locations by the same user who could not have traveled that distance in the time between the events.

70. B. DLL injection forces a process to load and run code from a dynamically linked library (DLL) that was not originally used by the application or software. This can be used to modify behaviors of the program or to perform malicious actions through the application. WinBuff, SYRINGE, and memory traversal were all made up for this question.

71. B. Access control lists (ACLs) allow or deny traffic based on rules that include protocol, IP addresses, ports, and other details. They do not understand packet content and simply assess traffic based on these basic rules. A HIPS is a host-based intrusion prevention system and is not installed between subnets. Least privilege is a concept, not an application or security tool, and VLANs are used to segment traffic but do not themselves control traffic this way. Instead, VLANs are often combined with ACLs to control network traffic and ensure segmentation.

72. D. Encryption is used to preserve confidentiality. Availability controls work to ensure that assets remain accessible and usable, and encryption can actually work against this in some circumstances, such as if a key is lost or the encrypted file becomes corrupted. Encryption is not used directly to preserve least privilege, nor does it preserve physical security.

73. B. Cross-site request forgery (XSRF or CSRF) sends fake requests to a website that purport to be from a trusted, authenticated user. Cross-site scripting (XSS) exploits the trust the user has for the website and embeds scripts into that website. Bluejacking is a Bluetooth attack. Nothing in this scenario requires or describes an evil twin, which is an attack that uses a malicious access point that duplicates a legitimate AP.

74. A. Both commercial and private threat feeds can be used by security tools like SIEM, EDR, and XDR systems to provide them with current information about indicators of compromise. A real-time blackhole list (RBL) and an IP reputation feed are examples of specific threat feeds but are not as broad as threat feeds. Vulnerability definitions are typically integrated with vulnerability scanners, but again are a narrower option than a threat feed.

75. B. Joseph is most likely fighting a virus, which is capable of copying itself to new locations. A Trojan is malware that is disguised to look like desirable software, a keylogger captures keystrokes, and a rootkit is intended to allow attackers to retain access to compromised systems.

76. D. Placing a larger integer value into a smaller integer variable is an integer overflow. Memory overflow is not a term used, and memory leak is about allocating memory and not deallocating it. Buffer overflows often involve arrays. Variable overflow is not a term used in the industry.

77. A. Until more is known, the best route for security administrators is to review the authentication logs in order to gather more information that can indicate whether an issue or security event has occurred. While Keith didn't indicate that he had failed login attempts, it's possible another user mistyped a user ID or that something else happened. Interviewing Keith might help but would provide less information if something malicious or accidental is happening, and the interview process would delay that analysis. Changing his password isn't immediately necessary as failed logins increase the time, not successful logins. Without more information, starting the incident response (IR) process may not be appropriate. If it can be shown that an attack occurred and was successful, the IR process should be started.

78. C. Environmental monitoring involves things like temperature, water or flood sensors, and other detection capabilities that help organizations know if a natural disaster or other environmental issue has occurred. Video cameras cannot detect many of these and are not typically deployed to places where they would detect things like under-floor leaks or floods. Intrusion alarm systems do not provide this type of detection, and log analysis would require environmental monitoring sensors.

79. A. Jack's team has created a shadow IT scenario by purchasing and using software without the awareness or engagement of central IT. They may be an inadvertent threat, but the term is not used to describe threat actors. They're not an intentional threat, and thus aren't an insider threat, and internal espionage actors is not a term used for the Security+ exam.

80. B. Security groups are used like firewall rules in Amazon Web Services (AWS), and since Amanda's system administrators are not effectively managing security groups, this is most likely to create a misconfiguration issue. Application programming interfaces (APIs) are provided by the vendor, and thus their security is typically a vendor issue or a misconfiguration issue. Malicious insiders are not mentioned, and security group misconfiguration does not drive multifactor authentication (MFA)-based attacks.

81. D. The Linux kernel is part of the operating system and needs to be handled with an OS patch. There is no application to patch, installing a HIPS might help, but the issue is dated 2018, meaning that a patch likely exists. If there wasn't a patch and this was a new vulnerability, segmentation might be a useful immediate response to reduce risk.

82. C. Collision attacks target hashes and attempt to produce a file that results in the same hash algorithm output but with different content that they can control.

83. C. The first step in securing a consumer-grade router is to change the default password. Once that has been completed, updating the firmware, turning off unneeded services, and running a vulnerability scan are all common steps. Routers typically do not have unnecessary software running.

84. B. Ensuring that any volume that is used in a virtual environment is encrypted when created will prevent reuse concerns because data will be unrecoverable even if encrypted data was accessible when drive space was reallocated. Firmware updates, cluster sizes, and reformatting do not properly address this issue.

85. C. Data exfiltration, blackmail, and financial gain are all common motivations for ransomware actors. Revenge is not a common ransomware actor motivation.

86. C. Botnets are often used to launch DDoS attacks, with the attack coming from all the computers in the botnet simultaneously. Phishing attacks attempt to get the user to give up information, click on a link, or open an attachment. Adware consists of unwanted pop-up ads. A Trojan horse attaches malware to a legitimate program.

87. B. Amanda has discovered an insider threat. Insider threats can be difficult to discover, as a malicious administrator or other privileged user will often have the ability to conceal their actions or may actually be the person tasked with hunting for threats like this! This is not a zero-day attack—no vulnerability was mentioned, there was no misconfiguration since this was an intentional action, and encryption is not mentioned or discussed.

88. B. Disinformation campaigns seek to achieve the goals of the attacker or owner of the campaign. They leverage social media using bots and groups of posters to support the ideas, concepts, or beliefs that align with the goals of the campaign. Impersonation is a type of social engineering attack where the attacker pretends to be someone else. A watering hole attack places malware or malicious code on a site or sites that are frequently visited by a targeted group. Asymmetric warfare is warfare between groups with significantly different power or capabilities.

89. B. Nation-state actors often have greater resources and skills, making them a more significant threat and far more likely to be associated with an advanced persistent threat actor. Unskilled attackers, also known as script kiddies, hacktivists, and insider threats, tend to be less capable and are all far less likely to be associated with an APT.

90. B. Amplification attacks typically use spoofed User Datagram Protocol (UDP) queries sent to servers to increase the volume of traffic sent in response to the target. Erica's process might involve identifying large DNS responses she can get with a small query, then spoofing a target system's IP address in the packets she sends to DNS servers. They would then respond with

the large responses, amplifying her requests and creating a distributed denial-of-service attack by using many servers to amplify her traffic. This doesn't require reversing an IP address, conducting an on-path attack, or spoofing the responses from the servers.

91. D. The fact that the website is defaced in a manner related to the company's public indicates that the attackers were most likely engaging in hacktivism to make a political or belief-based point. Scripts, nation-state actors, and organized crime actors don't account for the statements adverse to the company's policies, which is why hacktivism is the real cause.

92. B. Pretexting and impersonation are common elements in voice call–based attacks. Watering hole attacks leverage commonly visited websites, disinformation is when incorrect information is intentionally provided to change public opinion and could be part of a voice campaign but is not the most common element, and business email compromise (BEC) requires an email to be used, not a voice call.

93. C. Agentless software does not have an agent installed that can be targeted. That means that the server or control system is the only target for attackers. Agentless software can still consume resources as queries and actions are taken by the server or control plane. Client-based software often has better insights into systems, and may offer additional security features if it is a security tool. Client-based software and agentless software can both be patched to address security issues.

94. B. Password spraying is a specific type of brute-force attack that uses a smaller list of common passwords for many accounts to attempt to log in. Although brute forcing is technically correct, the best match here is password spraying. When you encounter questions like this on the exam, make sure you provide the most accurate answer, rather than one that fits but that may not be the best answer. Limited login attacks is a made-up answer, and spinning an account refers to changing the password for an account, often because of a compromise or to prevent a user from logging back into it while preserving the account.

95. B. A privilege escalation attack can occur horizontally, where attackers obtain similar levels of privilege but for other users, or vertically where they obtain more advanced rights. In this case, Charles has discovered a vertical privilege escalation attack that has allowed the attacker to obtain administrative rights. Cross-site scripting and SQL injection are both common types of web application attacks, and a race condition occurs when data can be changed between when it is checked and when it is used.

96. A. A zero-day exploit or attack occurs before the vendor has knowledge of it. The remainder of the answers don't accurately describe a zero-day attack—just because it has not yet been breached does not make it a zero-day, nor is a zero-day necessarily quickly exploitable. Finally, a zero-day attack does not specify how long the attacker may have access.

97. C. DNS poisoning occurs when false DNS information is inserted into legitimate DNS servers, resulting in traffic being redirected to unwanted or malicious sites. A backdoor provides access to the system by circumventing normal authentication. An APT is an advanced persistent threat. A Trojan horse ties a malicious program to a legitimate program.

98. D. Images can have data, including malware or exfiltrated organizational information using a technique called steganography that embeds data into images without losing the integrity of the image. Encryption, hashing, and forgery are not the direct driver of image-based threat vectors, although encryption is likely to be used as an additional layer to protect data from more advanced threat actors wishing to conceal what they are hiding.

99. A. In order to deliver a malicious update that uses a signing certificate, Eric will need to gain access to the private key for the signing certificate. The public key is exactly that—public—and having it will not allow Eric to sign the update. Hashes and collisions are not needed for this type of exploit.

100. B. This is an example of ransomware, which demands payment to return your data. A rootkit provides access to administrator/root privileges. A logic bomb executes its malicious activity when some condition is met. This scenario does not describe whaling, which is a type of phishing attack aimed at leaders in an organization.

101. C. Social engineering is about using people skills to get information you would not otherwise have access to. Illegal copying of software isn't social engineering, nor is gathering of discarded manuals and printouts, which describes dumpster diving. Phishing emails use some social engineering, but that is one example of social engineering, not a definition.

102. B. Unskilled actors are the least resourced of the common threat actors listed. In general, they flow from nation-state actors as the most highly resourced, to organized crime, to hacktivists, to inside actors, and then to unskilled actors, otherwise known as script kiddies, as the least capable and least resourced actors. As with any scale like this, there is room for some variability between specific actors, but for the exam, you should track them in that order.

103. D. Common email threats include phishing, email spoofing, and malware sent via email. Cross-site scripting is done via trusted websites where scripts are injected into user-visible code, causing the user to run the scripts using their credentials.

104. D. Rootkits provide administrative access to systems, thus the "root" in rootkit. A Trojan horse combines malware with a legitimate program. A logic bomb performs its malicious activity when some condition is met. A multipartite virus infects the boot sector and a file.

105. B. This question combines two pieces of knowledge: how botnet command-and-control works, and that IRC's default port is TCP 6667. Although this could be one of the other answers, the most likely answer given the information available is a botnet that uses Internet Relay Chat (IRC) as its command-and-control channel. 6667 is not a common alternate web traffic port, peer-to-peer network traffic is commonly done via HTTP or HTTPS in modern infections, and a remote access-Trojan is likely to behave differently and use another port as well.

106. A. Software updates for consumer-grade wireless routers are typically applied as firmware updates, and Susan should recommend that the business owner regularly upgrade their wireless router firmware. If updates are not available, they may need to purchase a new router that will continue to receive updates and configure it appropriately. This is not a default configuration issue nor an unsecured administrative account—neither is mentioned, nor is encryption.

107. B. The word you will need to know for the Security+ exam for phishing via SMS is "smishing," a term that combines SMS and phishing. Bluejacking sends unsolicited messages to Bluetooth devices, and phonejacking and text whaling were made up for this question.

108. A. Worms spread themselves via vulnerabilities, making this an example of a worm. A virus is software that self-replicates. A logic bomb executes its malicious activity when some condition is met. A Trojan horse combines malware with a legitimate program.

109. A. Directory traversal attacks attempt to exploit tools that can read directories and files by moving through the directory structure. The example would try to read the `config.txt` file three layers above the working directory of the web application itself. Adding common directory names or common filenames can allow attackers (or penetration testers) to read other files in accessible directories if they are not properly secured. The remainder of the options were made up for this question, although Slashdot is an actual website.

110. C. The Windows Security Account Manager (SAM) file and the `/etc/shadow` file for Linux systems both contain passwords and are popular targets for offline brute-force attacks.

111. B. Bluesnarfing involves accessing data from a Bluetooth device when it is in range. Blue-jacking involves sending unsolicited messages to Bluetooth devices when they are in range. Evil twin attacks use a rogue access point whose name is similar or identical to that of a legitimate access point. Nothing in this scenario points to a remote-access Trojan being the cause of the stolen data.

112. B. There are three common situations associated with race conditions: time-of-check (TOC), time-of-use (TOU), and target-of-evaluation. Time-of-change is not commonly associated with race conditions.

113. C. Relying on an outdated OS to confuse attackers is not a common isolation or segmentation option used to protect vulnerable legacy platforms. Many organizations have legacy platforms in place that cannot be patched or upgraded but that are still an important part of their business. Security professionals are often asked to suggest ways to secure the systems while leaving them operational. Common options include moving the devices to an isolated virtual LAN (VLAN), disconnecting the devices from the network and ensuring they are not plugged back in, and using a firewall or other security device to ensure that the legacy system is protected from attacks and cannot browse the Internet or perform other actions that could result in compromise.

114. B. TCP port 23 is typically associated with Telnet, an unencrypted remote shell protocol. Since Telnet sends its authentication and other traffic in the clear (clear/plain text), it should not be used, and Lucca should identify this as a configuration issue involving an insecure protocol.

115. A. Linux privileges can be set numerically, and 777 sets user, group, and world to all have read, write, and execute access to the entire `/etc` directory—a very insecure, and thus open or weak permission. Setting permissions like this is a common workaround when permissions aren't working but can expose data or make binaries executable by users who should not have access to them. When you set permissions for a system, remember to set them according to the rule of least privilege: only the permissions that are required for the role or task should be configured.

116. C. Concurrent sessions can be relatively common in some applications, so additional data is important when assessing if the event is an IoC. If the event occurs in two different locations, particularly if travel between them would be classified as impossible travel it would more likely be an indicator of compromise or misuse.

117. A. Angela has impersonated an actual employee of the delivery service to gain access to the company. Company uniforms are a very useful element for in-person social engineering. Whaling is a type of phishing attack aimed at leaders in an organization. A watering hole attack deploys malware or other attack tools at a site or sites that a target group frequently uses. Prepending is not a common security term.

118. C. Frank's best option is to review the anti-denial-of-service and other security tools that his cloud hosting provider provides and to make appropriate use of them. The major infrastructure-as-a-service (IaaS) providers have a variety of security tools that can help both detect and prevent DoS attacks from taking down sites that are hosted in their infrastructure. Calling the cloud service provider's ISP will not work because the ISP works with the cloud provider, not with Frank! It is possible the cloud service provider might be able to assist Frank, but they are most likely to instruct him to use the existing tools that they already provide.

119. C. The most common motivation for hacktivists is to make a political statement. Reputational gains are often associated with unskilled attackers/script kiddies, whereas financial gain is most commonly a goal of organized crime or insider threats. Gathering high-value data is typical of both nation-state actors and organized crime.

120. B. Configuration reviews, either using automated tool or manual validation, can be a useful proactive way to ensure that unnecessary ports and services are not accessible. Configuration management tools can also help ensure that expected configurations are in place. Neither passive nor active network packet capture will show services that are not accessed, meaning that open ports could be missed, and log review won't show all open ports either.

121. C. This is an example of typo squatting. The website is off by only one or two letters, and the attacker hopes that users of the real website mistype the URL and are taken to their fake website. Session hijacking is taking over an authenticated session. Cross-site request forgery sends fake requests to a website that purport to be from a trusted, authenticated user. Clickjacking attempts to trick users into clicking on something other than what they intended.

122. B. A logic bomb performs malicious actions when a specific condition or conditions are met. A boot sector virus infects the boot sector of the hard drive. A buffer overflow occurs when the attacker attempts to put more data in a variable than it can hold. A sparse infector virus performs its malicious activity intermittently to make it harder to detect.

123. A. While malicious hardware does exist, few organizations face it as a common threat due to the complexity of the attack and the fact that most hardware providers want to avoid the reputational harm that compromised hardware would create. Malicious firmware and software added to the OS image as well as an inability to deliver hardware in a timely manner are all common concerns with hardware providers.

124. D. A mobile device management (MDM) solution will allow settings and software to be managed centrally, allowing Helen to both control sideloading permissions and to prevent unwanted applications from being installed. Disabling either the hardware vendor or Google's store does not prevent sideloading from an external media like a microSD card, which can reduce the functionality of devices. An EDR is helpful to identify malicious software but doesn't manage devices and prevent sideloading.

125. A. Rootkits are designed to help retain control of and access to a system without users noticing. That means that obtrusive behaviors like network scanning, displaying ransom notices, or deletion of files are unusual for rootkits to perform. Other malware components beyond the rootkit may perform these as part of a malicious actor's toolkit.

126. A. A HIPS may block legitimate traffic if the traffic matches an existing rule or if a threat feed is used and has a detection that matches that traffic. That means that organizations that deploy HIPS in datacenters where disruptions could cause significant outages are careful about what rules they put in place and how threat feed data is used. A HIPS doesn't prevent least privilege and typically doesn't interact with application allow lists, and segmentation should not impact a HIPS.

127. B. Nation-state actors are typically the most sophistical adversaries organizations will face. Organized crime is the second most sophisticated actor in general, with hacktivists, then shadow IT following.

128. C. Malware is the most common threat vector involving files. Business email and phishing-related compromises that occur through files are typically due to malware. Cross-site scripting relies on embedding code in web pages that users will run when they view them, taking action as their logged-in account.

129. C. The first step for most organizations when addressing a known vulnerability is to check whether a patch is available. Organizations will also assess the potential risks associated with the patch: has it been widely deployed and tested, are there known issues, and is there a likelihood of disruption due to patching? If there are known issues, other solutions like isolation or deploying additional security controls such as a host-based firewall or firewall rule, or even disabling the service if possible, may be employed.

130. B. Systems are typically removed from management when they are shut down and before disks are wiped. Once they're off and will not return to service, they are wiped and then removed from inventory. Memory wipes and removal are not typical steps in decommissioning processes.

131. D. TCP 1433 is the default service port for Microsoft SQL. Joe will want to take appropriate actions to protect his SQL server, including patching, properly configuration, firewall rules, and network segmentation.

132. D. Encryption prevents resource reuse attacks from occurring because the data will not be accessible to attackers after resources are released and reallocated to third parties. VM escape attacks target the underlying VM infrastructure and could still occur if it was vulnerable. Pass-the-hash attacks are used against authentication systems when a hash can be captured and sent to validate a session, and birthday attacks leverage the likelihood of finding a valid collision more quickly by guessing than by moving linearly through a solution set for a hash.

133. D. Tyler has encountered spyware, software that gathers information to send back to a third party. While spyware is less outright malicious than other types of malware and may even have asked users to agree to release information as part of a click-through during installation, it is still considered malware because it sends information about users, systems, and networks to third parties that is not intended or desired. Trojans are intended to appear like desirable or legitimate software but are malicious; bloatware is preinstalled software that is not needed and takes up disk space, CPU, and memory; and keyloggers capture keystrokes from a keyboard to retain locally or send to a malicious actor.

134. A. The application log typically contains information about software that is installed on a Windows workstation, including errors that Eden is trying to identify. The security log contains security events like logins and file deletions. The setup log contains information about the installation of Windows, and the system log contains system-related events like bootup errors.

135. B. DNS hijacking can occur in a number of ways, including via the registrar, by changing your organization's DNS servers, or via changes to a local hosts file. DNS-based DoS attacks seek to disable or prevent DNS from working, whereas DNS-based DDoS attacks tend to be amplified and reflected by sending spoofed DNS queries with large results that will bog down the network connection of a targeted system or organization.

136. B. The `auth.log` or `secure` file contains authentication logs for Linux systems and will have such information as user ID, authentication time, and the IP address that the user connected from. Giovanni can use the IP addresses and times along with a geo-IP system to check for impossible travel. `/messages` contains general log messages, and `cron.log` contains `cron` job information. `/travel` is not a typical Linux log file.

137. B. Intune and Jamf provide a wide range of hardening functionality, including configuration enforcement.

138. B. Misinformation is incorrect information, but not purposefully so like disinformation. This is true regardless of the way the information is provided. Phishing is used to gather credentials and other sensitive information, and brand impersonation attacks focus on appearing like a legitimate brand or company.

139. A. Requiring callers to validate their identity using non-public information can help to prevent impersonation attacks. Not publishing a support number externally means that internal users will still have it and that it can be leaked or found. Requiring users to provide a callback number only works if business numbers are used, and this tends to prevent support from being effective for traveling users and others who may not be at a desk or able to use a soft phone due to technology issues. User awareness training won't protect the help desk staff from making mistakes.

140. B. TCP port 515 is the LPR port, commonly used for print services. Bob knows that exposing printers to the Internet is not a common practice and should recommend that the print server be segmented away from the Internet so that only internal systems that need to can send print jobs to it.

141. B. The Security+ exam outline expects test takers to be familiar with three types of attacks: downgrade attacks that request weaker encryption types; collision attacks, which focus on finding collisions in hashes, allowing arbitrary changes to files that would normally be verified with hashes; and birthday attacks, which allow nonlinear guesses to be more likely to find a solution than simply progressing through key space. Magic key attacks were made up for this question.

142. A. This is a remote-access Trojan, malware that opens access for someone to remotely access the system. A worm would have spread itself via a vulnerability, whereas a logic bomb runs when some logical condition is met. Finally, a rootkit provides root or administrative access to the system.

143. A. Ethical concerns are typically associated with hacktivists and some insider threats. APTs are typically nation-state actors and are commonly associated with war, data exfiltration, and espionage operations.

144. C. DLL injection requires that a DLL be loaded dynamically, and the ability to place a malicious DLL where it will be loaded is critical to the success of this type of attack. That means that using fully qualified DLL paths can help prevent the attack from succeeding. Preventing DLLs from being loaded by users and the programs they run or entirely avoiding using DLLs will cause functional issues for Windows, DLL vulnerability scanners are not a common solution, and avoiding the use of DLLs is not a common practice since DLLs are a key part of Windows systems.

145. A. Firmware providers often provide digitally signed firmware that can be validated before it is installed. Mackenzie should ensure that her organization's practices include validating firmware signatures before installation. Antivirus will typically not detect malicious code in firmware files, encrypted firmware without a digital signature does not provide the same protection as digitally signed firmware, and firmware updates should be installed to prevent vulnerabilities from being exploited.

146. D. Zoie's best option is to review web application server logs to identify session IDs that are the same coming from different IP addresses. She will not see session IDs in firewall, AV, or authentication logs.

147. B. Isolating the system is the best option for Valerie to select until she can investigate the system. Isolation will prevent the system from impacting other systems and will also prevent attackers from getting to it. Antimalware and patching are useful options further into the investigation and response process. Changing default passwords and checking for unexpected user accounts is a good practice but won't help protect other systems if the system is compromised.

148. A. Preventing fallback options from being used for encryption may stop some clients from connecting but will most effectively prevent downgrade attacks. Current browsers may be needed for this, but requiring that does not prevent attackers from using a downgrade attack if fallback options are allowed. Current web server software does not prevent settings from being weak. An IDS can detect downgrade attempts but cannot stop them.

149. B. Buffer overflow attacks cram more data into a field or buffer than they can accept, overflowing into other memory locations and either crashing the system or application or potentially allowing code to be inserted into executable locations. Bluesnarfing and bluejacking are both Bluetooth attacks. Cross-site scripting attacks allow attackers to inject scripts into pages viewed by other users.

150. B. Cross-site request forgery (XSRF or CSRF) sends forged requests to a website, supposedly from a trusted user. Cross-site scripting (XSS) is the injection of scripts into a website to exploit the users. A buffer overflow tries to put more data in a variable than the variable can hold. Directory traversal attempts to change directories through URL manipulation to access files that should not normally be accessible to the web server or application.

151. D. Disk encryption does not prevent malware attacks under most circumstances. Use of endpoint detection and response tools, antivirus tools, and limiting administrative access are all common ways to counter malware.

152. B. Spyware and adware are both common examples of unwanted programs. Though not directly malicious, they can pose risks to user privacy as well as create annoyances like pop-ups or other unwanted behaviors. Trojans appear to be legitimate programs or are paired with them, RATs provide remote access and are a subcategory of Trojans, and ransomware demands payment or other actions to avoid damage to files or reputation.

153. C. Olivia has encountered a resource reuse issue. It is likely that the drive was reallocated without being securely wiped and that the previous user did not encrypt their drives. While this is unlikely with major cloud service providers now, it has been observed in the past and could still occur. There is no indication that a VM escape occurred that would run software on the host hypervisor, and no procedural issues around chain of custody or legal hold are described in the question.

154. A. While attachments are a common vector for BEC attacks, deleting all attachments is not a common practice. Instead, users should be taught to be careful about clicking on and opening attachments, particularly on unsolicited email. Using two-factor authentication, reviewing suspicious emails for potential indicators of BEC, and not clicking on URLs but instead visiting sites manually are all common anti-BEC practices.

155. A. Pretexting is a type of social engineering that involves using a false motive and lying to obtain information. Here, the penetration tester lied about their role and why they are calling (impersonation), and then built some trust with the user before asking for personal information. A watering hole attack leverages a website that the targeted users all use and places malware on it to achieve their purpose. Phishing is the process of attempting to gain credentials or other information, typically via email or similar means. Shoulder surfing involves looking over an individual's shoulder or otherwise observing them entering sensitive information like passwords.

156. C. Watering hole attacks target groups by focusing on common shared behaviors like visiting specific websites. If attackers can compromise the site or deliver targeted attacks through it, they can then target that group. Watercooler, phishing net, and phish pond attacks were all made up for this question.

157. D. If access is not handled properly, a time-of-check (TOC)/time-of-use (TOU) condition can exist where the memory is checked, changed, then used. Memory leaks occur when memory is allocated but not deallocated. A buffer overflow is when more data is put into a variable than it can hold. An integer overflow occurs when an attempt is made to put an integer that is too large into a variable, such as trying to put a 64-bit integer into a 32-bit variable.

158. B. Local on-path attacks typically involve responding to ARP requests with a different gateway MAC address before the gateway itself can respond or through modification of local hosts files. External DNS should not be resolving local network DNS information. Encrypted traffic using a less secure algorithm is a downgrade attack. Website URLs being modified might be an example of typo squatting or another attack.

159. C. Session IDs should be unique for distinct users and systems. A very basic type of session replay attack involves providing a victim with a session ID and then using that session ID once they have used the link and authenticated themselves. Protections such as session timeouts and encrypting session data, as well as encoding the source IP, hostname, or other identifying information in the session key, can all help prevent session replay attacks.

160. C. End users cannot add applications that are not on the allow list to their workstations in environments using an application allow list. Since Andy is an end user, not an administrator, he cannot install applications as an administrator, nor can he add the application to the allow list. Andy will need to request that the application be added and then administrators will need to install the application. Jailbreaks are used for mobile devices, not workstations.

161. C. Evil twins are threats for wireless networks, not wired networks. Frank should consider how to keep all his traffic secure, likely by using a VPN that tunnels all his traffic to a trusted network exit point, and both worms and network-based attacks are possible from infected or malicious systems.

162. B. The malware in this example is a Trojan horse—it pretends to be something desirable, or at least innocuous, and installs malicious software in addition to or instead of the desired software. A rootkit gives root or administrative access, spyware is malware that records user activities, and a boot sector virus is a virus that infects the boot sector of the hard drive.

163. C. The former employee is threatening to release data making this blackmail. Espionage—including both nation-state driven and corporate—typically involves theft of data or other information, and there is no description of revenge or an attempt to disrupt services.

164. B. Sideloading can be as simple as loading files on the phone, although some bundles and applications require installers or other tools. Jailbreaking, disabling antimalware protection, or even installing a package manager are not required to sideload applications for Android but may be done. Jailbreaking and package managers are commonly used for iOS devices.

165. D. If this query is successful, it will match all categories because it looks for categories that match customers or TRUE which is how OR 1=1 resolves. That means that any category will match, providing Jill with a list of all users, not just all customers or customers with specific userIDs.

166. D. Disabling unnecessary ports and protocols reduced a device or system's attack footprint. The fewer targets attackers have, the less likely they are to be successful at finding a viable target. Reducing ports and protocols will speed up port scans and will reduce the number of logged events, but this is not the primary purpose of the change. Default ports are set for services based on common practice, and ports and protocols are not disabled to save default ports.

167. D. Attackers are increasingly relying on keyloggers that can capture information entered at a keyboard and send it to them, allowing them to quickly use the information to log in before the user can use an MFA code. Viruses, worms, and logic bombs are not designed to provide this functionality.

168. A. Organized crime actors are typically external rather than internal actors. They are often well resourced and sophisticated.

169. D. Package managers like Cydia and Sileo are used to add applications and other functionality to jailbroken iPhones. If the phone is an organizationally owned phone or contains organizational data, Valerie may need to take action based on organizational policies. Cydia and other package managers do not open up remote management tools by default and are not malware, although they may not be permitted software for many organizational devices.

170. B. Simple SQL injection attacks often rely on the single quote or Boolean conditions like OR 1=1 as part of their attack. While these are simple examples and more complex options exist, Isaac's organization is wise to prevent simple attacks. Buffer overflow attacks target memory locations or variables, replay attacks re-send legitimate traffic, and directory traversal attacks attempt to access other file structures.

171. C. Sending email from a user's personal email account to them is not a common BEC exploit, but using compromised accounts, spoofing email with slightly modified email addresses, and using malware to gain access to accounts and send email are all common techniques.

172. B. An application allow list provides the greatest control over what applications are installed on devices. Application deny lists are useful for preventing specific software from being installed but cannot handle the breadth of possible applications that users may find and use. Access control lists (ACLs) are used like firewall rules to apply rules to network traffic, and segmentation is used to separate systems based on various factors like data sensitivity or trust levels.

173. B. Ron wants to deny any source port to systems on the 10.10.20.0/24 network with a service port of TCP 22 for SSH.

174. A. Sam is using blocked content logging to determine what systems may be compromised and attempting to connect to malicious domains and if users are trying to access those IP addresses or domains. This can help Sam intervene with individual users and can also help identify infected systems. Resource inaccessibility is typically an unintentional indicator rather than a result of a security measure as described here. No logs are missing, and there is not a specific indicator of compromise that was described or published listed in the question.

175. D. While resource consumption alone may not indicate a compromise, unexpected consumption of resources may indicate unexpected or unwanted activity. Christina should look for other indicators of compromise to determine if she needs to declare a security incident. Resource inaccessibility would require the resource to not be available or working, and at 80% full a Linux filesystem will still work. There is no description of the content, and no content access was prevented, so this is not blocked content. Impossible travel occurs when logins or other resource usage occur in two locations at times that do not allow for travel between the locations.

176. B. Bloatware is a general term used to describe the unnecessary and unwanted programs that are installed on many PCs by manufacturers. Spyware is more harmful, sending information about the user, their browsing habits, or the computer back to the software's vendor or other organizations. Logic bombs are malware that take action under specific circumstances like a time, date, or other trigger, and firmware is the software that runs on top of hardware to provide basic underlying functionality.

177. C. The ability to run a program as a privileged user like an administrator from an unexpected or uncommon location is a common indicator of a privilege escalation attack. A buffer overflow would push data into a variable to attempt to cause it to take a desired action, a Trojan would look like a wanted or desirable file but would be malware, and a replay attack would send successful authentication or other information again to gain access to a system.

178. D. This is a directory traversal attack. The characteristic / . . / . . / is the first indicator you should pay attention to. The %00 is a null byte, meaning that many applications will stop reading when they encounter it. You might not know that detail as you take the exam, but you should know that attackers would look for the `passwd` file, not a PNG of a password!

179. B. VLANs are commonly used to provide segmentation for networks by placing them in separate logical networks. Encryption doesn't require or use VLANs, impossible travel describes logins and other activities from disparate physical locations in a time frame that would be impossible for travel to occur during, and a HIPS is a host intrusion prevention system.

180. C. Horizontal privilege escalation occurs when users at a similar level are able to use privileges or accounts belonging to peer users. Here, Mark's coworker is able to act as another similar user. Vertical privilege escalation focuses on greater privileges like administrative rights. Replay attacks re-send traffic to authenticate or otherwise repeat a transaction. Forgery attacks like cross-site request forgery (XSRF) leverage trusted sessions to allow malicious apps to take action due to the trust between a browser and a web application.

181. C. This is most likely a distributed denial-of-service (DDoS) attack since it is coming from many different IP addresses. Using small requests to generate large responses is an example of a resource exhaustion attack. Since this is coming from many addresses rather than one or a small number, it is more properly called a DDoS than a simple denial-of-service (DoS) attack. There is no indication that the service is vulnerable, the requests are small and no mention is made of a specific payload other than a HTTP GET for a file, and there is no traffic redirection as you would expect in an on-path attack.

182. C. Allowing all TCP 80 traffic to any internal system is a common misconfiguration for firewalls when troubleshooting. Placing an overly broad rule in a firewall ruleset, particularly when it is processed early (at the top) of a ruleset is dangerous, even though it happens more than security practitioners want to think about! Jailbreaks are done on iOS-based mobile devices to bypass security; race conditions occur when the time-of-check (TOC) and time-of-use (TOU) of a variable, memory location, or other resource allows for changes when it shouldn't; and injection attacks are typically conducted against memory, code, or other resources, not firewall rules.

183. B. File-level encryption will allow Brian's organization to encrypt individual files rather than entire disks or volumes and will protect files even when they are not in transit, unlike transport encryption using TLS.

184. B. Intune, formerly known as Microsoft Endpoint Manager and SCCM, provides configuration management, mobile app management, and other central system, software, and device management capabilities. It does not detect and respond to malware, but it can deploy configurations for Defender. It is not a code repository and versioning tool like `git`, and it does not provide web application firewalling.

185. A. Data exposure is typically a more significant risk than downtime, particularly when the downtime is limited to hours. SaaS vendors do not typically sell or deliver hardware, as they provide services. Software vulnerabilities may exist, but without a known impact, compromise leading to data loss remains the most significant issue.

186. D. In a DLL injection, the malware attempts to inject code into the running process of a library in memory. This is a rather advanced attack. A logic bomb executes its misdeed when some condition is met. Session hijacking is taking over an authenticated session. Buffer overflows are done by sending more data to a variable than it can hold.

187. D. Locking the resource until the action is completed is a common method of preventing TOC/TOU issues. Deleting the resource after each use doesn't allow resources to be persistent, preventing applications from using them on an ongoing basis. Running a single instance of the process will heavily limit the ability for Annie's business to scale the service. Making multiple copies doesn't allow for a shared resource.

Chapter 3: Domain 3.0: Security Architecture

1. A. Organizations set recovery point objectives (RPOs) which describe how much data is acceptable to lose in a data loss event, and recovery time objectives (RTOs), which describe the maximum amount of time that it should take to recover data. Together these two objectives help guide backup strategy and infrastructure design and implementation. MTBF (mean time before failure) describes the mean time before a device like a hard drive, power supply, or network switch will fail, typically described in hours of powered-on operation. RFBT was made up for this question.

2. A. When an intrusion detection system (IDS) or antivirus/antimalware mistakes legitimate traffic for an attack, this is called a false positive. A false negative is when the IDS mistakes an attack for legitimate traffic. It is the opposite of a false positive. Options C and D are both incorrect. Although these may be grammatically correct, these are not the terms used in the industry. In military operations, false flag operations attempt to transfer blame to another organization or adversary, thus a "false flag."

3. B. Air gapping refers to the server not being on a network. This means literally that there is "air" between the server and the network. This prevents malware from infecting the backup server. A separate virtual local area network (VLAN) or physical network segment can enhance security but is not as effective as air gapping. A honeynet is used to detect attacks against a network, but it doesn't provide effective defense against malware in this scenario.

4. C. SCADA, or supervisory control and data acquisition systems, are commonly used to manage facilities like power plants. The remaining options were made up.

5. C. Geoff is looking for a warm site, which has some or all of the infrastructure and systems he needs but does not have data. If a disaster occurs, Geoff can bring any equipment that he needs or wants to the site along with his organization's data to resume operations. A hot site is a fully functional environment with all the hardware, software, and data needed to operate an organization. They are expensive to maintain and run but are used by organizations that cannot take the risk of downtime. A cold site is a location that can be brought online but does not have systems; cold sites typically have access to power and bandwidth but need to be fully equipped to operate after a disaster since they are just rented space. An RTO is a recovery time objective, and it measures how long it should take to resume operations; it is not a type of disaster recovery site.

6. B. If Olivia wants to ensure that third parties will be unable to modify the operating system for Internet of Things (IoT) devices, requiring signed and encrypted firmware for operating system updates is an effective means of stopping all but the most advanced threats. Setting a default password means that a common password will be known. Checking the MD5sum for new firmware versions will help administrators validate that the firmware is legitimate, but signed and encrypted firmware is a much stronger control. Finally, regular patching may help secure the devices but won't prevent OS modifications.

7. B. Maria should implement ongoing auditing of the account usage on the SCADA system. This will provide a warning that someone's account is being used when they are not actually using it. Host-based antivirus/antimalware is almost never a bad idea, but this scenario did not indicate that the compromise was due to malware, so antimalware may not address the threat. Since the engineer has access to the SCADA system, a network intrusion prevention system (NIPS) is unlikely to block them from accessing the system, and full-disk encryption (FDE) will not mitigate this threat because the system is live and running, meaning that the disk will be decrypted in use.

8. C. A snapshot is an image of the virtual machine (VM) at some point in time. It is standard practice to periodically take a snapshot of a virtual system so that you can return that system to a last known good state. Sandboxing is the process of isolating a system or software. The hypervisor is the mechanism through which the virtual environment interacts with the hardware, and elasticity is the ability for the system to scale.

9. D. Serverless architectures do not require a system administrator because the provider manages the underlying function-as-a-service (FaaS) capability. It can also scale up or scale down as needed, allowing it to be very flexible. Serverless architectures are typically not ideal for complex applications and instead tend to work better for microservices.

10. B. Software-defined networking (SDN) makes the network very scalable. It is relatively easy to add on new resources or remove unneeded resources, and it helps with high availability efforts. SDN does not stop malware, detect intrusions, or prevent session hijacking.

11. A. A microservice architecture builds applications as a set of loosely coupled services that provide specific functions using lightweight protocols. It doesn't specifically define the size of the systems, but it is not a tightly coupled environment. Protocol choice is often open standards–based, but the emphasis is on lightweight protocols. There is not a requirement that services be in-house or third party exclusively.

12. C. The correct answer is to implement IaC. Infrastructure as code (IaC) is the process of managing and provisioning computer datacenters through machine-readable definition files, rather than physical hardware configuration or interactive configuration tools. Whether the datacenter(s) use physical machines or virtual machines, this is an effective way to manage the datacenters. Although datacenter managers may be needed, that won't necessarily provide consistent management across the enterprise. Software-defined networking (SDN) will not fix this problem, but it would help if Abigail needed to configure and manage her network based on usage and performance. Finally, this issue is not just about provisioning; it is about management.

13. C. Using secure firmware, as well as using an RTOS with time and space partitioning, are both common methods to help ensure RTOS security. Unlike traditional operating systems, real-time operating systems are used in applications where they need to deal with inputs immediately. That means that adding additional load like firewalls and antimalware is not a typical component in RTOS applications. For similar reasons, you're unlikely to find a web browser on most devices running an RTOS.

14. D. Embedded systems can bring a broad range of security implications, many of which are driven by the limited capabilities of the processors and hardware they are frequently built with. Low-power consumption designs may lack computational power and thus have challenges implementing strong cryptography, network connectivity, and other similar problems. Patching embedded systems can be challenging both because of where they are deployed and because of a lack of connectivity for them—in fact, in many environments, you may not want the devices to be connected to your network. Since many don't have a screen, keyboard, or a network connection, authentication is also a problem. Few embedded devices, however, need bulk storage, making the lack of bulk storage a problem that typically isn't a major concern.

15. D. Differential backups back up all of the changes since the last full backup. An incremental backup backs up all changes since the last incremental backup. A snapshot captures machine state and the full drive at a bitwise level, and full backups are a complete copy of a system but typically do not include the memory state.

16. B. Elasticity is a cloud computing concept that matches resources to demand to ensure that an infrastructure closely matches the needs of the environment. Scalability is the ability to grow or shrink as needed but does not directly include the concept of matching to workload. Normalization is a code development concept used to ensure that data is in a consistent form.

17. A. An uninterruptable power supply (UPS) should be Nathaniel's first priority. Ensuring that power is not disrupted during an outage and can be maintained for a short period until alternate power like a generator can come online is critical, and a UPS can provide that capability. A generator alone will take longer to come online, resulting in an outage. Dual power supplies can help to build resilience by allowing multiple power sources and avoiding issues if a power supply does fail, but that is not the focus of the question. A managed power distribution unit (PDU) provides remote management and power monitoring but will not prevent power loss in an outage.

18. C. Separating the SCADA (supervisory control and data acquisition) system from the main network makes it less likely that the SCADA system can be affected from the main network. This includes malware as well as human action. Software-defined networking (SDN) would make isolating the SCADA system easier but would not actually isolate it. Patch management is always important, but in this case, it would not have prevented the issue. Encrypted data transmissions, such as TLS, would have no effect on this situation.

19. D. Transport Layer Security (TLS) provides a reliable method of encrypting web traffic. It supports mutual authentication and is considered secure. Although Secure Sockets Layer (SSL) can encrypt web traffic, TLS was created in 1999 as its successor. Although many network administrators still use the term SSL, in most cases today what you are using is actually TLS, not the outdated SSL. Point-to-point Tunneling Protocol (PPTP) and Internet Protocol Security (IPSec) are protocols for establishing a VPN, not for encrypting web traffic.

20. B. Nora has established a cold site. A cold site is a location that can be brought online but does not have systems; cold sites typically have access to power and bandwidth, but they need to be fully equipped to operate after a disaster since they are just rented space. Warm sites have some or all of the infrastructure and systems Nora needs but does not have data. A hot site is a fully functional environment with all of the hardware, software, and data needed to operate an organization. They are expensive to maintain and run but are used by organizations that cannot take the risk of downtime. A MOU is a memorandum of understanding and is not a type of disaster recovery site.

21. C. Data sovereignty refers to the concept that data that is collected and stored in a country is subject to that country's laws. This can be a complex issue with multinational cloud services and providers that may store data in multiple countries as part of their normal architecture. It may also create compliance and other challenges based on differences in national laws regarding data, data privacy, and similar issues.

22. A. Low-power devices typically have limited processor speed, memory, and storage, meaning that encryption can be a challenge. Fortunately, solutions exist that implement low-power cryptographic processing capabilities, and continued advances in processor design continue to make lower-power processors faster and more efficient. Legal limitations do not typically take into account whether a device is a low-power device, and public key encryption can be implemented on a wide range of CPUs and embedded systems, so factoring prime numbers is unlikely to be an issue.

23. B. A generator is the most appropriate answer to a multi-hour outage. Although a hot site would allow her organization to stay online, the cost of a hot site is much higher than that of a generator. A PDU, or power distribution unit, is used to manage and distribute power, not to handle power outages. Finally, UPS systems are not typically designed to handle long outages. Instead, they condition power and ensure that systems remain online long enough for a generator to take over providing power.

24. D. Network load balancers distribute traffic among systems, allowing systems to be added or removed, and making patching and upgrades easier by draining connections from systems and removing them from the pool when work needs to be done on them. They can also help monitor systems for performance, report on issues, and ensure that loads match the capabilities of the systems that they are in front of. Firewalls are used for security, switches are a network device used to transfer traffic to the correct system, and a horizontal scaler was made up for this question.

25. B. Nathaniel has created an air gap, a physical separation that will require manual transport of files, patches, and other data between the two environments. This helps to ensure that attackers cannot access critical systems and that insiders cannot export data from the environment easily. A screened subnet, also known as a demilitarized zone (DMZ), is a separate network segment or zone that is exposed to the outside world or other lower trust area. A vault is a secured space or room. Hot and cold isles are equipment arrangements used in server rooms or datacenters to efficiently circulate air and keep server racks and other equipment cool.

26. B. The option that best meets the needs described is PEAP, the Protected Extensible Authentication Protocol. PEAP relies on server-side certificates and on tunneling to ensure communications security. EAP-MD5 is not recommended for wireless networks and does not support mutual authentication of the wireless client and network. LEAP, the Lightweight Extensible Authentication Protocol, uses WEP keys for its encryption and is not recommended due to security issues. Finally, EAP-TLS, or EAP Transport Layer Security, requires certificates on both the client and server, consuming more management overhead.

27. C. Olivia should make her organization aware that a failure in one of the active nodes would result in less maximum throughput and a potential for service degradation. Since services are rarely run at maximum capacity, and many can have maintenance windows scheduled, this does not mean that the load balancers cannot be patched. There is nothing in this design that makes the load balancers more vulnerable to denial-of-service than they would be under any other design. Having two active nodes will typically increase throughput over a single node.

28. C. Least connection–based load balancing takes load into consideration and sends the next request to the server with the least number of active sessions. Round-robin simply distributes requests to each server in order, whereas weighted time uses health checks to determine which server responds the most quickly on an ongoing basis and then sends the traffic to that server. Finally, source IP hashing uses the source and destination IP addresses to generate a hash key and then uses that key to track sessions, allowing interrupted sessions to be reallocated to the same server, and thus allowing the sessions to continue.

29. D. The safest and most secure answer is that Ramon should simply implement TLS for the entire site. Although TLS does introduce some overhead, modern systems can handle large numbers of simultaneous TLS connections, making a secure website an easy answer in almost all cases.

30. D. A firewall has two types of rules. One type is to allow specific traffic on a given port. The other type of rule is to deny traffic. What is shown here is a typical firewall rule. Options A, B, and C are incorrect. The rule shown is clearly a firewall rule.

31. D. Unlike IPSec's tunnel mode, IPSec transport mode allows different policies per port. The IP addresses in the outer header for transport mode packets are used to determine the policy applied to the packet. IPSec doesn't have a PSK mode, but WPA2 does. IKE is used to set up security associations in IPSec but doesn't allow this type of mode setting.

32. C. Global Positioning System (GPS) data and data about local Wi-Fi networks are the two most commonly used protocols to help geofencing applications determine where they are. When a known Wi-Fi signal is gained or lost, the geofencing application knows it is within range of that network. GPS data is even more useful because it can work in most locations and provide accurate location data. Although Bluetooth is sometimes used for geofencing, its limited range means that it is a third choice. Cellular information would require accurate tower-based triangulation, which means it is not typically used for geofencing applications, and of course USB is a wired protocol.

33. A. A Transport Layer Security (TLS) VPN is frequently chosen when ease of use is important, and web applications are the primary usage mode. RDP is a remote access tool, not a VPN tool, and ICMP is used for things like ping, not for VPN. IPSec VPNs are used for site-to-site VPNs and for purposes where other protocols may be needed, because they make the endpoint system appear to be on the remote network.

34. A. Binary data is a form of non-human-readable data. Encrypted data may be in binary format, but not all binary data is encrypted. Binary data is not human-readable, nor is it masked, which hides elements of data to allow for it to be used without exposing the underlying data.

35. D. Load balancers provide a virtual IP, or VIP. Traffic sent to the VIP is directed to servers in the pool based on the load-balancing scheme that that pool is using—often a round-robin scheme, but other versions that include priority order and capacity tracking or ratings are also common. The load balancer's IP address is normally used to administer the system, and individual IP addresses for the clustered hosts are shielded by the load balancer to prevent traffic from consistently going to those hosts, thus creating a failure or load point.

36. A. Port security filters by MAC address, permitting allow listed MAC addresses to connect to the port and blocking block listed MAC addresses. Port security can be static, using a predetermined list or dynamically allowing a specific number of addresses to connect, or it can be run in a combination mode of both static and dynamic modes.

37. C. Authentication headers (AHs) provide complete packet integrity, authenticating the packet and the header. Authentication headers do not provide any encryption at all, and authentication headers authenticate the entire packet, not just the header.

38. A. Network taps copy all traffic to another destination, allowing traffic visibility without a device inline. They are completely passive methods of getting network traffic to a central location. Port mirroring would get all the traffic to the network-based intrusion prevention system (NIPS) but is not completely passive. It requires the use of resources on switches to route a copy of the traffic. Incorrect switch configurations can cause looping. Configuring loop detection can prevent looped ports. Putting a network NIPS on every segment can be very expensive and require extensive configuration work. Setting up a NIPS on each segment would also dramatically increase administrative efforts.

39. B. Internet key exchange (IKE) is used to set up security associations (SAs) on each end of the tunnel. The security associations have all the settings (i.e., cryptographic algorithms, hashes) for the tunnel. IKE is not directly involved in encrypting or authenticating. IKE itself does not establish the tunnel—it establishes the SAs.

40. A. The NIPS is not seeing the traffic on that network segment. By implementing port mirroring, the traffic from that segment can be copied to the segment where the NIPS is installed. Installing a network IPS on the segment would require additional resources. This would work but is not the most efficient approach. Nothing in this scenario suggests that the NIPS is inadequate. It just is not seeing all the traffic. Finally, isolating the segment to its own VLAN would isolate that network segment but would still not allow the NIPS to analyze the traffic from that segment.

41. D. Load-balancing the cluster will prevent any single server from being overloaded. And if a given server is offline, other servers can take on its workload. A VPN concentrator, as the name suggests, is used to initiate virtual private networks (VPNs). Aggregate switching can shunt more bandwidth to the servers but won't mitigate the threat of one or more servers being offline. SSL accelerators are a method of offloading processor-intensive public key encryption for Transport Layer Security (TLS) and Secure Sockets Layer (SSL) to a hardware accelerator.

42. B. The correct answer is to encrypt all the web traffic to this application using Transport Layer Security (TLS). This is one of the most fundamental security steps to take with any website. A web application firewall (WAF) is probably a good idea, but it is not the most important thing for Ryan to implement. While a network-based intrusion prevention system (NIPS) or network-based intrusion detection system (NIDS) may be a good idea, those should be considered after TLS is configured.

43. C. Claire's best option is to deploy a detection and fix via her web application firewall (WAF) that will detect the SQL injection (SQLi) attempt and prevent it. An intrusion detection system (IDS) only detects attacks and cannot stop them. Manually updating the application code after reverse-engineering it will take time, and she may not even have the source code or the ability to modify it. Finally, vendor patches for zero days typically take some time to come out even in the best of circumstances, meaning that Claire could be waiting on a patch for quite a while if that is the option she chooses.

44. A. Session persistence makes sure that all of a client's traffic for a transaction or session goes to the same server or service. The remaining options do not properly describe how session persistence works.

45. D. Although next-generation firewalls (NGFWs) provide may defensive capabilities, SQL injection (SQLi) is an attack instead of a defense. In addition to geolocation, intrusion detection system (IDS) and intrusion prevention system (IPS), and sandboxing capabilities, many next-generation firewalls include web application firewalls, load balancing, IP reputation and URL filtering, and antimalware and antivirus features.

46. C. UTM, or unified threat management, devices commonly serve as firewalls, intrusion detection system (IDS)/intrusion prevention system (IPS), antivirus/antimalware, web proxies, web application and deep packet inspection, secure email gateways, data loss prevention

(DLP), security information and event management (SIEM), and even virtual private networking (VPN) devices. They aren't mobile device management (MDM) or universal endpoint management devices, however, since their primary focus is on network security, not systems or device management.

47. A. IDSs, or intrusion detection systems, can only detect unwanted and malicious traffic based on the detection rules and signatures that they have. They cannot stop traffic or modify it. An IPS, or intrusion prevention system, that is placed in line with network traffic can take action on that traffic. Thus, IDSs are often used when it is not acceptable to block network traffic, or when a tap or other network device is used to clone traffic for inspection.

48. C. Although insider threats are a concern, they're not any different for containers than any other system. Ensuring container host security, securing the management stack, and making sure that network traffic to and from containers is secure are all common container security concerns.

49. A. This is an example of using geographic restrictions to protect data. Fred has rules that require additional authentication for those who are off-site and also those who may be performing impossible travel. Time is not part of both rules, there's no role description, and supervisory control is not a term used for this.

50. D. 802.1X is the IEEE standard for port-based network access control. This protocol is frequently used to authenticate devices. Challenge Handshake Authentication Protocol (CHAP) is an authentication protocol but not the best choice for device authentication. Kerberos is an authentication protocol but not the best choice for device authentication. 802.11i is the Wi-Fi security standard and is fully implemented in WPA2 and WPA3. It is not a device authentication procedure.

51. D. Anomaly-based detection systems build a behavioral baseline for networks and then assess differences from those baselines. They may use heuristic capabilities on top of those, but the question specifically asks about baselined operations pointing to an anomaly-based system. Heuristic-based detections look for behaviors that are typically malicious, and signature-based or hash-based detections look for known malicious tools or files.

52. A. Mila should select a hash because a hash is designed to be unique to each possible input. That means that multiple files could have the same checksum value, whereas a hashing algorithm will be unique for each file that it is run against.

53. A. Tabletop exercises are used to talk through a process. Unlike walk-throughs, which focus on a step-by-step review of an incident, Mila will focus more on how her team responds and on learning from those answers. A tabletop exercise can involve gaming out a situation. A simulation actually emulates an event or incident, either on a small or a large scale. Drills are not defined as part of the Security+ exam outline.

54. D. High-availability designs are less expensive because they attempt to minimize service interruptions, whereas fault-tolerant designs seek to avoid service interruptions almost entirely, and thus cost significantly more. Both focus on service availability and typically use both hardware and software tools to meet their goals.

55. D. Geographic dispersion is intended to help with availability by ensuring that a single disaster does not take multiple datacenters or other facilities offline. It does not directly impact confidentiality or integrity, and assurance is not part of the CIA triad.

56. A. Masking replaces some characters with an alternate character, allowing tasks like validating credit card numbers without exposing all of a data field. Tokenization replaces values with a replacement value allowing data to be accessed without exposing the actual value. Steganography hides data in images and is not a useful solution in this scenario. Hashing is a mathematical technique that analyzes a file and computes a unique fingerprint, known as a message digest or hash, for that file.

57. C. Datacenters should have a fail over process that can be manually executed in case of emergency. Mateo should use that process to fail over to his organization's fail over site. Turning off every system in a datacenter is not recommended as this may lead to other unexpected failures. Simulation is not a fail over test, and creating an outage of a critical system typically will not cause an entire datacenter to fail over.

58. A. Trade secrets are intellectual property that is commercially valuable and is limited to a small group of individuals. Regulated information is controlled by law or has legal requirements around it. Financial information involves things related to monetary transactions or accounts. Public information is not controlled and is available to the public or could be without causing harm or concern.

59. B. Implementing Transport Layer Security (TLS) to encapsulate Simple Mail Transfer Protocol (SMTP) would allow the traffic to be encrypted in transit, protecting it from being read. Sender Policy Framework (SPF) and DomainKeys Identified Mail (DKIM) are both used to prevent spoofing, and Exchangeable Image File Format (EXIF) is information found in an image file.

60. B. Jump servers are used to access secured zones and are typically carefully controlled and monitored because they are the single point of entry from untrusted environments. A Unified Threat Management (UTM) is a security device that combines firewall features with a variety of other security functions. ICS stands for Industrial Control System. This is not an ICS, although the IoT devices it allows connections to may be a form of ICS. VPNs, or virtual private networks, encapsulate and protect network traffic as it moves through untrusted networks.

61. C. IPSec virtual private networks are commonly established to tunnel through public or untrusted networks. A RTOS, or real-time operating system, is used for embedded systems. SHA-1 is a hashing algorithm, and RSA is an encryption algorithm that is used for IPSec as part of its authentication process. IPSec tunnels themselves commonly use AES, but may use other algorithms as well.

62. B. Intellectual property that would have value to competitors and that is kept confidential to preserve it for competitive advantage is a trade secret. Legal information is typically related to contracts, regulations, or similar matters. Regulated data is covered by law, and classified data is used by governments.

63. A. A unified threat management (UTM) device combines multiple security services including firewall, IDS or IPS, antivirus/antimalware, email filtering, WAF, and similar services into a single solution. An FWSM, or firewall service module, is an older Cisco chassis-based firewall; a WAF is a web application firewall; and an ELB is Elastic Load Balancer, a load-balancing service available via AWS.

64. A. Tabletop exercises do not involve an actual technical system and instead are gamed out in a room. This means they're least likely to cause disruptions. Fail over and parallel processing exercises can have actual impact to live systems, and simulation exercises require care because simulated calls and actions may inadvertently become real if staff are not fully aware of the scenario being an exercise or accidentally execute a command that can cause actual impact.

65. B. Data sovereignty is a new concern for organizations that host services and data outside of their local area, including across state or national boundaries. Recovery point objectives (RPOs), recovery time objectives (RTOs), and power resilience are all common concerns for on-premises datacenters.

66. D. Disk encryption is used to protect data at rest, not data in use or data in transit. TLS, VPNs, and file encryption can all be used to protect files that are sent via a network.

67. B. A TLS-enabled proxy between the devices and server doesn't require anything else to be installed on the devices, which is typically impossible with SCADA devices. That means the VPN connection and the X.509 certificates are unlikely to work. SD-WAN helps to manage external connectivity, not to directly protect traffic in this scenario.

68. C. Simulations try to avoid causing potential outages and work to simulate a scenario. They may validate that notification processes communication systems and procedures all work.

69. C. Geolocation is used to control where data can be accessed from but does not protect data in transit. Encrypting data, encapsulating via TLS, or use of a VPN are all common methods to protect data in transit.

70. B. Next-generation firewalls (NGFWs) typically provide the ability to inspect traffic at both the transport layer (layer 4) and the application layer (layer 7). This means an NGFW will best fit the need. Web application firewalls also work at this level, but only focus on web applications, which does not fully meet the broad application inspection requirement in the question. Stateful firewalls and packet filters both operate at layer 4 only.

71. C. A load balancer can help handle individual web server failures gracefully by moving load to the functioning web servers in a cluster. In scalable environments, this can also result in more servers being instantiated. Platform diversity helps to protect against failures or vul-nerabilities in a single vendor, platform, or system. Multi-cloud systems could help in this case but are much more complex than required by the relatively simple need to handle an individual web server's failure. A warm site would be suited to a datacenter failure, not a single web server failing.

72. A. In-line network taps are typically configured to fail-open since they are used to create a copy of the network traffic. Devices that provide in-line security like IPS systems may be configured to fail-closed because their failure removes critical security functionality. Fail over describes the ability to fail to another device, which is not a common function for an in-line tap. Fail-reset was made up for this question.

73. D. Software-defined wide area networks (SD-WANs) are the core component of secure access, secure edge technology. Additional tools like zero trust functionality, cloud access security brokers, and firewalls are all combined to build a complete SASE implementation.

74. A. Network access control (NAC) has the ability to both profile device security and validate that a given user is authorized to plug a device into a specific Ethernet jack makes this the best solution for Mikayla's use case. Port security's list of recognized MAC addresses is both potentially vulnerable to MAC spoofing and does not meet the device security check requirements described. An IPS can help prevent network attacks but does not control port-level access, and jump servers are used to allow access to secured network segments, not to protect individual network jacks.

75. C. Version control will allow staff from Mark's organization to identify a bad version and revert to a previous known-good version if needed. Threat modeling, least privilege, and artifact signing are all common best practices for IaC, but don't directly impact version changes.

76. A. PaaS vendors are responsible for the underlying service and platform, including the networks, systems, and infrastructure that it runs on, including their security. Customers are responsible for their use of the platform, including endpoints, users, and applications built on the platform, again including their security.

77. B. The biggest issue for resilience is that placing backups in the same facility as the devices or systems they are backing up means that a single disaster could destroy both. Nick should consider off-site backup storage. Tape recovery can be slow, but this is a restoration time-frame issue, not a resilience issue. Tape lifetime is typically quite long, and backups are usually rolled over in time periods shorter than a year for most organizations. Finally, validation of backups can be a concern, but there is no description in the question that would lead to conclusions about testing.

78. B. AES-256 is the current mainstream standard for encryption. AES 128 and 192 are both less secure, and AES-512 is not an implemented or commonly used standard.

79. C. While RTOS issues with vulnerabilities, the inability to install security tools. and a lack of patches for RTOS-based devices are all common security concerns, they are not as frequently targeted by malware infections.

80. B. Tokens should not be easily reversible. Instead, they should require access to the original tokenization function or a mapping to the original data. Tokens should not have intrinsic meaning or value, and frequently rely on hash functions as part of their generation process to ensure this.

81. B. Replication is typically the fastest means to recovery since the replica system is running and ready to take over. Snapshot recovery is normally the next fastest, followed by restoration from other storage. Journaling can introduce additional slowdowns depending on how

long it has been since the last backup, as the journal is replayed from the time that occurred to the time of failure.

82. D. The Security+ exam outline recognizes three data states: data at rest, data in transit, and data in use. When Henry accesses the data and it is transferred via the network, it is data in transit. When he is working with the data, including modifying or otherwise using it, it is data in use. When it resides on the drives the database is stored in, it is data at rest. Data on the wire is not a common term for this—data in motion and data in transit are both common in industry usage, and the Security+ exam outline uses data in transit.

83. C. Data sovereignty means that governments have the ability to control data within their borders via law and regulations. Theresa's organization will need to comply with the laws of each country they operate in. Obfuscation refers to making something difficult to understand or read. Legal holds are used to require preservation of data when legal action is occurring or pending. Geographic restriction is used to limit where data can be accessed from and is a technical control used by organizations as part of data security efforts.

84. A. Hrant's use of an IPS means he wants to be in-line to allow him to block traffic. Since he prefers that a failure remain secure rather than potentially allowing attacks through, he should select a fail-closed implementation.

85. C. Physical isolation requires the creation of an air gap. This means unplugging the device from the network. A secure VLAN won't accomplish this, nor will 802.1X. Unplugging the device from power isn't required for physical isolation.

86. A. Path diversity ensures that the connectivity to the facility does not take the same path. This helps to prevent the moment network managers dread when a single accident—or construction equipment in the wrong place—tears up multiple fiber or copper paths, taking organizations offline. Diversity of the cabling type is not a requirement or need, SD-WAN does not directly address physical disasters, and geographic dispersion is not possible at a single site.

87. D. Carlos is using a jump server that is used to connect from an untrusted or lower trust zone from outside of a firewall. A network tap is used to provide copies of network traffic for analysis. SASE combines SD-WAN and other security technologies to provide network security services regardless of where systems are for enterprises. SD-WAN (software-defined wide area networking) is used to manage network connectivity through commodity Internet providers and other services.

88. B. Capacity planning for disaster operations needs to take the impact on staff themselves into account. While modern operations can frequently be conducted remotely, reducing the number of staff required to be physically able to reach the site, staff members may not have power, Internet access, or even housing in disaster scenarios. The remote site's ability to operate is not directly a staff capacity planning issue, nor is how generators will be fueled.

89. A. Typical exercise types for most organizations include simulations that emulate an actual incident response process, walk-throughs that guide staff through an event, and tabletop exercises that are gamed out without taking actual action. Drills are classified as more focused on specific actions or functions, and they are less common because they can result in inadvertent action or mistakes and do not cover the breadth of an incident.

90. D. Comparing hashes is an effective way of determining if a file is different from the original. While file length may be the same and metadata can be modified, hashes will still show changes. Encrypting the files does not compare them, and should not be used for this purpose.

91. B. Off-site backup locations are typically chosen so that they will not be impacted by the same disaster. That means that recovery may be slow if the backups either need to be physically retrieved or must be downloaded via an Internet connection. Backup integrity is typically verified as part of the backup process, and this can be checked easily. Off-site backups are typically updated as part of the backup process, and this should not be an issue.

92. B. Load balancers are commonly used to help provide resilience by allowing applications and servers to be clustered. Cross-training staff is a people- or staff-based capacity planning solution. Both geographically diverse datacenters and UPS are examples of infrastructure resilience options.

93. C. The European Union's (EU) General Data Protection Regulation (GDPR) is a privacy regulation, and thus, data covered by the GDPR is regulated data. The GDPR does include language that addresses not adversely impacting the rights of others, including intellectual property rights, particularly in terms of software, but the best answer remains that this is regulated data. Trade secrets and legal information are not broad enough to describe this data.

94. B. Journaling replays transactions, which can take an extended period of time if the time between the last backup and the data loss event was longer and there was a high volume of transactions. Journals typically minimize the amount of transaction data that is lost; they can be encrypted, although care must be taken to ensure that they can be recovered; and journaling is used with live databases to ensure transactions are recoverable to as close to the point in time of a data loss event as possible.

95. C. Using UPS with generators will allow systems to remain online during a power outage even if the power outage extends for some time. Generators alone will not spin up fast enough to avoid an outage, and UPS systems will run out of battery power in extended outages. A warm site requires setup time to bring it online, resulting in an outage.

96. A. Masking may be conducted in client-side code, resulting in potential exposures of data. Secure designs require masking to occur in server-side code rather than in the client-side web application. Tokenization typically relies on a separate database or field, making it less likely to be a problem. Encryption and hashing are both unlikely to have problems with client side tampering, making them less secure.

97. C. Top Secret and Secret are examples of government classifications. Businesses typically use classifications like sensitive, confidential, and public.

98. D. Compute is rarely a significant concern for embedded systems. They're designed to function for long periods of time performing a specific function and do not have additional software or functions added. How easy they are to deploy, if they can be patched and updated, and the support lifespan as guaranteed or promised by the vendor, and risk transference by engaging third-party vendors are all likely concerns for a major industrial control system (ICS) deployment that Malia can control through the selection process.

99. B. Layer 7 is the application layer. In order the layers are: 1 – physical, 2 – data link, 3 – network, 4 – transport, 5 – session, 6 – presentation, and 7 – application. The Security+ exam outline only focuses on Layer 4 and Layer 7 in the context of network security devices that can operate at those layers.

100. C. These are all examples of embedded systems, computers built into devices to allow them to function. Other examples include computers built into cars, digital cameras, and thermostats. They often receive fewer (or no) updates, and are required to function for long periods of time as part of other devices or systems.

101. D. Microservices are loosely coupled and fine-grained, and they are intended to be easy to deploy without significant overhead or dependencies. They rely on lightweight protocols like HTTP to make them easier to deploy in common infrastructures. Containers are used to allow applications to be easily deployed without moving a complete operating system but with the required libraries and components to function. The Internet of Things (IoT) describes Internet-enabled devices of all sorts, including embedded systems. Software-defined infrastructure is commonly used for cloud services.

102. A. Incremental backups only include the data that has changed since the last full backup. To restore a backup using incremental backups, the full backup is restored, then incremental backups are applied in order from oldest to most recent. Partial backups describe a backup of only certain data or parts of a system. Daily backups are just that—daily—and may be full or incremental. Snapshots are point-in-time images of a system's or a device's data and memory.

103. C. Sharon is most likely part of a simulation exercise, where organizations test how they would respond to a scenario without taking actual actions. This is safer than a fail over or parallel processing test but is closer to a real event than a tabletop exercise.

104. A. Generators are used by organizations that need to handle extended power outages. They are commonly paired with UPS systems that handle the immediate power outage, allowing the generator to start and stabilize. Solar power alone is not a good solution without a significant battery system, and datacenter-scale battery systems paired with solar are not yet common. PDUs (power distribution units) are used to distribute and control power in a datacenter but do not provide power generation or backup capabilities.

105. C. Physically isolating the network for the SCADA and ICS systems can prevent attacks from outside of the network. In critical infrastructure like power generation stations, this is a common technique to ensure that external attacks cannot cause outages to critical physical infrastructure. Separate VLANs is a common logical control, but attacks against the network or using VLAN hopping techniques can allow attackers to bypass the separation. TLS is useful for protecting traffic but does not meet the security requirement described, and SDN is useful for managing networks but again does not meet the enhanced security requirements in the question.

106. D. Hardware addresses, known as MAC addresses, are used for port security to determine which systems can connect to a port. Their IP address, the network card manufacturer, and the user's password are not used by port security.

107. C. Generators are typically sized to the datacenter they support, so capacity is rarely a primary concern. Fuel availability, maintenance and maintenance cycles for extended runs, and ensuring physical redundancy so that a secondary generator can take over during maintenance cycles for long outages are all common concerns.

108. B. Geographic restrictions are rarely helpful for insider threats because insiders are likely to already be in the same location as authorized users in most organizations. Encryption, tokenization, and permission restrictions can all be used to ensure that only authorized users gain access to the data.

109. C. Use of encryption through secure enclaves and restricted processing environments, controlling access to the data, and limiting where data is processed are all useful controls. Hashing the data does not leave it in a usable form since hashes transform the data, and thus is not a useful solution.

110. B. UPS systems are perfectly suited to handling short power outages and temporary undervoltage events. They sit between systems and grid power, ensuring clean, reliable power is available. Generators take time to start, meaning that a UPS + generator solution is used for longer outages. PDUs (power distribution units) are used to distribute and manage power in datacenters. Solar power is increasingly used by datacenters to help offset their power consumption but is not a solution during nighttime hours.

111. A. Containers do not include an operating system, but do contain applications, libraries, and configuration files.

112. C. SD-WAN, or software-defined wide area network, is a virtual wide area network architecture that relies on a software-based controller to manage multiple connections and connection types. MPLS, LTE, and broadband are commonly managed using SD-WAN technology. SASE, or Secure Access Service Edge, is used to provide end-to-end security in modern environments with systems and users spread throughout many locations and networks. SDN, or software-defined networking, is a code-based network management scheme. However, SD-WAN is the correct answer for wide area networks that rely on things like MPLS and broadband rather than on-premises networks. VSAN, or virtual SAN, is a virtual storage area network.

113. C. An IPS, or intrusion prevention system, can stop attacks based on behaviors and threat feed data. An IDS can detect attacks using the same information but cannot stop them. Proxy servers are used to filter content but do not meet this requirement, and jump servers are used for secure access into higher trust environments.

114. A. Contracts, nondisclosure agreements (NDAs), and statements of work (SOWs) are all examples of legal information. They may include trade secrets or financial information but do not have to. Regulated data is regulated by law and is not the same as legal information.

115. A. Using threat feeds allows administrators to have rules that automatically block new threats using IP reputation and other services. Those detections may rely on application awareness or deep packet inspection, but without the feed information new rules will have to be crafted to address specific new threats. High throughput allows NGFW devices to deal with significant load as well as the demands of deep packet inspection and application awareness.

116. C. IPSec VPNs provide encryption, which allows for confidentiality and integrity through hashing. They also provide authentication because both ends authenticate as part of the VPN connection process. Availability is not a feature of an IPSec connection, and it must be designed and built into the hardware and network infrastructure that the IPSec VPN relies on.

117. B. GPS and Wi-Fi are commonly used to enforce geofencing by determining where individual devices are. Bluetooth may be used in some cases as well, but Wi-Fi and GPS are the dominant options. DNS is not used as part of geographic restrictions, nor is encryption.

118. D. Infrastructure-as-a-service (IaaS) providers are responsible for the underlying infrastructure, including datacenters, networks, and physical hosts. In some cases, they may also be responsible for some operating systems, network controls, applications, and Identity and Access Management (IAM) infrastructure. Customers are always responsible for data and accounts, but may be responsible for applications, network controls, and operating systems as well.

119. C. Ensuring that third-party vendors are held to appropriate standards is best accomplished through contracts with direct suppliers. Since the third-party vendors sign contracts with Kirk's cloud provider, not with Kirk's organization, the only way to have influence over them is through the cloud service provider. Audits and vulnerability scans will typically not be allowed by organizations that do not have a contract with a vendor.

120. C. VPNs, or virtual private networks, are commonly established between two locations to provide a secure connection that can make the networks appear to be on the same network segment. A VLAN may then be used if desired, but a VLAN alone does not provide encryption and cannot be set up across a public connection. TLS encapsulating each service would provide security, but that would not make the two sites appear to be on the same network segment. Reclassifying the data does not secure the data or make the networks appear to be on the same segment, either.

121. B. Replication can be synchronous or asynchronous but focuses on keeping an up-do-date copy of live data. It does not require high-speed media but does require storage media that is fast enough to keep up with the speed of change from the production environment. Replication does not rely on journaling or snapshots.

122. B. NGFW devices are typically deployed where throughput and advanced security features are both needed. UTM devices are more common in small to mid-sized organizations where they can be set up and will often require less management and configuration. A WAF is appropriate for web services, but does not provide enough protection for an entire organization's Internet connectivity. A proxy server is useful for filtering traffic but has the same issues with limited functionality.

123. B. Barb needs to back up her data at least once every 6 hours to meet a 6-hour RPO, and Barb might even choose to run her backups slightly more often to ensure the RPO can be met. Running backups every hour significantly exceeds that target, and may have other implications on performance time to recover, so a more aggressive timeframe would need to be carefully reviewed. Every 12 or 24 hours would not meet the RPO set by Barb's company.

124. A. Since the data is not actively being moved between systems or via a network, and it is not being processed, it is data at rest. If the database was being actively accessed, the data might be in transit when it was sent to an application server and in use as the server processed it. Data sovereignty is the concept that countries can regulate data within their own borders.

125. D. Masking replaces some characters with an alternate character, allowing tasks like validating credit card numbers without exposing all of a data field. Encryption and hashing would transform the data, not replace it with an alternate character. Data classification is involved, but it's not a data obfuscation technique.

126. D. COOP plans address loss of access to some or all of a facility, personnel, or services. Other items may cause those losses, but the focus is on continued operations addressing the key components of an organization's business or purpose—facilities, staff, and services.

127. C. Switch Port Analyzer (SPAN) ports, also known as mirrored ports, configured on a network switch or router are active because the device is powered and are a monitor because they simply copy traffic rather than being inline.

128. B. A major advantage of WAFs is the ability to use thread and rule feeds from vendors that quickly respond to new threats and attacks. At the same time, Renee can also build WAF rules faster than it would take to deploy code fixes in many cases. Penetration testing and static code review are both slow processes and are not suited to the rapid respond described. SASE is used to protect diverse endpoints in many locations, not to counter SQL injection (SQLi) against a web service.

129. D. Many vendors offer a managed service that provides rules that stop trending and new attacks. Maria can subscribe to the service, but needs to be aware that sometimes rules may cause outages or issues if they block legitimate traffic accidentally. Manually deploying rules is slow and requires careful crafting. The Open Worldwide Application Security Project (OWASP) Top 10 is a short list and it is not updated quickly. Threat feeds are useful as a way to write rules but will be less effective than a managed service in most cases due to the variety of attacks and new threats.

130. B. Each network segment should be considered a separate security zone that can be managed and secured appropriately for its ongoing use. Networks are not typically considered fail-open or fail-closed—devices are. Data classification is used to label data.

131. D. Load balancers can help with availability by automatically removing failed notes from a load balanced group. They can help with responsiveness by distributing load to the least loaded systems in a load balanced pool, and they can help with scalability by allowing systems to transparently be added or removed from the pool. They don't directly help with risk transference since risk transference usually requires a contract or insurance.

132. D. When Angie logs in, her authentication data is processed, making it data in use. Data at rest is data that is stored and not in active use or processing. Data in storage and data in validation were made up for this question and are not typically considered data states.

133. B. A TLS-based VPN (often called an SSL-based VPN, despite SSL being outmoded) provides the easiest way for users to use VPN since it does not require a client. SSL VPNs also work only for specific applications rather than making a system appear as though it is fully on a remote network. HTML5 is not a VPN technology, but some VPN portals may be built using HTML5. Security Assertion Markup Language (SAML) is not a VPN technology. IPSec VPNs require a client or configuration and are thus harder for end users to use in most cases.

134. C. Device placement can matter due to physical risks or because of concerns about latency, access to services, or other considerations. Connectivity concerns focus on whether an organization can obtain a network connection and whether it meets the organization's needs, including throughput and reliability. Geographic dispersion refers to the distance between locations that helps to ensure that a single disaster does not take an organization offline. Attack surface is the set of services, ports, and physical access that an attacker could leverage.

135. B. Decentralized approaches can provide increased resilience since a failure or compromise of the management plane or services in a single location will not disrupt other locations. Unfortunately, this normally comes with increased cost and complexity. Increased complexity is not an advantage.

136. C. In an infrastructure as code (IaC) environment, updating the code that defines what a fully patched server is, then replacing servers in a cluster one at a time will be the least disruptive option while also ensuring that future instances will have the patches installed. Rebuilding a base image each time a patch comes out is not efficient, and manually patching is not a best practice in IaC environments and may lead to human error.

137. A. The data should not be released or exposed and could cause harm. This means that confidential best describes this data from the list of available terms. Restricted data is typically limited to a subset of staff, but that is not reflected in the question. The data is also not described as being critical to the operations of the organization; instead the emphasis is on confidentiality. Since this data must remain confidential, it is not public data.

138. A. Legacy devices typically cannot be purchased, so their cost becomes irrelevant. Whether they can be recovered, if patches are available, and the issues that lack of patching may cause are all common issues for legacy devices.

139. B. UTM devices commonly provide firewall, IPS, antivirus/antimalware, and a variety of other services. They are also commonly part of SD-WAN architectures, but do not themselves provide the SD-WAN service.

140. A. TLS VPNs are typically easier to set up and don't require clients to be installed, unlike an IPSec VPN. SD-WAN is used to manage external connectivity, and software-defined networking (SDN) is used to manage networks and their performance, not to allow remote access by users.

141. B. Moving devices to an isolated network segment that has appropriate controls in place to protect devices that may not be able to be secured or that may not receive regular patches is the best option available. Baselines, patching, and even scanning and remediation only help if the devices can be secured, patched, and otherwise protected. IoT devices are often not able to be secured this way, particularly as they age and both lighting and thermostats have relatively long useful lifespans.

142. B. Secure access service edge (SASE) deployments combine SD-WAN with a variety of cloud-hosted security services, including zero trust and CASB tools to replace VPNs. This provides an edge device–oriented security architecture with end-to-end security. SaaS is involved but is not a specific enough answer. SONET is a communication protocol used for fiber networks. Supply chain management (SCM) is not a term used in this context.

143. A. Fail over testing goes beyond parallel processing and completely takes over running services. This is the most complex and risky testing mode, but also the only one that completely tests failure scenarios in a real-world exercise. Simulations and tabletops are more abstract and would not test the site, instead focusing on practices and behaviors.

144. C. Cold sites are spaces that are ready to be used in a disaster but without equipment or other necessary items in place to quickly take over production if needed. A warm site would have some hardware ready to be used, but the hardware would not be configured or otherwise ready for immediate resumption of service. A hot site is prepared to take over processing for an organization immediately, and infrastructure is running in parallel with your production site. Geographic dispersion is used to ensure that a single disaster does not impact multiple sites.

145. C. Tabletop exercises are not simulations and typically do not involve simulated calls to resources. Simulations are a different type of exercise and have the potential for disruptions if staff are not aware of the exercise being conducted.

146. B. This type of architecture leverages the idea of platform diversity. Having multiple vendors and platforms helps to ensure that a single vendor's failure or vulnerability does not prevent an organization from continuing to function. Platform agnostic is not on the Security+ exam but typically means that organizations don't have a vested interest in which platform is selected or used. Multi-cloud environments run in multiple cloud vendors' tools, but this question involves physical router hardware. Parallel processing is a failure testing mode where two or more sites run at the same time during a test.

147. C. Kaito is using a weighted least connection load balancing approach, which distributes traffic based on both a server weight and connection number count. Source IP hashing uses a hash of the source and destination IP addresses to determine which server receives the connection. This also allows for interrupted sessions to go to the same server. Resource-based load balancing takes into account the availability of resources like CPU, memory, and network bandwidth for a server. Round-robin load balancing simply distributes connections as they come in by moving through a list of servers.

148. A. Attack surfaces are the potential points for an attack to occur. For devices, this is often the open services. For organizations, attack surfaces can include open ports and services, physical security concerns, and human vectors. Security zones are a way for organizations to categorize and manage different devices and systems based on security classification. Scalability describes whether a service or system can grow or shrink to handle demand or load. Resilience describes if a system or service can tolerate issues that might otherwise result in outages.

149. C. An infrastructure-as-a-service (IaaS) cloud-hosted model where a third-party provider focuses on scalability and administration of a containerization service will meet Geoff's needs. When scaling from low to very large load is a common event, the ability to grow or shrink in a cloud environment can also provide significant cost savings over paying for an on-premises option that can handle the full scaling event. Software as a service (SaaS) and platform as a service (PaaS) provide full applications or platforms, not containerization environments.

150. B. Financial data includes transactions, accounts, and many other types of information related to finances. Intellectual property is a broad category of data created by humans. Public information is information that is available to the public, and trade secrets are kept private to a limited number of individuals in a company for competitive advantage or other purposes.

151. B. Clustering involves using two or more systems to provide a service as though they're a single server. Load balancing spreads workloads across multiple independent systems while front-ending them with a load balancer device or service to distribute load. Fail-open means that if a network device fails, traffic continues to pass through it. Fail-closed devices stop traffic if they fail. Decisions about fail-open and fail-closed are made based on security in most cases, with fail-closed being more secure if the organization relies on the device for security.

152. C. PCI DSS is a credit card data security standard, meaning that Alaina is most likely dealing with financial information. PCI DSS does not directly address intellectual property or trade secrets, and it's not a regulation.

153. B. Snapshots are used to copy both the data and machine state for virtual machines. Journaling is used for databases and similar uses where replaying actions can be useful to recover if an issue occurs. Replication copies the data synchronously or asynchronously, allowing for a separate copy to be available at all times. Grandfather/Father/Son is a backup cycle commonly used for tape backup.

154. D. Parallel processing allows for systems to be tested without taking them offline. This means that in the event of an issue with the backup systems or facility, the primary facility can continue to operate. Parallel processing does allow for more throughput, but organizations should not rely on this as parallel processing environments need to be able to handle the full load for the organization if the primary or backup fails. Fail over does test redundant systems and does not require organizations to create a significant issue. Instead, manual fail over processes are used to conduct fail over tests.

155. D. Placing the IPS inline at position D will reduce the amount of traffic it has to filter while still allowing it to filter traffic bound for the datacenter. Points A, B, and C will all have more traffic, although point A will have the most, with reductions likely at points C and D.

156. B. Increased complexity can include jurisdictional challenges, increased cost, and regulatory challenges as well as visibility challenges, management overhead increases, and a wide range of additional challenges from operating in multiple locations and models.

157. D. In general, fail over connections should be able to handle an organization's full throughput. Overprovisioning for 100 Gbps will typically create significantly more cost not only for connectivity but also for network devices that can handle high speeds, and underprovisioning at 5 Gbps will mean that traffic would need to be reduced in a fail over scenario.

158. A. A hot site is prepared to take over processing for on organization immediately, and infrastructure is running in parallel with your production site. A warm site would have some hardware ready to be used, but the hardware would not be configured or otherwise ready for immediate resumption of service. Cold sites are spaces that are ready to be used in a disaster but without equipment or other necessary items in place to quickly take over production if needed. The term dispersion site is not commonly used, but the concept of geographic dispersion describes placement of sites with sufficient distance between them to make the likelihood of a single disaster impacting both quite low.

159. C. Geographic dispersion is unlikely for a single building's network core. Redundancy, power backups, and multiple connectivity options are commonly part of designing a highly available network.

160. C. The General Data Protection Regulation (GDPR), Health Insurance Portability and Accountability Act (HIPAA), Family Educational Rights and Privacy Act (FERPA), and the Gramm–Leach–Bliley Act (GLBA) are all regulations, meaning that data they cover is regulated data. Intellectual property is the result of human creativity, classified data is a designation used by governments, and trade secrets are proprietary data with limited access often used by organizations for competitive advantage.

161. A. Virtual machine (VM) escape attacks attempt to access or gain control of the underlying hypervisor through virtual machines. While uncommon, if this occurred it could result in serious issues due to the number of systems run on a single hypervisor host particularly in cloud or shared environments. The other options were made up for the question.

162. B. AH (Authentication Header), ESP (Encapsulating Security Payload), and IKE (Internet Key Exchange) are all important IPSec (Internet Protocol Security) protocols. ISA is not an IPSec protocol.

163. D. Intrusion detection systems are considered passive systems because they cannot block traffic. Active systems like firewalls, IPS, and proxies all have the ability to directly interact with and stop or allow traffic. Air gapped devices do not have a physical connection to a network, or they are on a separate network that is not connected to other networks. Fail-closed devices stop traffic when they fail. Most IPS systems are not deployed inline since they do not need to be interactive and having them inline only creates another potential failure point.

164. C. Hashing uses a one-way function and should not be able to be reversed. This means that you can use hashing to securely store a password because you can hash the password, then compare hashes without needing to know the password. If you hash a database field, however, there's no way to know what the original data was from the hash. Hashing should not be reversible, and it does not use symmetric or asymmetric encryption.

165. C. Tokenizing the data in a separate database will allow both the original unaltered database and a secured database to be used. This reduces risk while retaining data integrity where required. Steganography hides data in images and does not fit this use case. Masking only conceals data and does not protect it against attacks against the underlying application or database in many cases. Hashing the original database will transform the data, and using a single database remains risky.

166. C. SCADA and ICS systems often suffer from a lack of patches and updates. Cost is typically amortized over long periods of time, and SCADA and ICS systems are critical to organizational functions. Scalability is rarely a concern for embedded devices, and SCADA and ICS devices are designed for long life cycles and reliability.

167. C. In a SDN environment, the SDN controller provides manages and controls all the network devices, including switches and routers. That means that a compromise of the SDN controller would result in compromise of the entire network. No mention is made of SD-WAN in the question, so we don't know the connectivity or relative importance of SD-WAN in the scenario.

168. B. Third-party support availability is an example of risk transference where the support contract moves the risk to the contractor. Availability and responsiveness may be considerations for the contractor, but the ability to obtain support doesn't imply either of these. Compute is most commonly a concern where embedded devices or hardware solutions may not have sufficient computational power to meet new needs.

169. A. Network access control (NAC) tools that can allow for authentication and authorization based on user groups or roles and VLANs that separate groups based on those roles once they're on the network exactly fit the needs Yarif has. 802.1X can also be helpful with this, but containerization is used to allow applications to be deployed without worrying about the application environment. SDN and MAC address filtering doesn't account for user authentication and identities, just machine hardware addresses. SD-WAN is for external connectivity, not internal networks.

170. A. A simulation is the closest you can get to a real-world event without having one. A tabletop exercise has personnel discussing scenarios, whereas a walk-through goes through checklists and procedures. A wargame is not a common exercise type.

171. B. Serverless deployments remove the need to patch underlying infrastructure. They may still have vulnerable functions and should be logged. Cost savings is not a direct security advantage.

172. D. In a large-scale disaster scenario, personnel may be unwilling or unable to report to work. Organizations planning for disaster in an area where their personnel live and work often need to identify ways to ensure staffing in a scenario that impacts their staff. Lack of facility power is not a personnel issue. Authentication should be part of the hot-site capability. Insider threats are not a common concern during disasters.

173. D. ACLs, VLANs, and firewalls are all commonly used to implement network segmentation. Due to the operational challenges that air gaps create, they are far less commonly implemented and are only used when absolutely necessary.

174. C. Binary files like executable programs are examples of non-human-readable data. That's one of the reasons encoding schemes like XML were created for data files that can allow both machines and humans to read and interact with data. Restricted and confidential are both classification schemes that businesses may use to describe their organizational data.

175. D. Journaling tracks transactions as they occur. Unless the journal itself was lost, Melissa should be able to restore the backup, then replay the journal to ensure the organization loses very little data.

176. B. SCADA systems are often used to manage industrial control systems (ICSs). SDN and SD-WAN are used to manage networks and connectivity respectively, whereas Active Directory is used to manage Windows servers and workstations in a domain environment.

177. B. Encrypted backups require the encryption key, so Maria's organization will need to preserve and protect the recovery key in a secure manner that does not rely on the backups. This is often done via multiple physical copies of the key stored in secured locations with geographic diversity or using both physical and cloud secure storage like a key management system (KMS).

178. D. Replication is a continuous process and because of this it does not require restoration processes like restoring differential backups or journals to allow data to be used. Backups are periodic, and they typically require additional restoration work in order to be used.

179. D. Erin will need to restore the full backup, then apply the differential backups from each of the remaining three days for a total of four backups.

180. A. IPSec VPNs operate at the network layer instead of the transport layer. That means less information is visible to potential attackers. Both support strong encryption, IPSec VPNs do support tunneling, and not relying on tunneling is not an advantage in most use cases.

181. D. Vera can use a SD-WAN, or software-defined wide area network, to manage multiple connections dynamically, ensuring connectivity and performance for her organization. SASE is used to secure networks and device connectivity in modern organizations with complex and mobile boundaries. SDN is software-defined networking and manages networks as code. IPSec is a suite of protocols used to secure network traffic.

182. A. Embedded devices typically have minimal CPUs, memory, and storage. They prioritize responsiveness for their core functions, and thus availability and responsiveness are typically met with the device. Cost for embedded devices is typically associated with the larger device they're part of rather than the embedded device itself as they are there to monitor or operate the system.

183. C. Intellectual property is intangible creations by the human mind. Patents, copyrights, trademarks, and trade secrets are all examples of intellectual property. Intellectual property is not necessarily sensitive data, but it could be.

184. C. Storage capacity should be part of Jaime's infrastructure planning to ensure that large volumes of logs do not overwhelm her infrastructure. Compute is typically not an issue with logs, but it could be with log analysis later in her design process. People and power are not directly impacted by logging, but people might be needed for log analysis later as well.

185. B. This organization is using a decentralized model where there is no datacenter or primary hosting or operational facility. With remote workers making up much of the company, as well as flexible working locations, this design makes sense for the company but introduces additional complexity because endpoints will need to be secured wherever they are, regardless of what network they are on. A centralized design can somewhat simplify that, but modern application stacks and working conditions often make that less likely. This is not an on-premises design since workers and cloud tools are remote. There is no description of segmentation in the question.

186. B. Mobile device management (MDM) tools are often used to enforce geographic restrictions on devices by using GPS and Wi-Fi to determine where they are and to limit their access to sensitive systems or data if they are not in an allowed geographic boundary. This often matches being in a specific office building with known Wi-Fi for highly sensitive access or work hour requirements. Endpoint detection and response (EDR) is used to counter ransomware and other malicious software, 802.1X is used to control access to networks, and VPNs are used to provide site-to-site connectivity through untrusted networks as well as to location shift devices.

187. B. Round-robin load balancer algorithms spread load by assigning incoming connections to servers or services on a list. This helps to spread the load evenly even without awareness of the relative load each connection creates or that the server is under simply by relying on connections evening out over time. Load-based and capacity-based models use more knowledge of the state of the servers or services. User pinning is not a load balancing model.

188. C. Encryption is the most effective way to protect data at rest. Classification is useful to ensure data is handled in appropriate ways, but does not directly protect the data. Segmentation can help keep data in the right locations with appropriate controls around it, but again does not directly protect the data if the server or data store is accessible. Hashing is a one-way function and does not leave data in a usable state for most purposes that rely on the data being intact and in its original form.

189. C. Environmental sensor appliances are frequently deployed to datacenters and network closets to monitor for potential issues like high temperatures. Heating, ventilation, and air-conditioning (HVAC) systems monitor and control temperatures, but datacenters commonly add additional monitoring tools in case the HVAC system fails or other issues arise. UPS systems are not used for environmental monitoring, and load balancers are used to distribute load to servers and services.

190. B. Organizations typically deploy both a UPS and a generator (or generators!). Long power outages will drain the batteries that a UPS relies on. Since UPS systems are typically intended to run for minutes, rather than hours, for datacenters this should be Danielle's first concern. No generator was mentioned, and in fact the UPS is her only power resilience control. While a UPS may experience issues with surges when power resumes, temporary drops in voltage, and power outages are not uncommon even on well-maintained power grids, and UPS systems are designed to handle them under normal circumstances while protecting the systems they provide emergency power to.

191. C. An IPSec VPN is a common option for organizations that need to create a secure VPN tunnel between two locations. A VPN connection is established by network devices at both locations and traffic is able to travel securely over commodity Internet connections. TLS VPNs are more commonly used for individuals to connect to an organization's network. Web proxies are used to filter and control web traffic, not for this purpose. 802.1X is used to authenticate to networks and protect them from unauthorized connections, not to create secure, multisite tunnels.

192. C. Port security associates a list of allowed hardware (MAC) addresses with a port and only allows systems with permitted MAC addresses to connect to and send traffic through the network port. 802.1X uses authentication, which can include userIDs and multifactor. IP addresses are not a way that port security filters systems.

193. C. TLS VPNs provide an easier user experience from the browser without installing additional software or additional configuration like an IPSec VPN typically requires. A jump server is used for access to secure zones but isn't ideal for traveling and remote employees—often a VPN is used to access a jump server in scenarios like that. SD-WAN is useful to manage connectivity options, not for individual users.

194. A. The virtual machine's power state, memory state, and disk are all captured as part of a snapshot. The underlying hypervisor's configuration is not captured by a snapshot.

195. B. Data sovereignty concerns are driven by where the data resides, and geolocation can help understand the applicable law or regulations. Data can be at rest, in use, or in transit in any given location. Data criticality is determined by an organization, not by its location.

196. D. SCADA manages complex systems by combining central and local control systems with communication systems to manage large-scale industrial processes. The endpoint devices described may be embedded systems, Internet of Things (IoT), or real-time operating systems (RTOSs), but together they are a SCADA system.

197. D. Penetration tests will typically include vulnerability scanning as well as other activities that can provide a more complete view of an organization's Internet-facing attack surface. OSINT alone will not provide technical testing. Threat feeds do not provide information about a specific organization's attack surface, and vulnerability scanning may not reveal other issues like application issues.

198. A. IoT devices are typically deployed for long periods of time, meaning that over time the complexity of managing a multiple device and vendor environment is the largest concern. Initial concerns about ease of deployment would exist but could be overcome. Availability and resilience are both typically helped by platform diversity as outages or issues found with one device or vendor should not impact others.

199. B. A secure enclave is one way of protecting data in use. This relies on secured hardware that stores data that is in use and that only allows processes that run in the enclave from accessing data. Hashing, containerization, and using tunneling do not provide security for data in use.

200. B. There is no connection between the two network security zones in Model 2. This is an air gapped model with physical isolation. Logical segmentation would show VLANs or other logical segmentation options. Servers are shown, easily dismissing serverless as an option, and there is no indication of whether this is an on-premises or an off-site design.

201. C. Masking, encryption, and tokenization are all examples of data obfuscation methods that protect against data exposure. None of these are encryption or classification methods, and none of them are tagging methods, although classification often involves tagging data if it will be managed or monitored using automated methods.

202. B. IP hash relies on a hash of the client and server's IP addresses to associate them with a server. Even if you're not familiar with load-balancing techniques, you can rule out round-robin, which simply distributes sessions through a list in order; weighted least connection, which looks at which servers have the least traffic and a weight assigned to the server; and resource-based, which looks at how heavily loaded a server is.

203. A. 802.1X allows for authentication via EAP, then assignment to a VLAN based on a role or other attributes. EAP alone does not perform this function, port security leverages MAC addresses to determine if a system is allowed to connect, and VLAN tagging is part of how traffic is labeled for a specific VLAN but does not support authentication or role-based labels directly.

204. B. Logical segmentation uses software to define and create segmentation. VLANs are defined at the network layer using VLAN tags. Air gapping would remove network connectivity between a system or systems and other networks to prevent access via the network. Physical segmentation would require separate network infrastructure. Physical isolation typically means removing a system from a network.

205. A. Wi-Fi and other on premises network solutions are not typically part of an SD-WAN implementation. SD-WAN focuses on wide area networks, which are outside the on-premises network borders of organizations, and thus technologies like MPLS, broadband, and LTE are used with SD-WAN controllers.

206. A. Information that is available without restriction or authentication and that is available on an Internet-facing website should be considered public information. Internal, confidential, and restricted information all require additional controls and handling practices.

207. C. Identifying single points of failure is a common first step in network high availability designs. This allows network designers to plan for failures and how to avoid them. Configuring a hot site, implementing clustering, and purchasing redundant hardware all occur much further into the design process when needs are identified and prioritized.

208. A. Having artifacts signed after they have made it through the build and validation process helps ensure that they haven't been modified and that the artifact has had the organization's checks done. Container image scanning helps to find issues like malware and dependency issues. Dependency checks can validate things like open source tool risks or issues. Static analysis requires manual review of code.

209. C. A primary concern for organizations that encrypt their backups is whether the keys are available in a disaster. Ensuring that the keys are stored in a manner that ensures that they are recoverable if the backups are recoverable is critical. Modern backup encryption typically does not add a meaningful amount of time to backups, nor does it increase cost or space to such a significant degree that it is a primary concern.

210. C. Ransomware concerns are typically found with desktops, laptops, mobile devices, and servers instead of IoT devices. IoT devices often don't have patches or aren't patched, send data to third parties that may not be desired, and may not use secure communications.

211. C. In circumstances where a single vendor's outages are a major concern, multi-cloud deployments may be appropriate. This is more common when the application is containerized or otherwise easily portable. The more customized to the current cloud vendor the application or service is, the more difficult it is to move to other cloud vendors and the more costly the move will be. In addition, multi-cloud can drive additional costs for overhead services, making multi-cloud a choice organizations undertake cautiously. Deploying in multiple AZs or regions will not avoid an outage if the IaaS vendor has a cloud-wide issue, and contractual obligations won't stop outages—they will typically just provide penalties if there is an outage longer than the contract allows.

212. C. Meeting both resilience and performance requirements can be best addressed in this scenario by contracting with two separate network service providers. This allows for both resilience and the possibility of sending traffic through both connections for greater performance. Both a generator and a UPS can help with power resilience, but the focus of this question is network connectivity.

213. A. Segmentation of data separates data based on factors like use cases, sensitivity, roles, and types or classifications of information. Obfuscation attempts to conceal or hide information. Masking replaces information with other data like asterisks or X's when displayed, allowing partial data to be displayed for business purposes. Tokenization replaces data with an alternate value, often based on a hashing algorithm that allows the alternate value to be used as an index or reference without the actual data visible.

214. C. Mandatory access control (MAC) is used in scenarios where users should not have the ability to grant access to files. Role-based access control and rule-based access control both provide more flexibility, and they are more commonly used than mandatory access control in cases where that is desired. Discretionary access control (DAC) allows users to grant access to other users and does not fit the requirements either.

215. B. A proxy server is likely to be used in an environment where the ability to filter searches may be required, such as a library with public workstations. A jump server is used to access more secure zones, a load balancer is typically used to allow multiple systems to provide a service, and a DLP system is used to prevent unauthorized data exfiltration.

216. A. In platform-as-a-service (PaaS) environments, customers and providers typically share responsibility for identity and directory infrastructure, applications, and network controls. Customers are responsible for data, devices, and accounts, and the provider is responsible for the underlying systems, including operating systems and physical infrastructure.

217. C. A microservices design will allow for each component or service to be separate and lightweight, allowing them to be developed independently and thus easier to fix without complex dependencies. Containerization would allow for easy deployment of applications to different service environments, but the focus for containerization is on portability, not on the design requirements listed. Virtualization requires even more resources because operating systems are virtualized, but it suffers from the same lack of a direct means of addressing the needs explained in the question. SCADA stands for supervisory control and data acquisition and is used to manage complex industrial or controls' environments, not service environments like the question describes.

218. D. The biggest advantage of a monitoring port over an inline network tap is that if the monitoring port fails, it will not impact the network traffic flow. If an inline device fails, it may impact the network traffic even if it is designed to avoid that scenario. Inline taps don't have to rely on the performance of the switch, meaning that they are often higher performance; they can be passive, meaning that they cannot be attacked like a switch's operating system can be; and since inline passive devices simply copy traffic, they are often easier to configure since you merely plug them in.

219. A. Embedded systems are often used for long periods of time, use relatively low-power CPUs and have limited memory and storage, and are typically not user configurable or manageable in meaningful ways. They typically don't have the ability to install additional software as they are purpose-built to serve a specific need.

220. A. Containerization technologies bundle the needed libraries and other components for an application together in a lightweight package format that can easily be deployed to a provider's containerization service. Snapshots are used to capture a virtual machine's state and data at a given point in time. Embedded systems are computers that are built into a device or system. Segmentation is the concept of dividing a network or system into separate parts, often with security and other boundaries between them.

221. D. Data sovereignty is the right of nations to pass laws that control the use of data within their borders. This means that organizations must follow each country's laws when they store, process, or otherwise handle data in the country they operate in. Data classification is a process of classifying data to set handling or other processes and practices around it. Treaties are not covered by the Security+ exam.

222. B. This is an example of air gapped design where there is no network connectivity. This prevents network-based attacks from being possible against the high-value certificate authority server. Port security is used to enable or disable network ports. Defense-in-depth is a design concept that relies on layers of defenses to ensure security. Zero trust requires continuous authentication and rights verification to provide ongoing security for a network or system architecture.

223. B. A large-scale denial-of-service attack that is using resources can be costly. Microsoft's cloud will be able to scale to meet the demand, but Jayne's organization may spend large amounts of money without benefiting any legitimate customers. Loss of data is unlikely because the application is being heavily used without any underlying issue for the application's data. Log files will still be created, but the size and scale of the logs may drive cost. There is nothing in the scenario that demonstrates a vulnerability, and resource exhaustion attacks do not require a vulnerability to be successful.

224. B. EAP (Extensible Authentication Protocol) is used for 802.1X authentication before the port is enabled for other traffic. EAP does not permit vulnerability or port scanning, nor does it provide system security status validation.

225. B. The functions shown are typical of a proxy server. The proxy can be used to apply content controls and to conceal the IP addresses of internal users. A web application firewall filters web traffic but is specifically targeting attacks and malicious behavior. A jump server is used between a low-trust and a higher-trust area to provide access, and this is not shown or described in the image or question. A load balancer is used to distribute traffic load between servers, and this is not shown in the image or reflected in the question.

226. B. While blocking single quotes won't stop all SQL injection, it will stop many basic injection attacks. Preventing the use of SQL or AND and OR statements may break some applications, although secure web applications should be using stored queries.

Chapter 4: Domain 4.0: Security Operations

1. A. While all of these are best practices, moving the device's administrative interface to a protected VLAN will provide the most significant improvement in security since there are no known issues or vulnerabilities at the moment. If there were, patching or disabling services would quickly move up the list.

2. B. Threat hunting is the process of searching for threats, often using IoCs, threat intelligence, technological tools, and expertise to identify threats that might impact an organization. IoC creation involves documenting and defining an indicator of compromise. Root cause analysis looks for the underlying cause of an issue or event, and eradication is the complete removal of a threat or artifacts of malicious activity.

3. A. The simplest way to ensure that APIs are only used by legitimate users is to require the use of authentication. API keys are one of the most frequently used methods for this. If an API key is lost or stolen, the key can be invalidated and reissued, and since API keys can be matched to usage, Cynthia's company can also bill customers based on their usage patterns if they want to. A firewall or IP restrictions may be able to help, but they can be fragile; customer IP addresses may change. An intrusion prevention system (IPS) can detect and prevent attacks, but legitimate usage would be hard to tell from those who are not customers using an IPS.

4. C. Greg can clone a legitimate Media Access Control (MAC) address if he can identify one on the network. Greg can do this by checking for a MAC label on some devices or by capturing traffic on the network if he can physically access it.

5. B. Screened subnet designs use a firewall with three interfaces, one for the Internet or an untrusted network, one for a protected but front-facing network, and one for a shielded or protected network. ACLs (access control lists) use rules to control access. This design may use ACLs, but an ACL alone does not describe it. Binary firewalls were made up for this question, and while an NGFW may be multihomed, "multiroute" is not a term used to describe this design.

6. B. The Common Vulnerabilities and Exposures (CVE) list has entries that describe and provide references to publicly known cybersecurity vulnerabilities. A CVE feed will provide updated information about new vulnerabilities and a useful index number to cross reference with other services.

7. A. This is an example of a false positive. A false positive can cause a vulnerability to show that was not actually there. This sometimes happens when a patch or fix is installed but the application does not change in a way that shows the change, and it has been an issue with updates where the version number is the primary check for a vulnerability. When a vulnerability scanner sees a vulnerable version number but a patch has been installed that does not update it, a false positive report can occur. A false negative would report a patch or fix where there was actually a vulnerability. Automatic updates were not mentioned, nor was a specific Apache version.

8. B. All of these protocols are unsecure. FTP has been replaced by secure versions in some uses (SFTP/FTPS), whereas Telnet has been superseded by SSH in modern applications. RSH is outmoded and should be seen only on truly ancient systems. If you find a system or device exposing these protocols, you will need to dig in further to determine why they are exposed and how they can be protected if they must remain open for a legitimate reason.

9. B. OSINT, or open source intelligence, is intelligence information obtained from public sources like search engines, websites, domain name registrars, and a host of other locations. OPSEC, or operational security, refers to habits such as not disclosing unnecessary information. STIX is the Structured Threat Intelligence Exchange protocol, and IntCon was made up for this question.

10. A. Proprietary, or closed threat, intelligence is threat intelligence that is not openly available. OSINT, or open source threat intelligence, is freely available. ELINT is a military term for electronic and signals intelligence. Corporate threat intelligence was made up for this question.

11. C. Bug bounties are increasingly common and can be quite lucrative. Bug bounty websites match vulnerability researchers with organizations that are willing to pay for information about issues with their software or services. Ransoms are sometimes demanded by attackers, but this is not a ransom since it was voluntarily paid as part of a reward system. A zero-day disclosure happens when a vulnerability is disclosed and the organization has not been previously informed and allowed to fix the issue. Finally, you might feel like $10,000 is a payday, but the term is not used as a technical term and doesn't appear on the exam.

12. C. A false negative occurs with a vulnerability scanning system when a scan is run and an issue that exists is not identified. This can be because of a configuration option, a firewall, or other security setting or because the vulnerability scanner is otherwise unable to detect the issue. A missing vulnerability update might be a concern if the problem did not specifically state that the definitions are fully up-to-date. Unless the vulnerability is so new that there is no definition, a missing update shouldn't be the issue. Silent patching refers to a patching technique that does not show messages to users that a patch is occurring. A false positive would have caused a vulnerability to show that was not actually there. This sometimes happens when a patch or fix is installed but the application does not change in a way that shows the change.

13. B. Threat hunting can involve a variety of activities such as intelligence fusion, combining multiple data sources and threat feeds, and reviewing advisories and bulletins to remain aware of the threat environment for your organization or industry. Incident response happens once an incident has occurred, penetration testing tests security from an attacker's perspective, and vulnerability scanning seeks to identify vulnerabilities using testing through technical means like connecting to services or checking local version information.

14. C. Since Frank is using the cloud service provider's web services, he will need to review the logs that they capture. If he has not configured them, he will need to do so, and he will then need a service or capability to analyze them for the types of traffic he is concerned about. Syslog and Apache logs are both found on a traditional web host, and they would be appropriate if Frank was running his own web servers in the infrastructure-as-a-service (IaaS) environment.

15. C. Although it may be tempting to immediately upgrade, reading and understanding the CVEs for a vulnerability is a good best practice. Once Charles understands the issue, he can then remediate it based on the recommendations for that specific problem. Disabling PHP or the web server would break the service, and in this case, only newer versions of PHP than 5.4 have the patch Charles needs.

16. D. Although 80 and 443 are the most common HTTP ports, it is common practice to run additional web servers on port 8080 when a nonstandard port is needed. SSH would be expected to be on port 22, RDP on 3389, and MySQL on 3306.

17. C. A network device running SSH on port 22 and a web server on TCP port 443 is a very typical discovery when running a vulnerability scan. Without any demonstrated issues, Carolyn should simply note that she saw those services. Telnet runs on port 21, an unencrypted web server will run on TCP 80 in most cases, and Windows file shares use a variety of ports, including TCP ports 135–139 and 445.

18. C. A test server should be identical to the production server. This can be used for functional testing as well as security testing, before deploying the application. The production server is the live server. A development server would be one the programmers use during development of a web application, and predeployment server is not a term typically used in the industry.

19. C. Staging environments, sometimes called preproduction environments, are typically used for final quality assurance (QA) and validation before code enters the production environment as part of a deployment pipeline. Staging environments closely mirror production, allowing realistic testing and validation to be done. Development and test environments are used to create the code and for testing while it is being developed.

20. C. Application programming interface (API) keys are frequently used to meet this need. An API key can be issued to an individual or organization, and then use of the API can be tracked to each API key. If the API key is compromised or abused, it can be revoked and a new API key can be issued. Firewall rules written to use public IP addresses can be fragile, since IP addresses may change or organizations may have a broad range of addresses that may be in use, making it hard to validate which systems or users are using the API. Credentials, including passwords, are not as frequently used as API keys.

21. A. Baseline configurations, per NIST 800-53: "Baseline configurations serve as a basis for future builds, releases, and/or changes to information systems. Baseline configurations include information about information system components (e.g., standard software packages installed on workstations, notebook computers, servers, network components, or mobile devices; current version numbers and patch information on operating systems and applications; and configuration settings/parameters), network topology, and the logical placement of those components within the system architecture. Maintaining baseline configurations requires creating new baselines as organizational information systems change over time. Baseline configurations of information systems reflect the current enterprise architecture."

22. A. Indexing encrypted files will mean that an unencrypted index is stored, potentially exposing the content of encrypted files. Disabling the indexing service for encrypted files helps to protect them. There is no denial-of-service scenario for this unless a vulnerability in the indexing service is discovered and none is mentioned. The service is not exposed via the network, and dark web access is not accomplished via indexing services.

23. D. OAuth is a common authorization service used for cloud services. It allows users to decide which websites or applications to entrust their information to without requiring them to give them the user's password. OpenID is frequently paired with OAuth as the authentication layer. Kerberos is more frequently used for on-site authentication, and SAML is Security Assertion Markup Language.

24. A. Fingerprint reader systems are the most widely accepted biometric systems in common use for entry access and other purposes today. Facial recognition systems are increasingly in use and are also likely to be more accepted by user populations based on their broad deployment in phones, but they are not listed as an option. Both retina and iris scans are less likely to be accepted, whereas voice systems are both relatively uncommon and more disruptive for frequent usage.

25. C. Static codes are typically recorded in a secure location, but if they are not properly secured, or are otherwise exposed, they can be stolen. Brute-force attempts should be detected and prevented by backoff algorithms and other techniques that prevent attacks against multifactor authentication systems. Collisions exist with hashing algorithms, not with static multifactor codes, and clock mismatch issues occur for time-based one-time password (TOTP) codes.

26. C. The best answer from this list is DLP, or data loss prevention technology. DLP is designed to protect data from being exposed or leaking from a network using a variety of techniques and technology. Stateful firewalls are used to control which traffic is sent to or from a system, but will not detect sensitive data. OEM is an original equipment manufacturer, and security information and event management (SIEM) can help track events and incidents but will not directly protect data itself.

27. A. Social login is an example of a federated approach to using identities. The combination of identity providers and service providers, along with authorization management, is a key part of federation. AAA (authentication, authorization, and accounting) is typically associated with protocols like RADIUS. Privilege creep occurs as staff members change jobs and their privileges are not adjusted to only match their current role. IAM is a broader set of identity and access management practices. Although IAM may be involved in federated identity, this question does not directly describe IAM.

28. A. Although it may seem like Charles has presented two factors, in fact he has only presented two types of things he knows along with his identity. To truly implement a multifactor environment, he should use more than one of something you have, something you know, and something you are.

29. B. A site survey is the process of identifying where access points should be located for best coverage and identifying existing sources of RF interference, including preexisting wireless networks and other devices that may use the same radio frequency spectrum. By conducting a site survey, Naomi can guide the placement of her access points as well as create a channel design that will work best for her organization.

30. C. Mobile device management (MDM) suites often provide the ability to manage content on devices as well as applications. Using content management tools can allow Charlene to provision files, documents, and media to the devices that staff members in her organization are issued. Application management would be useful for apps. Remote wipe can remove data and applications from the device if it is lost or stolen, or an employee leaves the organization. Push notifications are useful when information needs to be provided to the device user.

31. C. In this scenario, Denny specifically needs to ensure that he stops the most malware. In situations like this, vendor diversity is the best way to detect more malware, and installing a different vendor's antivirus (AV) package on servers like email servers and then installing a managed package for PCs will result in the most detections in almost all cases. Installing more than one AV package on the same system is rarely recommended, since this often causes performance issues and conflicts between the packages—in fact, at times AV packages have been known to detect other AV packages because of the deep hooks they place into the operating system to detect malicious activity!

32. C. The application includes input validation techniques that are used to ensure that unexpected or malicious input does not cause problems with the application. Input validation techniques will strip out control characters, validate data, and perform a variety of other actions to clean input before it is processed by the application or stored for future use. This validation may help prevent buffer overflows, but other techniques described here are not used for buffer overflow prevention. String injection is actually something this helps to prevent, and schema validation looks at data to ensure that requests match a schema, but again this is a narrower description than the broad range of input validation occurring in the description.

33. A. WPA3 supports SAE, or simultaneous authentication of equals, providing a more secure way to authenticate that limits the potential for brute-force attacks and allows individuals to use different passwords. WPA is not as secure as WPA2, and WEP is the oldest, and least secure, wireless security protocol. WPA2 is not as secure as WPA3 but remains in use due to broad deployment.

34. B. The correct answer is to use a sandboxed environment to test the malware and determine its complete functionality. A sandboxed system could be an isolated virtual machine (VM) or an actual physical machine that is entirely isolated from the network. Leaving the malware on a production system is never the correct approach. You should test or analyze the malware to determine exactly what malware it is, allowing you to respond to the threat properly. A honeypot is used for luring and trapping attackers, not for testing malware.

35. D. Isaac knows that trusting client systems to be secure is not a good idea, and thus ensuring that validation occurs on a trusted client is not an appropriate recommendation. Ensuring that validation occurs on a trusted server, that client data is validated, and that data types and ranges are reasonable are all good best practices for him to recommend.

36. C. Isaac can configure a geofence that defines his corporate buildings and campus. He can then set up a geofence policy that will only allow devices to work while they are inside that geofenced area. Patch management, IP filtering, and network restrictions are not suitable solutions for this.

37. A. Static code analysis can help identify business logic issues by leveraging expert knowledge and understanding of the business process and logic involved. Fuzzing is a technique whereby the tester intentionally enters incorrect values into input fields to see how the application will handle it but doesn't directly test business logic. Baselining is the process of establishing security standards, and version control simply tracks changes in the code—it does not test the code.

38. B. Endpoint detection and response (EDR) focuses on identifying anomalies and issues, but it is not designed to be a malware analysis tool. Instead, the ability to search and explore data, identify suspicious activities, and coordinate responses is what makes up an EDR tool.

39. A. Mandatory access control (MAC) is the correct solution. It will not allow lower privileged users to even see the data at a higher privilege level. Discretionary access control (DAC) has each data owner configure their own security. Role-based access control (RBAC) could be configured to meet the needs, but it's not the best solution for these requirements. Security Assertion Markup Language (SAML) is not an access control model.

40. B. An agent-based, preadmission system will provide greater insight into the configuration of the system using the agent, and using a preadmission model will allow the system configuration to be tested before the system is allowed to connect to the network. Agentless NAC uses scanning and/or network inventory techniques and will typically not have as deep a level of insight into the configuration and software versions running on a system. Postadmission systems make enforcement decisions based on what users do after they gain admission to a network, rather than prior to gaining admission, allowing you to quickly rule out two of these options.

41. C. CYOD, or choose your own device, allows users to choose a device that is corporate owned and paid for. Choices may be limited to set of devices, or users may be allowed to choose essentially any device depending on the organization's deployment decisions. BYOD allows users to bring their own device, whereas COPE, or corporate-owned, personally enabled, provides devices to users that they can then use for personal use. VDI uses a virtual desktop infrastructure as an access layer for any security model where specialized needs or security requirements may require access to remote desktop or application services.

42. C. If Claire is using Simple Network Management Protocol (SNMP) to manage and monitor her network devices, she should make sure she is using SNMPv3 and that it is properly configured. SNMPv3 can provide information about the status and configuration of her network devices. Remote Authentication Dial-In User Service (RADIUS) might be used to authenticate to the network, but Transport Layer Security (TLS) and SSH File Transfer Protocol (SFTP) are not specifically used for the purposes described.

43. B. Containerization will allow Eric's company's tools and data to be run inside of an application-based container, isolating the data and programs from the self-controlled bring your own device (BYOD) devices. Storage segmentation can be helpful, but the operating system itself as well as the applications would remain a concern. Eric should recommend full-device encryption (FDE) as a security best practice, but encrypting the container and the data it contains can provide a reasonable security layer even if the device itself is not fully encrypted. Remote wipe is helpful if devices are lost or stolen, but the end user may not be okay with having the entire device wiped, and there are ways to work around remote wipes, including blocking cellular and Wi-Fi signals.

44. B. Data loss prevention (DLP) tools allow sensitive data to be tagged and monitored so that if a user attempts to send it, they will be notified, administrators will be informed, and if necessary, the data can be protected using encryption or other protection methods before it is sent. Full-disk encryption (FDE) would protect data at rest, and S/MIME and POP3S would protect mail being retrieved from a server but would not prevent the SSNs from being sent.

45. A. Attribute-based access control (ABAC) looks at a group of attributes, in addition to the login username and password, to make decisions about whether or not to grant access. One of the attributes examined is the location of the person. Since the users in this company travel frequently, they will often be at new locations, and that might cause ABAC to reject their logins. Wrong passwords can certainly prevent login, but are not specific to ABAC. ABAC does not prevent remote access, and a firewall can be configured to allow, or prohibit, any traffic you wish.

46. B. Single sign-on (SSO) is designed specifically to address this risk and would be the most helpful. Users have only a single logon to remember; thus, they have no need to write down the password. OAuth (Open Authorization) is an open standard for token-based authentication and authorization on the Internet. It does not eliminate the use or need for multiple passwords. Multifactor authentication helps prevent risks due to lost passwords, but does not remove the need for multiple passwords by itself. Security Assertion Markup Language (SAML) and Lightweight Directory Access Protocol (LDAP) do not stop users from needing to remember multiple passwords.

47. D. Rule-based access control applies a set of rules to an access request. Based on the application of the rules, the user may be given access to a specific resource that they were not explicitly granted permission to. MAC, DAC, and role-based access control wouldn't give a user access unless that user has already been explicitly given that access.

48. D. Both the Windows and Linux filesystems work based on a discretionary access control scheme where file and directory owners can determine who can access, change, or otherwise work with files under their control. Role-based access controls systems determine rights based on roles that are assigned to users. Rule-based access control systems use a series of rules to determine which actions can occur, and mandatory access control systems enforce control at the operating system level.

49. A. Restricting each faculty account so that it is only usable when that particular faculty member is typically on campus will prevent someone from logging in with that account after hours, even if they have the password. Usage auditing may detect misuse of accounts but will not prevent it. Longer passwords are effective security, but a longer password can still be stolen. Credential management is always a good idea, but it won't address this specific issue.

50. C. Password complexity requires that passwords have a mixture of uppercase letters, lowercase letters, numbers, and special characters. This would be the best approach to correct the problem described in the question. Longer passwords are a good security measure but will not correct the issue presented here. Changing passwords won't make those passwords any stronger, and SSO will have no effect on the strength of passwords.

51. B. Mandatory access control (MAC) is based on documented security levels associated with the information being accessed. Role-based access control (RBAC) is based on the role the user is placed in. Discretionary access control (DAC) lets the data owner set access control. BAC is not an access control model.

52. A. Discretionary access control (DAC) allows data owners to assign permissions. Role-based access control (RBAC) assigns access based on the role the user is in. Mandatory access control (MAC) is stricter and enforces control at the OS level. Attribute-cased access control (ABAC) considers various attributes such as location, time, and computer in addition to username and password.

53. A. OS hardening is the process of securing an operating system by patching, updating, and configuring the operating system to be secure. Configuration management is the ongoing process of managing configurations for systems, rather than this initial security step. Both security uplift and endpoint lockdown were made up for this question.

54. D. Secure Lightweight Directory Access Protocol (LDAPS) uses port 636 by default. DNS uses port 53, LDAP uses 389, and secure HTTP uses port 443.

55. B. Role-based access control (RBAC) grants permissions based on the user's position within the organization. Mandatory access control (MAC) uses security classifications to grant permissions. Discretionary access control (DAC) allows data owners to set permissions. Attribute-based access control (ABAC) considers various attributes such as location, time, and computer, in addition to username and password.

56. A. Security groups are a virtual firewall for instances, allowing rules to be applied to traffic between instances. Dynamic resource allocation is a concept that allows resources to be applied as they are needed, including scaling up and down infrastructure and systems on the fly. Virtual private cloud (VPC) endpoints are a way to connect to services inside of a cloud provider without an Internet gateway. Finally, instance awareness is a concept that means that tools know about the differences between instances, rather than treating each instance in a scaling group as the same. This can be important during incident response processes and security monitoring for scaled groups, where resources may all appear identical without instance awareness.

57. B. If the system maintains a password history, that will prevent any user from reusing an old password. Password complexity and length are common security settings but would not prevent the behavior described. Multifactor authentication helps prevent brute-force attacks and reduces the potential impact of stolen passwords but would not help with this scenario.

58. A. Setting login time restrictions is a common method to control when a system can be used. Turning off a system does not prevent it from being turned back on. Guards are expensive compared to a simple technical control limiting logins, and disabling remote login does not prevent local login.

59. A. Security Assertion Markup Language (SAML) is an XML-based, open standard format for exchanging authentication and authorization data between parties. OAuth allows an end user's account information to be used by third-party services, without exposing the user's password. RADIUS is a remote access protocol. New Technology LAN Manager (NTLM) is not XML-based.

60. A. Backups are considered to be the least volatile type of storage since they change at a much slower pace and, in fact, may be intentionally retained for long periods of time without changing. In this list, CPU cache will change the most frequently, then RAM, then local disk contents.

61. C. After eradication of the issue has been completed, recovery can begin. Recovery can include restoration of services and a return to normal operations.

62. C. The MITRE ATT&CK framework focuses on techniques and tactics. CIS Benchmarks are security configuration baselines, the Dark Web Analysis Project was made up for this question, and the CVSS standard is a vulnerability scoring system and is not a useful framework for analyzing malware and attacks.

63. D. To properly preserve the system, Ted needs to ensure that it does not change. Turning off the system will cause anything in memory to be lost, which may be needed for the investigation. Removing the drive while a system is running can cause data to be lost. Instead, live-imaging the machine and its memory may be required. Allowing users to continue to use a machine will result in changes, which can also damage Ted's ability to perform a forensic investigation.

64. D. Windows does not log network traffic at a level of granularity that will show if a file has been uploaded. Basic traffic statistics can be captured, but without additional sensors and information-gathering capabilities, Jessica will not be able to determine if files are sent from a Windows system.

65. C. The chain of custody in forensic activities tracks who has a device, data, or other forensic artifact at any time, when transfers occur, who performed analysis, and where the item, system, or device goes when the forensic process is done. Evidence logs may be maintained by law enforcement to track evidence that is gathered. Paper trail and digital footprint are not technical terms used for digital forensics.

66. B. The `-c` flag for `grep` counts the number of occurrences for a given string in a file. The `-n` flag shows the matched lines and line numbers. Even if you're not sure about which flag is which, the syntax should help on a question like this. When using `grep`, the pattern comes before the filename, allowing you to rule out two of the options right away.

67. B. Network flows using NetFlow or sFlow would provide the information that Eric wants, with details of how much traffic was used, when, and where traffic was directed. A firewall or data loss prevention (DLP) would not show the bandwidth detail, although a firewall may show the connection information for events. Packetflow was made up for this question and is not a technology used for this purpose.

68. D. Hashing using MD5 or SHA1 is commonly used to validate that a forensic image matches the original drive. Many forensic duplicators automatically generate a hash of both drives when they complete the imaging process to ensure that there is a documentation chain for the forensic artifacts. A third image may be useful but does not validate this. Directory listings do not prove that drives match, and photos, though useful to document the drives and serial numbers, do not validate the contents of the drives.

69. B. Nessus is a popular vulnerability scanning tool. It is not a fuzzer, web application firewall (WAF), or protocol analyzer.

70. D. Red Hat stores authentication log information in /var/log/secure instead of /var/log/auth.log used by Debian and Ubuntu systems. Knowing the differences between the major distributions can help speed up your forensic and incident investigations, and consistency is one of the reasons that organizations often select a single Linux distribution for their infrastructure whenever it is possible to do so.

71. C. Cuckoo, or Cuckoo Sandbox, is a malware analysis sandbox that will safely run malware and then analyze and report on its behavior. strings is a command-line tool that retrieves strings from binary data. scanless is a tool described as a port scraper, which retrieves port information without running a port scan by using websites and services to run the scan for you. Sn1per is a pen test framework.

72. C. Metadata viewing tools will allow Lucca to view the metadata that is embedded in the file itself. Metadata is not downloaded separately or available via the hash for a JPEG file.

73. B. When artifacts are acquired as part of an investigation, they should be logged and documented as part of the evidence related to the investigation. Artifacts could include a piece of paper with passwords on it, tools or technology related to an exploit or attack, smartcards, or any other element of an investigation.

74. D. Forensic reports should include appropriate technical detail. Analysis of a system does not include a picture of the person from whom the system was acquired.

75. C. The browser cache, history, and session information will all contain information from recently visited sites. Bookmarks may indicate sites that a user has visited at some point, but a bookmark can be added without visiting a site at all.

76. C. Organizations define retention policies for different data types and systems. Many organizations use 30-, 45-, 90-, 180-, or 365-day retention policies, with some information required to be kept longer due to law or compliance reasons. Susan's organization may keep logs for as little as 30 days depending on storage limitations and business needs. Data classification policies typically impact how data is secured and handled. Backup policies determine how long backups are retained and rotated and may have an impact on data if the logs are backed up, but backing up logs are a less common practice due to the space they take up versus the value of having logs backed up. Legal hold practices are common, but policies are less typically defined for legal holds since requirements are set by law.

77. C. A quarantine process or setting will preserve malicious or dangerous files and programs without allowing them to run. This allows defenders to retrieve them for further analysis as well as to return them to use if they are determined not to be malicious, or if the malicious components can be removed from needed files. Purging, deep-freezing, and retention are not terms used to describe this behavior or setting.

78. C. Chuck should recommend a mobile device management (MDM) system to ensure that organizational devices can be managed and protected in the future. Data loss prevention (DLP) will not stop a lost phone from being a potential leak of data, isolating the phones is not a realistic scenario for devices that will actually be used, nor is containment because the phone is out of the organization's control once lost.

79. B. The most important action Charles can take while working with his forensic artifacts to provide nonrepudiation is to digitally sign the artifacts and information that he is creating in his evidence records. Encrypting the output will ensure its confidentiality but will not provide nonrepudiation by itself. MD5 checksums for images are commonly gathered but must then be signed so that they can be validated to ensure they have not been modified.

80. A. The best way to capture a virtual machine from a running hypervisor is usually to use the built-in tools to obtain a snapshot of the system. Imaging tools are not typically capable of capturing machine state, and dd is not designed to capture VMs. Removing a server's drives can be challenging due to possible RAID and other specific server configuration items, and doing so might impact all other running VMs and services on the system.

81. A. Law enforcement is not typically part of organizational incident response teams, but incident response teams often maintain a relationship with local law enforcement officers. Security analysts, management, and communication staff as well as technical experts are all commonly part of a core incident response team.

82. A. Even if you're not familiar with `iptables`, you can read through these rules and guess which rule includes the right details. DROP makes sense for a block, and you should know that SSH will be a TCP service on port 22.

83. A. A packet capture will show attempts to connect to the service and will help Maria determine if there is unexpected traffic to the system. A network firewall could stop the traffic, but analyzing the actual traffic itself is best done with a packet capture. Logs may be useful as part of the analysis, but again, packet captures will provide more information. A forensic disk image is not useful for reviewing network traffic.

84. A. Incident response plans don't stop incidents from occurring, but they do help responders react appropriately and prepare the organization for incidents, and may be required for legal or compliance reasons.

85. D. Degaussing a drive uses strong magnetic fields to wipe it and is the least likely to result in recoverable data. Deleted files can often be recovered because only the file index information will be removed until that space is needed and is overwritten. Quick formats work in a similar way and will leave remnant data, and files that are overwritten by smaller files will also leave fragments of data that can be recovered and analyzed.

86. D. Henry's most likely use for the video is to document the forensic process, part of the chain of custody and provenance of the forensic data he acquires. The order of volatility helps determine what devices or drives he would image first. There is no crime being committed, so establishing guilt is not relevant to this scenario, and the video will not ensure data is preserved on a drive during a forensic process.

87. B. IPSec is not a tool used to capture network flows. sFlow, NetFlow, and IPFIX are all used to capture network flow information, which will provide the information Charlene needs.

88. B. PRTG and Cacti are both network monitoring tools that can provide bandwidth monitoring information. Bandwidth monitors can help identify exfiltration, heavy and abnormal bandwidth usage, and other information that can be helpful for both incident identification and incident investigations. If you encounter a question like this on the exam, even if you're not familiar with either tool, you can use your knowledge of what Simple Network Management Protocol (SNMP) is used for to identify which of the categories is most likely correct.

89. A. A variety of configuration changes could be pushed to mobile devices to help: setting passcodes, enabling full-disk encryption (FDE) on mobile devices via organizationally deployed mobile device management (MDM), or even preventing some sensitive files from being downloaded or kept on those devices could all help. Firewall rules, data loss prevention (DLP) rules, and URL filters will not prevent a stolen device from being accessed and the data being exposed.

90. B. The Security+ exam outline talks about seven incident response process steps: Preparation, Detection, Analysis, Containment, Eradication, Recovery, and Lessons Learned.

91. C. Jill wants the least possible changes to occur on the system, so she should instruct the user to not save any files or make any changes. Rebooting the system will not create a memory dump, and may cause new files to be written or changed if patches were waiting to install or other changes are set to occur during a reboot. Turning off Secure Delete or making other changes will not impact the files that were deleted prior to that setting change.

92. B. The IR process used for the Security+ exam outline is Preparation, Detection, Analysis, Containment, Eradication, Recovery, and Lessons Learned. Veronica should move into the lessons learned phase.

93. C. Quick formatting merely deletes file indexes rather than removing and overwriting files, making it inappropriate for sanitization. Physical destruction will ensure that the data is not readable, as will degaussing and zero wiping.

94. D. Microsoft Office places information like the name of the creator of the file, editors, creation and change dates, and other useful information in the file metadata that is stored in each Office document. Bart can simply open the Office document to review this information, or he can use a forensic or file metadata tool to review it. Filenames may contain the creator's name, but this would only be if the creator included it. Microsoft Office does not create or maintain a log, and the application log for Windows does not contain this information.

95. B. Windows Defender Firewall operates on a per-application model and can filter traffic based on whether the system is on a trusted private network or a public network. Nathaniel should allow Chrome by name in the firewall, which will allow it to send traffic without needing to specify ports or protocols.

96. B. Building a timeline, particularly from multiple systems, relies on accurately set system clocks or adding a manually configured offset. Disk hashing and acquisition does not need an accurate system clock, and file metadata can be reviewed even without an accurate clock, although accurate clock information or knowing the offset can be useful for analysis.

97. B. Data breach notification laws often build in a maximum length of time that can pass before notification is required. They also often include a threshold for notification, with a maximum number of exposed individuals before the state or other authorities must be notified. They do not include a maximum number of individuals who can be notified, nor do they typically have specific requirements about police involvement in forensic investigations or certification types or levels.

98. C. A data loss prevention (DLP) tool that can scan and review emails for SSN style data is the most effective tool listed here. Naomi may want to set the tool to block all emails with potential SSNs, and then review those emails manually to ensure that no further emails leave while allowing legitimate emails to pass through. An intrusion detection system (IDS) might look tempting as an answer, but an IDS can only detect, not stop, the traffic, which would allow the SSNs to exit the organization. Antimalware and firewalls will not stop this type of event.

99. C. Email headers contain a significant amount of metadata, including where the email was sent from. The from: field lists a sender but does not indicate where the email was actually sent from. The to: field lists who the email was sent to, and footers are not used to store this information for email.

100. C. NXLog is a log collection and centralization tool. IPFIX, NetFlow, and sFlow all gather data about network traffic, including source, destination, port, protocol, and amount of data sent to be collected.

101. D. SQL injection (SQLi) attempts are sent as HTTP or HTTPS requests to a web server, meaning that Valerie will be able to see the attacks in the web server log. Domain Name System (DNS) logs, if available, will not show these. Auth logs show logins, not web or SQL Server queries or requests. Unlike Windows, there is no security log file for Linux, although there is a secure log for some systems.

102. C. A legal hold notice will inform the company that they must preserve and protect information related to the case. None of the other items are terms used in this process.

103. B. A quarantine setting will place a malicious or suspect file in a safe location and will keep it there until a set timeframe has passed or until an administrator takes action to deal with it. This can allow you to further analyze the file or to restore it if it was an incorrect identification or if the file is needed for another purpose. Containment is used to limit the extent of an incident or attack, isolation keeps a system or device from connecting to or accessing others, and deleting a file wouldn't keep it around.

104. C. The recovery phase often involves adding firewall rules and patching systems in addition to rebuilding systems. Although preparation may involve configuring firewall rules or regular patching, it does not do so in response to an incident. Detection attempts to identify events and issues, and analysis involves investigating the events.

105. C. Tim should look at the trend information for malware detections to check to see if there are more infections being detected than during recent weeks. This can be a useful indicator of a change, due to a new malware technique or package; a successful attack that has resulted in staff members clicking malicious links or opening malicious emails; or other paths into the organization. Tim could then check with users whose systems reported the malware to see what had occurred. Alerts might show the infections but would not show the data over time as easily as trends. Sensors will show individual places data is gathered, and bandwidth dashboards can show useful information about which systems are using more or less bandwidth, but the trends dashboard remains the right place for Tim to look in this situation.

106. B. The Center for Internet Security (CIS) benchmarks provide recommendations for how to secure an operating system, application, or other covered technology. Michelle will find Windows-specific security configuration guidelines and techniques.

107. C. A single point of failure (SPOF) is a single weakness that can bring down an entire system and prevent it from working. Cloud computing allows the delivery of hosted service over the Internet. Load balancing spreads traffic or other load between multiple systems or servers. Virtualization uses a system to host virtual machines that share the underlying resources such as RAM, hard drive, and CPU.

108. C. Asset management policies typically include all stages of an asset's life cycle, and asset tags like those described are used to track assets in many organizations. Change management, incident response, and acceptable use policies do not require asset tagging.

109. D. The diagram shows a fully redundant internal network with pairs of firewalls, routers, and core switches, but with a single connection to the Internet. This means that Megan should consider how her organization would connect to the outside world if that link was severed or disrupted. There is no indication whether this is a wired or wireless link, and the image does not show a redundant link.

110. B. Support tools typically require additional steps or integrations to take action on a ticket and a human is often involved to ensure that legitimate emails do not result in the creation of unwanted rules or responses. Juan's team could use the ticketing system to track whether emails are dealt with, to correlate them, and potentially to trigger additional actions.

111. D. The Sender Policy Framework (SPF) lists IP addresses of systems allowed to send email in DNS TXT records for a domain. DKIM (DomainKeys Identified Mail) validates a domain's identity using a public key pair, validating the authenticity of the sender. DMARC (domain-based message authentication, reporting, and conformance) controls how unauthenticated messages are handled by mailbox providers, including quarantining, rejecting, or rejecting messages. STP is not an email security framework.

112. D. The packet capture shows a high volume of SYN packets, indicating a potential SYN flood, a type of denial-of-service attack. There is no information to indicate SMTP traffic for a phishing campaign, nor is there HTTP traffic for SQL injection against an application. While SYN traffic is commonly seen when a connection is lost, this traffic is repeated at a rapid pace rather than a typical reconnection attempt.

113. D. Endpoint detection and response (EDR) tools combine behavior-based detection capabilities with centralized dashboards and advanced response capabilities. Intrusion prevention systems (IPSs) can detect network threats but aren't well suited to detecting behaviors on endpoint systems. NAC (network access control) is used to limit who can connect to a network. Data loss prevention (DLP) systems monitor for data exfiltration as well as data that is sent both inadvertently and on purpose outside the organization that shouldn't be.

114. C. Tabletop exercises involve teams sitting down to talk through an exercise. Teams don't perform actions or even simulate them, third-party penetration testers are not reviewing their data, and no actual fail overs occur.

115. B. Root cause analysis is a process used to determine the underlying cause of an issue such as why attackers were able to successfully take down Michelle's web server cluster. Threat hunting is used to proactively look for threats using a variety of techniques, including OSINT and leveraging indicators of compromise. Lessons learned processes look for takeaways from events and incidents to allow organizations to improve their processes and procedures. Recovery is part of the incident response process but focuses on restoring the organization to normal operation.

116. D. Jailbreaking is not a typical hardening process and is instead used to bypass device security to allow additional control of the device. While individuals may jailbreak devices, organizations rarely permit it. The NSA provides a guide to mobile device security practices at `https://media.defense.gov/2021/Sep/16/2002855921/-1/-1/0/MOBILE_DEVICE_BEST_PRACTICES_FINAL_V3%20-%20COPY.PDF`, which includes many practices such as disabling Bluetooth, using strong passwords, and keeping device software up-to-date.

117. C. WPA3 Enterprise is the most secure option. It provides for central authentication as well as encryption. WPA4 has not yet been released. WPA2 and WPA3 Personal are not centrally managed, giving Lucca's organization less control over who connects.

118. B. The EF (exposure factor) for an asset is the value of the asset that would be lost in the event of a loss or damage scenario. Depreciation is a financial term that writes down the cost of a capital item over a given lifespan; annualized loss expectancy is a risk-related term, not annual loss event; and asset valuation adjustment was made up for this question.

119. B. Derek's team needs to carefully consider what alerts should be sent, why, and how often. That will require alert tuning. Simply setting alert thresholds may miss critical events, disabling alerts will not achieve the goal of enabling this type of notification, and moving the alerts to email will typically result in a less timely response.

120. B. Jill can build a signature if she has an example of the SQL code. IPS signatures require data to match against potential attack traffic. A source IP address would only match specific potential attackers instead of the many different potential sources. A hash of the attack would detect one specific version of the attack, but a SQL injection (SQLi) attack may have multiple versions or configurations. The source port will vary with each request and isn't useful in most cases.

121. A. While all of these are potential problems, Jack's account should not be provisioned to match Erin. Instead, provisioning based on role is an IAM best practice. Jack's seniority, the staff he works with, and file access should all be determined by his role.

122. A. Hardware tokens provide the greatest security because they need to be physically present to be used. Application-based tokens are more secure than SMS in many cases because SMS can be redirected or accessed through SIM-swapping and other attacks. Extending password length does not provide a second factor and is the least secure of these options by far.

123. A. The lack of consistency could be addressed by enforcing baselines across the organization. Gurvinder should emphasize this, then explain the other common benefits of security automation, including scaling in a secure manner, improving reaction time, automation's impact as a workforce multiplier, efficiency, employee retention advantages, and the ability to more easily standardize infrastructure configurations.

124. C. The Five Why's process is well suited to interviews because it asks "Why" each time an answer is provided to get to a root cause. The Five W's are a common reference in journalism to who, what, when, where, and why—not a root cause analysis tool. Fishbone diagrams are commonly used for RCA, but are not as useful for an interview process. They're more likely to be used after the interview to see how answers and events fit together. Recursion analysis is not an RCA process.

125. B. Amanda has conducted a simulation, or walk-through, where actual recovery actions are simulated to ensure that recovery plans will work as expected. A fail over test moves production to a backup environment like a hot site, and a plan review is just that—a review of the response plan. A tabletop exercise involves discussions about the scenario and what would be done without taking any actual action.

126. B. Legal holds require organizations and individuals to preserve data related to pending or active litigation, regardless of its normal data life cycle once the hold notice is received. This means that Liam needs to identify and preserve the data and that normal processes like wiping drives or reusing backup media may not be possible. It does not necessarily mean that Liam's company must engage a lawyer to preserve the data, and law enforcement is not typically involved in legal holds.

127. A. OAuth is an open standard widely supported by cloud identity providers. Kerberos is used for internal use rather than for external integrations; LDAP is used for some services but is no longer a common choice for this type of integration with cloud service providers compared to options like OAuth, SAML, and OpenID-based integrations; and Active Directory is used by Microsoft but is not as interoperable.

128. B. Attribute-based access control (ABAC) provides access based on attributes like location, age, rank, or other attributes of a user. Rule-based access control uses defined rules to make access decisions. Role-based access control uses a user's role in an organization to make access control decisions, and mandatory access control (MAC) enforces access control using centralized control.

129. C. Security keys are commonly used for passwordless authentication since they can provide both a physical token and cryptographic login credentials that are unlocked using a password, fingerprint reader, or camera. A password manager does not provide this but does securely store and manage passwords. RFID cards are simply something you have, and biometrics are typically not tokens—they're data stored to match a user's biometric signature.

130. B. Older, insecure services like chargen, daytime, echo, time, rsh, and telnet are all managed by inetd in Linux distributions. Disabling these services is a common item in security hardening benchmarks like the CIS benchmarks. These services are not Windows services, they are not SQL-related, and disabling them is not a type of patching.

131. A. Bring your own device (BYOD) leaves the choice of device in the hands of the end user. Since the device is the end user's device, it often means that the organization has less, if any, control over the device. Corporate-owned, personally enabled (COPE) allows users to use organizationally owned devices for their own use. Choose your own device (CYOD) lets users choose a device that the organization owns. COBO, or company-owned, business-only, is a model that only allows business use of business-provided devices.

132. D. The `Secure Cookie` attribute is intended to keep cookies secure in transit. That means that it requires secure cookies be sent only via HTTPS. It does not encrypt the cookie at rest, store it on the server instead of the remote system, nor does it remove the cookie after it has been used.

133. B. Code signing uses the signing organization or individual's private key to sign a hash of the code. This allows the code to be verified using the organization's or individual's public key. Signing code does not involve encrypting it.

134. C. Without an inventory, organizations may misplace, lose, or even have devices stolen. That may result in data breaches or simply loss of assets. A hardware life cycle process is an operational concern; manufacturer support is typically tied to individual devices; and vulnerability scans are possible without an inventory, but Naomi may not know what the device itself is until she physically locates it.

135. C. Static analysis processes for code involve reviewing the source code itself. Dynamic analysis processes use running code. Agile is a project management framework, and internal review is not a term used to describe this.

136. A. Sites accessible using TOR are considered part of the dark web. Information-sharing organizations like ISACs share information in an industry vertical or among other organizations that participate. Proprietary information is provided by vendors, typically as part of a contract or service. Threat feeds may be public or private and provide information about threats in a digestible format for use with security tools.

137. A. A lessons learned session is commonly conducted at the end of an incident response process. Once eradication and recovery are complete, incident response processes are typically over and the response effort can be reviewed. The lessons learned are then leveraged as part of the preparation process to be ready for the next incident. That may involve more training, tabletop exercises, or additional detection methods.

138. A. The CVSS environmental score's impact metric takes into account confidentiality, integrity, and availability risks, with each rated between high, medium, and low levels. It is not a direct rating of network, disk, memory, severity, likelihood, probability, or cost.

139. D. The Security Content Automation Protocol (SCAP) is frequently used to allow for monitoring and measurement of NIST 800-53-based controls. SAML is used for authorization and authentication, and CVE and CVSS are used to identify and rank vulnerabilities.

140. A. WPA3 Enterprise uses Advanced Encryption Standard (AES) and can use 128-, 192-, and 256-bit keys. It does not support 3DES, and both SHA-1 and SHA-256 are hashing algorithms.

141. A. Kerberos is one of a small number of commonly used AAA protocols for network devices. SAML and OpenID are more commonly used for federated services, and TKIP is an encryption method.

142. C. Vulnerability scanners are perfectly suited to this type of task and can be configured to specifically test the web servers that are part of the IoT devices to increase the speed of the scan. A WAF is used to protect web applications and servers, not to assess vulnerabilities and security issues. Pentesting can identify these problems but is typically not fast or scalable. Port scanners identify open ports and service but don't identify vulnerabilities as effectively as a dedicated vulnerability scanning tool will.

143. B. DMARC, or Domain-based Message Authentication, Reporting, and Conformance, controls how unauthenticated messages are handled by mailbox providers, including quarantining, rejecting, or rejecting messages. SPF (Sender Policy Framework) lists IP addresses of systems allowed to send email in DNS TXT records for a domain. Domain-Keys Identified Mail (DKIM) validates a domain's identity using a public key pair, validating the authenticity of the sender. TLS (Transport Layer Security) is used to encrypt data in motion.

144. D. In most organization, Wayne's next steps should be to document the exemption due to the criticality of the server and its extenuating circumstances. Removing the server from scans will prevent it from being effectively impacted by a denial-of-service attack each time a scan occurs, but this also means that compensating controls should be implemented if possible. Reporting the server as vulnerable and suggesting it be replaced does not remediate the server or protect it, and will continue to allow it to fail based on future scans. Disabling the device's network connection will also cause a service outage. Insurance will not prevent service outages or protect the device.

145. B. Identity proofing is used to validate a user's claim to an identity. Here, Valentine's company uses information that only a legitimate owner of that identity should have easy access to. Provisioning is the process of creating an account and providing it with appropriate resources and rights. Deprovisioning removes accounts and rights. Social identity is the process of using existing user accounts like those found through Facebook or Google to create accounts for existing users at other organizations like Valentine's.

146. C. Organizations often immediately rescan a system after patching to ensure that the patching worked. While this isn't an absolutely certain means of validating the patch, it helps to quickly ensure that patching was effective across many machines. Noting false positives may occur if the patch was successful, but systems continue to show as vulnerable. Rebooting may be done but doesn't necessarily validate the patching installation's success, and performing an audit may be done but is a less common next step.

147. A. Third-party audit documentation is a common practice for organizations that want to attest to their customers that they have a secure environment. Rescanning systems and providing vulnerability scans is not a common practice, nor is allowing customers to conduct their own scans of production systems.

148. B. TCP port 1433 is the minimum port requirement for a Microsoft SQL server connection. TCP 3389 is used for Remote Desktop Protocol (RDP). TCP 8080 is a common alternate port for web servers, and TCP 139 and 445 are used for SMB connections.

149. A. Baselining is the process of establishing a standard for security. A change from the original baseline configuration is referred to as baseline deviation. Security evaluations or audits check security but don't establish security standards. Hardening is the process of securing a given system, but it does not establish security standards. Normalization is the process of removing redundant entries from a database.

150. B. COPE, or company-owned, personally enabled, models allow staff to use organizationally owned devices for reasonable personal use. CYOD, or choose your own device, allows users to pick their company-owned device from a list of approved devices. COBO, or company-owned, business-only, is just that—users can only use the devices for business purposes. BYOD asks users to bring their own device, often leaving organizations with limited or no control of the device.

151. B. Process auditing involves reviewing processes to identify unknown or unexpected processes. During incident response scenarios, this is often initially done via the Task Manager. Dynamic analysis is a code review process that uses running code. CVSS matching was made up for this question, and vulnerability scanning tests open services and doesn't involve the Task Manager.

152. B. Email security gateways are appliances or software virtual appliances that provide anti-spam, anti-phishing, and other email security–related services. They're purpose-built to deliver exactly the capabilities that Ujama is looking for. A WAF (web application firewall) is used to protect web applications. DKIM and DMARC are both email security frameworks, but they're not implemented as appliances themselves.

153. D. A SIEM (security information and event management) tool is designed to aggregate, analyze, correlate, alert on, and report on log entries. MDM (mobile device management) is used to manage mobile devices, jump servers provide access from less secure zones to more secure zones, and SDN is software-defined networking.

154. A. Leveraging automation and scripting to increase employee happiness and retention as well as improving efficiency and realizing time savings is a common strategy in situations like this. Deploying fewer devices only works if the organization needs fewer devices, baselines are most useful when paired with automation and scripting for deployment, and a physical endpoint device typically can't be moved to the cloud.

155. B. Authenticated scans can identify vulnerabilities that are not visible to unauthenticated scans. Penetration testers may not be able to obtain access equivalent to authenticated scans, so an authenticated scan is more likely to provide detailed data. Port scans do not provide deep vulnerability data.

156. C. Quarantine and isolation are both commonly used in the containment phase of an incident to ensure that impacted systems are unable to impact other systems or parts of the organization. Files may also be quarantined to prevent further impact from malware. Detection and analysis typically do not involve quarantine and isolation, but quarantine and isolation may carry through into the eradication phase before systems are returned to normal operation.

157. C. Linux permissions are read left to right for user, group, and other. With r's at each location, this means everyone can read the contents of the directory. Only the user can write and execute files in the directory.

158. A. A set of rules that defines who can access the data has determined if Beena is granted access. Here, rules assess her role, the time of day, and the workstation's status. This is not accomplished using a classification or clearance system like MAC uses, and it does not rely on just an attribute like Beena's location or other information about her.

159. A. Trend analysis is commonly used as part of behavior-based detections, which can help identify new attacks. Signatures require knowledge of existing attacks to match signatures. IP- and port-based detection is useful for known attacks but not typically useful for unknown attacks.

160. D. Heatmaps are used to show signal strength and coverage, allowing organizations to identify areas where there may be poor coverage or where multiple signals may conflict. War walking (and war driving) are techniques used to map wireless access points to geographic locations. Spectrum analysis and SSID plots are not terms used for this type of activity.

161. C. The concept of least privilege is that only the minimum rights or privileges required to accomplish a role or task are provided. Zero trust requires continuous authentication and authorization, and least privilege is part of a zero trust environment, but zero trust goes beyond least privilege. Provisioning and deprovisioning are part of the account life cycle, and provisioning should respect the concept of least privilege.

162. D. Automation provides many advantages for the provisioning process, including improving consistency, decreasing the potential for mistakes, and providing faster provisioning. It does not specifically address auditability in ways that manual processes cannot. Regardless of how provisioning is done, audit logs and trails should be created for all events, not just automated ones.

163. B. Bug bounty programs are frequently part of responsible disclosure programs intended to provide a way for third parties to report security issues and to be incentivized to report them in responsible ways. Bug bounties can help identify flaws, but they're not typically part of contracted penetration testing engagements. Third-party bounty is not a typical way of describing them, and trusted threat programs were made up for this question.

164. D. Even if you're not familiar with specific Cisco IOS commands and configuration you can quickly determine that this is a Network Time Protocol (NTP)-related setting. Authenticating NTP and ensuring a trusted key is enabled would help to ensure that network time is trusted and secure. This prevents attackers from conducting attacks that rely on modifying network time or the switch recording incorrect time in its logs. There is no Network Terminal Protocol, this does not impact logs, and network time traffic is not encrypted.

165. C. Using a VPN is a best practice over any untrusted or potentially untrusted network connection. Patching the phone and deploying a security baseline are good for the phone's security, but they won't help directly with the security of data in transit.

166. C. ISACs, or Information Sharing and Analysis Centers, are information-sharing organizations established to connect organizations in verticals like health care, government, utilities, and higher education. While it may provide OSINT information, they go far beyond that. They are not typically found via the dark web and don't require TOR to access their information, and they are not commercial or proprietary threat data sources.

167. A. Attestation is the verification of ownership or that a person matches who they claim to be. In this case, Mark presents his driver's license to attest to his own identity. Provisioning is the creation of accounts and the granting of rights, and deprovisioning is the removal of accounts and rights for accounts. SSO is single sign-on.

168. D. Bluetooth devices can be fingerprinted relatively easily, making it easy to identify individual users who have Bluetooth turned on. Modern Bluetooth traffic is encrypted, its relatively short range is not a security concern, and Bluejacking sends unwanted spam, which isn't a direct data security issue.

169. D. PAM tools provide a variety of capabilities, including just-in-time permissions, password vaulting, and ephemeral credentials. Password persistence was made up for this question and is not a typical feature.

170. A. Port scans can help with enumeration of assets when an inventory does not exist. They do not provide OSINT; OSINT is a passive information-gathering process and a scan is an active process. Version tracking via port scans is inaccurate and does not provide full information. Identifying assets via port scans is a reasonably common part of asset management, particularly for initial discovery.

171. C. Fingerprints are biometric factors and are something you are. Something you know is a knowledge factor like a password or PIN. Something you have is a hardware token, RFID card, or other similar factor. Somewhere you are is a geographic factor based on location such as GPS coordinates.

172. C. Dependency checking for open source software is a common best practice to help ensure that underlying components do not have known security vulnerabilities. There are dependency security checking applications and tools available that Dana could use to help with this process. Software source code escrow is often used to ensure that organizations can obtain the software code if a company goes out of business or other adverse events occur that might endanger the company relying on the code. Reviewing the source code for an entire application is outside of the scope and capability of the majority of organizations, particularly when other dependencies are included. Purchasing software from a known vendor can help, but does not necessarily ensure that the software is secure and dependencies don't introduce or include known issues.

173. B. Sharon knows that Enterprise mode authentication is typically done with 802.1X. LDAP and Kerberos are not typically used for this, and SAML is more frequently part of federated and cloud services.

174. C. Windows supports both password history and a minimum password age to help prevent users from simply resetting their password over and over again until they can reuse their preferred password. This does not prevent attackers from resetting passwords or using brute-force attacks and doesn't ensure password expiration.

175. B. CVSS scores are based on base metrics like the attack vector; complexity; scope; user interaction required and privileges required; the temporal group, which includes exploit code maturity, remediation level, and report confidence; and the environmental group, including confidentiality, availability, and integrity requirements. While scope, impact, risk, and threat all play into these elements, CVSS calls the three metric groups Base, Temporal, and Environmental.

176. B. In scenarios where the data needs to be guaranteed to be unrecoverable, physical destruction is a common choice. Zero wiping and reformatting both leave remnant data on SSDs, and sanitization processes are reasonably secure but cannot always be guaranteed to result in total data removal.

177. A. IoT devices often have very limited security options, if any. That means that hardening them using built-in tools and configurations is limited, if not impossible. IoT devices typically use their own OS; benchmarks are rarely available, not just out-of-date; and central management for many IoT devices is frequently not available.

178. C. Reviewing any baseline to determine its fit for the organization and how the organization's systems and services operate is an appropriate next step after selecting a benchmark. Deploying SELinux may be necessary for some features depending on the distribution in use, but nothing in the question indicates that this is required. Once the benchmark has been modified to purpose and suitability, it can be tested, and further modifications can be made if necessary. Finally, it can be deployed and managed.

179. B. EAP-TLS provides TLS-based Transport Layer Security as part of a secure authentication implementation. LEAP is the Lightweight Extensible Authentication Protocol, which was in use before 802.11i but is now largely outdated. EAP-PSK uses a preshared key for mutual authentication and does not rely on public key encryption, but it is not supported in WPA3 deployments. EAP-PWD uses a shared password for authentication and, like EAP-PSK, is not supported by WPA3.

180. C. DLP systems often rely on classification, tagging, and metadata to help them identify sensitive data that the organization handles and which could be exfiltrated or sent inadvertently outside of the organization. Hashing and creating signatures is more commonly associated with filesystem-monitoring tools. Encrypting the data is not required by a DLP and may actually make it harder for the DLP to identify the data. Applying a mandatory access control scheme to the data is not a typical step in preparing for DLP-based protection.

181. D. File integrity monitoring tools use hashes to validate that files match their original content. If the files change, the hashes will not match, allowing the tool to alert administrators that a change has occurred. Drive encryption and file encryption both protect the confidentiality of data but don't indicate changes without a signature. File availability monitoring is not a typical tool, although system or service availability monitoring is.

182. A. Endpoint detection and response (EDR) tools are most likely to use hashing to match known malicious files like this. Firewalls may provide the capability, but system logs do not, ruling out the "all of the above" option.

183. B. Group Policy is the most common way of deploying baselines throughout Windows organizations. Group Policy Objects (GPOs) are set and managed across the entire Active Directory organization, allowing them to be modified for groups or specific purposes while inheriting most settings from the top of the organizational structure. PowerShell is a scripting tool, and both PowerShell and Group Policy are commonly used for specific purposes, but GPOs are typically preferred at scale. Manual configuration is not recommended for an entire organization.

184. B. A common technique to ensure that traffic sent via unsecure protocols remains secure is to wrap it using TLS. SD-WAN is used to manage external connectivity, and there is no mention of files, only of an unsecure protocol. Even if files were encrypted, the rest of the traffic might leak information. Hashing does not leave data recoverable, making it unusable for this type of use in almost all cases.

185. B. Passwordless authentication avoids making users provide a password or PIN by using a proof of identity from a device or token. Windows Hello, cell-based authenticator applications, and FIDO2 security keys all support this, but entering a PIN does not.

186. B. Since ICS and SCADA devices need connectivity as part of their design, Laura knows that using segmentation to place the devices in a secure network is likely her best hardening option. Isolating the devices would break the functionality of ICS/SCADA systems. Neither ICS nor SCADA devices typically have support for host-based firewalls or host-based IPS.

187. B. The detection and analysis phases of the incident response process both commonly leverage IoCs to detect and then correlate information to identify incidents. Preparation might involve setting up threat feeds and building automations to help notify security administrators of issues. Containment and eradication may leverage threat data to help understand common actions taken by threat actors, but the SIEM detecting and correlating events is not typically part of containment or eradication.

188. A. Enabling DNS filtering based on the URL from the email is the most effective option listed. Disabling the organization's Internet connection will result in additional disruption. Blocking the email's source IP for an already received email will not be effective, nor will enabling reputation services for email after the email has already been received.

189. B. Successful authentications will not be logged based on these settings. Having access to both successes and failures can be useful when investigating incidents, particularly if attackers have stolen credentials. Text-based log files take up minimal space on most workstations and servers and should not be a significant concern. While the message notes that the policy may be overridden, Nick's primary concern should be missing log data.

190. B. CVSS scores range from 0 to 10.0, with 10.0 being the most critical. A score of .1–3.9 is considered a low rating, meaning that Brian can take his time to review and remediate the risk. Scores of 4.0–6.9 are medium, 7.0–8.9 are high, and 9.0–10.0 are critical.

191. A. DKIM (DomainKeys Identified Mail) validates a domain's identity using a public key pair, validating the authenticity of the sender. DMARC (Domain-based Message Authentication, Reporting, and Conformance) controls how unauthenticated messages are handled by mailbox providers, including quarantining, rejecting, or rejecting messages. The Sender Policy Framework (SPF) lists IP addresses of systems allowed to send email in DNS TXT records for a domain. STP is not an email security framework. The Simple Mail Transfer Protocol (SMTP) is the default email protocol.

192. C. SELinux is a Linux kernel module that provides a variety of security capabilities and access control methods, including support for MAC (mandatory access control) for Linux systems. Group Policy is a Windows tool, the CIS benchmarks provide security configuration recommendations for systems but do not directly provide mandatory access control, and containerization is used to make application installations portable.

193. B. Package monitoring tools review the dependencies and packages that make up open source tools to identify vulnerable components. Static analysis is manual review of code. Fagan testing is a formal code analysis process. Port scanning is not used to monitor for dependency security.

194. B. SaaS environments allow customers to manage information, data, devices, accounts, and identities. That means that ensuring least privilege is used is possible through use of accounts and identities. Host-based firewalls, OS configurations, and physical security are all the responsibility of the SaaS provider.

195. A. Unlike the other controls listed, insurance simply transfers the risk to another organization at a cost. It does not take any action to prevent the risk from occurring. Patching, segmentation, and firewalling are all technical controls.

196. D. Sanitization is part of decommissioning and disposal processes, not asset management. Tracking data classification used on systems, identifying owners, and documenting acquisition dates for warranty and life-cycle tracking are all common parts of this process.

197. C. Enterprise password managers provide functionality just like this, allowing passwords to be stored securely and tracked on use. EAP is an authentication protocol; multifactor authentication adds one or more factors, increasing security, but doesn't provide the functionality described; and passwordless isn't designed for a checkout and reset function.

198. B. Using threat data from reputation tools will best fit Selah's needs. Agent-based web filtering is used when systems will be mobile or connected to networks that are not controlled centrally. Centralized web filtering proxies and URL scanning are useful general controls, but reputation tools answer the specific need more directly.

199. A. ACLs are interpreted in the order they are listed. This ACL is not properly written if it is intended to block HTTPS because the ACL order includes a rule that allows any traffic after the rule that blocks HTTP is processed. This means that traffic will first be checked to see if it is HTTP traffic. If it is not, it will be allowed, and thus will bypass the HTTPS block. It will not prevent web application attacks since HTTPS can pass the ACL, and no specific configuration is set for inspection of web traffic.

200. A. User and entity behavior analytics (UEBA) tools are specifically designed to use behavior-based analytic tools leveraging machine learning and algorithmic analysis. SIEM is used to correlate events and log data as part of ongoing monitoring. EDR focuses on malicious behavior detection on endpoints. DMARC is used for email security.

201. C. Password history is intended to prevent password reuse in Windows. It is commonly paired with a minimum password age to prevent users from simply resetting their password multiple times until they can reuse their password, and a longer history is used to make this more difficult too. It does not influence password length or complexity.

202. C. This script will stop and disable the Windows Defender service on a system with IP address 10.1.1.101. You can identify both the `Stop-Service` and `StartupType Disabled` values in the script to determine what it is likely to do. It does not start Windows Defender, nor does it enable the service.

203. B. Since Batu has been asked to consider the lifespan of the scripts, ensuring that they're supportable in an ongoing manner is the biggest concern. Initial cost is typically small compared to the ongoing benefit of scripts like these. Existing technical debt is not a major concern for automated ticket creation with a new tool, and while having a single point of failure can be a concern, automated ticket outages are a point-in-time concern not a lifetime-centered concern.

204. A. Alex has used a compensating control because he cannot remediate the underlying vulnerability. This reduces the risk by preventing the devices from being available on the network to untrusted devices and users. He cannot patch, no insurance was purchased, and no exemption was granted or registered.

205. C. Eradication efforts focus on completely removing all artifacts of a compromise or event. Wiping drives to ensure that no remnant malware or other artifacts remain, then reinstalling using known good media are examples of eradication processes. Restoring the system to service after it has been remediated occurs after eradication. Containment efforts attempt to limit the potential spread or ongoing impact of an incident, and root cause analysis is used to determine the underlying causes of an issue, incident, or event. Root cause elimination is not a commonly used term for this.

206. A. Certification of destruction can include photographic evidence, logs, and other data that demonstrate the disposal contract was followed. Data retention policies are applied internally, not to third-party companies that are contracted for disposal.

207. C. CVSS environmental scores help organizations take their own requirements and risks into account. That means that Sally can use numeric scores to prioritize risk while using her organization's needs and unique threat model. Qualitative and quantitative risk assessments are useful, but they are not as well suited to leveraging data from a vulnerability scanner in a timely manner.

208. A. Password expiration polices help reduce the length of time a password could be exposed for. Henry knows that if his staff change their password periodically that it can help avoid issues with reuse on other sites. He also knows that multifactor is a more effective solution and that he should focus his time there as well. Password length and complexity don't matter if the password was compromised elsewhere, and minimum age policies are used to prevent reuse in the organization by resetting passwords over and over again to return to an original desired password. Note that policies like this don't stop reuse outside of a user's organization on 3rd party sites!

209. D. Fuzzing, the process of feeding unexpected and random input to programs to see how they behave, is an example of dynamic analysis where the code is actually run to test it. Static analysis involves reviewing the code, as does code review. Fuzzing is typically done as part of software testing rather than penetration testing, but it may be used by pentesters.

210. B. Ensuring supply chain security can be challenging, but buying directly from a vendor can remove opportunities for devices to be modified. Trusted value-added resellers are the second best choice. Buying from the gray market or a reseller typically adds additional opportunities for device modification.

211. B. Increasing password length makes it harder to crack. Decreasing the password length would make passwords easier to crack. History and expiration do not influence brute-force attacks unless the expiration happens to land during the time the password cracking was attempted.

212. C. IDS and IPS devices are the only network security device in this list. Other common logs used to identify potential DDoS attacks include network logs and firewall logs. Application and web server logs may be useful if the DDoS is associated with an application. OS-specific security logs, endpoint logs, and authentication logs are not typical places to find useful information for a network-based DDoS attack.

213. A. SAE (Simultaneous Authentication of Equals) provides a secure authentication mode that replaced WPA2's preshared key session key negotiation process. PKI is public key encryption and is not the solution in use. TLS is Transport Layer Security, used to encrypt data in motion, and EAP is an authentication protocol.

214. D. Embedded systems typically have few, if any hardening options because of their purpose-built functionality. Benchmarks are rarely available for them, and most are not designed for central management or adding on security software.

215.   B. Identity proofing uses information about a user to prove that they are who they claim to be. A state or nationally issued ID is a better proof than a Facebook or Google account which can be created under any name without validation. Credit cards are not a form of identity.

Chapter 5: Domain 5.0: Security Program Management and Oversight

1.   C. This description does not include any risk to availability since there is no information about systems or services being down or offline. This scenario would likely result in reputational, financial, and data loss impacts for Scott's company.

2.   D. KRIs, or key risk indicators, need to be actionable so that the organization can use them to control or manage risk, they need to be measurable so that they can be assessed, and they must be relevant to the risks that they measure. They don't necessarily have to be inexpensive, as organizations may make choices about costs based on their risks and business models.

3.   A. A recovery time objective (RTO) is set by organizations to describe how long restoring systems or services to normal function after a disruption can take. Mean time to repair (MTTR) is the average time it takes to repair a system or device. A recovery point objective (RPO) describes how much data can be lost in the event of an outage or issue, and the mean time between failures (MTBF) is a measure of the reliability of a system. It is the expected amount of time that will elapse between system failures.

4.   B. Acceptable use policies (AUPs) describe how and what users can use organizational resources, systems, and services for. Business continuity policies describe how an organization approaches business continuity, and incident response policies focus on how organizations respond to incidents. A standard acts as the rules to achieve an intent, while policies describe the organization's intent. This policy describes intent, not specific implementations.

5.   D. Angie has conducted passive reconnaissance. She did not perform a scan or otherwise take direct active action to gather her information. Instead, she used the existing Shodan engine to gather information. While Shodan is a commercial product and does gather information using scans, databases like Shodan are considered passive reconnaissance, and the Security+ exam objectives recognize two types of reconnaissance: active and passive.

6.   C. Data processors do just that—they process the data on behalf of a data controller, who determines how data is processed and what purposes it is used for. They do not own the data, and they are typically contracted to process the data rather than contracting with third parties themselves.

7.   D. Ginger is a data subject, a person who can be identified by her personally identifiable information (PII). Data owners are responsible for protection, usage, and quality of datasets. Data controllers determine how data will be used, and processors do the actual data processing.

8. C. Qualitative risk assessment uses knowledge and expertise to assess risk rather than assigning numeric values and calculations like a quantitative assessment process would. Ad hoc risk assessment is done when risks need to be assessed for a specific, immediate need unlike the planned, regular risk assessments described. Continuous risk assessment is ongoing, whereas this is conducted regularly.

9. A. Qualitative risk assessments measure likelihood on a descriptive scale like high, medium, or low. Quantitative assessments measure likelihood on a numeric scale using known event occurrence rates where possible.

10. A. Boards often include external members who may have industry or other experience and expertise that will benefit the organization, and they are sometimes, but not always, paid as part of their work on the board. Committees are frequently composed of internal staff; government-based governance occurs through laws or as part of public service. Market-based is not a type of governance outlined by the Security+ exam objectives.

11. A. Risk transfer options move the costs of risks to another organization such as through insurance. Acceptance involves management acknowledging that the risk and its impacts may occur, and that the organization will move forward despite that chance. Avoidance seeks to prevent the risk from occurring. Mitigation works to limit the impact of a risk.

12. C. Boards provide strategic oversight and direction for organizations. Boards may form subcommittees to accomplish specific tasks or to provide oversight over specific areas. Regulators oversee an industry based on law. Activist investor's groups are not covered by the exam, but typically they own stock in an organization and seek to direct the organization through their activism and stock ownership.

13. C. This governance approach is a decentralized approach with each unit or area providing their own governance. While flexible, this can be problematic because of a lack of consistency and overhead due to unique circumstances and requirements. Centralized designs do not delegate authority and instead place authority in a central place, organization, or individual. There is no mention of a board or committee.

14. B. A one-time risk assessment that addresses the acquisition will best meet Sharon's needs. Ad hoc assessments are less formal, and they are often used to quickly assess a system or other potential risk. There is no requirement listed for third-party assessment, and they can be both expensive and time-consuming. Continuous risk assessment efforts are typically built into ongoing processes and are not suited to this type of one-time review.

15. C. Data processors process data on behalf of controllers. Data subjects are the individuals or organizations that data describes. Data owners create and are responsible for data, and data administrator is not a broadly or consistently used term in this context.

16. D. Right-to-audit clauses provide customers with the right to have an audit of their vendor like an SOC 2, Type 1 assessment performed. SOC 2, Type 1 reports are not penetration testing reports, vulnerability scan reports, or risk assessment reports.

17. A. Data owners are responsible for data, including classifying it, protecting it, overseeing the use of it, and ensuring the quality of the overall data. They are not, however, responsible for directly processing the data.

18. B. Risk exceptions are granted when a risk is accepted by the organization, despite not following typical organizational policies or processes. This is not a transfer or mitigation, and simply documenting the risk does not cause it to be accepted.

19. C. Data owners classify, protect, oversee the use of, and ensure the quality of data. Controllers are responsible for the procedures and purposes of data use, often described as the why and how. Custodians are the staff and teams who handle data, and processors work with data on behalf of a controller.

20. C. There are four commonly used business impact analysis (BIA) measures that are part of the Security+ exam objectives: recovery time objectives (RTOs), recovery point objectives (RPOs), mean time to repair (MTTR), and mean time between failures (MTBF). ARO, or annual rate of occurrence, is associated with risk assessment, not BIA.

21. B. Data processors process data for data controllers. In this scenario, Julie or a member of her staff is the data controller and the third-party organization is a processor. They do not own the data, and they are not custodians who are responsible for the data on an ongoing basis.

22. D. Service level agreements (SLAs) set forth the expected service level as well as penalties for nonperformance. A master services agreement (MSA) is a broad agreement that additional work may be performed under. An NDA, or nondisclosure agreement, sets forth what information may and may not be shared or disclosed. The mean time between failures (MTBF) is a measure of the reliability of a system. It is the expected amount of time that will elapse between system failures.

23. D. Data controllers determine the purpose and methods of data processing. They may be individuals, groups, or organizations. This is defined by the General Data Protection Regulation (GDPR). That may involve how data flows, and the formats or other details of data, but the best—and legally defined—role of a controller is the one set by the GDPR.

24. B. Augie is a data custodian. In this role he is responsible for data's use in the business, including storing and properly handling data. Data owners are responsible and accountable for data as well as ensuring that custodians and others are handling the data appropriately. Data processors do actual data processing, and may be an individual, organization, or group. Data subjects are the people who the data describes or is about.

25. C. Sanctions are typically applied to countries rather than companies or individuals. Fines and loss of license are typically aimed at companies and individuals, and mandatory reporting is not a penalty included in the Security+ exam.

26. A. Terms used for risk appetite in the Security+ exam objectives include conservative, neutral, and expansionary. Intentional is not a term used for risk appetite.

27. B. Data stewards are responsible for the data in their charge. That means they carry out data usage and security policies and ensure that data is handled appropriately. Creating data is typically done by data owners, who also explain and set data security policies. Multiple roles oversee data throughout its life cycle, not just a data steward.

28. A. Data controllers determine what data is used and how it is processed. Supervisory authorities are public authorities in the European Union (EU) that monitor for compliance with the General Data Protection Regulation (GDPR). Data protection officers are required by the GDPR and oversee data protection strategies and their implementation. Data processors do just that—they process the data on behalf of a data controller who determines how data is processed and what purposes it is used for. They do not own the data, and are typically contracted to process the data rather than contracting with third parties themselves.

29. C. Avoidance seeks to prevent the risk from occurring. In this case, the WAF is a method of preventing the attack, thus avoiding the risk. Risk transfer options move the costs of risks to another organization such as through insurance. Acceptance involves management acknowledging that the risk and its impacts may occur and that the organization will move forward despite that chance. Mitigation works to limit the impact of a risk.

30. B. HTTPS using TLS is a form of encryption for data in motion. Encryption standards often require specific ways to use encryption, encryption algorithms, settings or configurations for encryption, or times and places where encryption must be used. Access control standards focus on how access is controlled, by whom, and who is impacted. Password standards define settings and requirements related to passwords, and physical security standards address physical security requirements.

31. A. Cloud vendors rarely agree to right-to-audit clauses, instead choosing to provide their own third-party audit results. This reduces the chances of an audit or assessment causing issues with their other customers. Third-party audit costs covered by right-to-audit clauses are often borne by the customers, not the vendor. Not passing an audit is unlikely for major vendors, regulatory requirements are more likely to require audits, and regulations rarely limit auditability.

32. A. Access control standards often define how and when users can access or use systems and services. Defining user access to only be allowed during working hours is an example of an access control standard. Encryption standards often require specific ways to use encryption, encryption algorithms, settings or configurations for encryption, or times and places where encryption must be used. Password standards define settings and requirements related to passwords, and physical security standards address physical security requirements.

33. C. The Advanced Encryption Standard (AES) is the most commonly accepted and used encryption standard as of this writing. Selecting a longer key length like 256 over a 128-bit option provides greater resistance to brute-force attacks. SHA-1 and SHA-2 are hashing algorithms, not encryption algorithms.

34. D. Agile, along with continuous integration/continuous delivery (CI/CD) pipelines, describes a software development life cycle. Business continuity, disaster recovery, and incident response policies may mention the Agile process and impacts on the CI/CD pipeline, but it is not the primary focus of those types of policies.

35. C. Change management practices often include options for preapproved changes, emergency changes, and standard changes. Changes required by legislation or other external factors are not typically built into most change management processes.

36. B. A business impact analysis (BIA) is a formal process used to identify mission-critical functions and to ensure that critical systems that support those functions are identified and assessed. Risk assessment seeks to identify risks and their probability and impact, and a penetration test attempts to emulate how attackers might gain access to or otherwise impact systems and services.

37. C. Policies are a statement of organizational intent. Standards are defined to help organization achieve that intent through the use of rules. Policies are typically defined by an organization, and standards may be adopted from third parties or created by the organization itself. Policies might be defined by law but are not required to be defined that way.

38. A. Service level agreements set forth the expected service level as well as penalties for nonperformance. That means that Sophie needs to determine whether her vendor is meeting their promised delivery levels or availability levels and to claim appropriate penalties as defined in the contract if they are not met. KPIs may be involved but would be measured against her vendor's performance, not her team's performance. Security levels and supply chain availability levels are not the only potential items covered by an SLA.

39. C. Probability and impact are used to describe risk. ALE is the annual loss expectancy, or how much risks will likely cost an organization per year, and SLE is the single loss expectancy, or how much a single risk will cost if it occurs. Acceptance is a risk-handling process, not a way of describing risks.

40. B. The only active reconnaissance task listed here is the nmap scan. Looking up information in Shodan, querying local DNS, and using public records are all examples of passive information gathering that does not actively probe the organization.

41. B. Data owners are responsible for categorizing, overseeing the usage of, and protecting data, but are typically not directly responsible for processing it.

42. B. Knowledge-based authentication information is often easily available via social media or searches. Thus, using it as part of password recovery processes is problematic for organizations. Users will typically remember answers to knowledge-based authentication questions. While knowledge-based authentication isn't typically used for multifactor, something you know is a legitimate option, and knowledge-based authentication information could be recovered from compromised organizations, but this is not a common threat model.

43. D. Mitigation works to limit the impact of a risk, such as by taking action like segmenting the network to prevent further malware spread. Avoidance seeks to prevent the risk from occurring. Risk transfer options move the costs of risks to another organization such as through insurance. Acceptance involves management acknowledging that the risk and its impacts may occur, and that the organization will move forward despite that chance.

44. A. Password standards typically include elements like the NIST 800-63B recommendations, not using password hints, not expiring passwords, storing passwords in a secure way, and establishing a minimum password length of at least 8 characters for user-generated passwords.

45. B. Organizations that focus on reducing risk and that have significant compliance requirements are likely to adopt a conservative risk appetite. Expansionary risk appetite is rare when compliance and risk reduction are primary goals of the organization. Authoritarian and legislative are not typically used terms to describe risk appetite.

46. C. Detailed guides to organization practices for security events are called playbooks. In this case, Jack received the organization's ransomware playbook. A policy would include high-level statements of intent, cookbooks are not a typical term used for documents like these, and this situation involves ransomware, not a disaster recovery scenario.

47. D. Regulations most commonly have fines and sanctions as their primary punishments levied against noncompliant organizations. Data breaches and reputational damage may occur, but are they are not enforced by regulation. Contractual impacts may occur, but again are not directly enforced by regulations.

48. A. Playbooks are detailed documents describing how to respond to a type of incident or event. An example is the CISA's Cybersecurity Incident and Vulnerability Response playbook, which includes steps like identifying anomalous activity, identifying root cause, and analyzing for common adversary TTPs (**www.cisa.gov/sites/default/files/publications/ Federal_Government_Cybersecurity_Incident_and_Vulnerability_ Response_Playbooks_508C.pdf**). They are not legal documents, are detailed instead of high-level like a policy, and are more detailed than a general IR process document.

49. B. Nondisclosure agreements (NDAs) are used to protect sensitive data. Service level agreements (SLAs) determine service levels and penalties if they are not met. Master service agreements (MSAs) are foundational documents determining how organizations will work together as a foundation for specific work covered in SOWs (statements of work). BPAs (business partners agreements) are used when two organizations want to do business as a partnership.

50. C. Onboarding processes commonly include things like new employee orientation, creation of user accounts and provisioning of rights for the employee's account, and ensuring the employee has completed security training. Identity proofing may be part of that process, but was not mentioned here. Mandatory access control is an access control model, and biometric enrollment involves capturing information about an individual's biometric markers or profile.

51. A. The GDPR provides the right to be forgotten, which allows individuals to request that their data be deleted. The rights to deletion, privacy, and ownership were made up for this question.

52. B. Acceptance involves management acknowledging that the risk and its impacts may occur, and that the organization will move forward despite that chance. Risk transfer options move the costs of risks to another organization such as through insurance. Avoidance seeks to prevent the risk from occurring. Mitigation works to limit the impact of a risk, such as by taking action to prevent further malware spread.

53. B. Sending organizational data with a departing employee is not a common practice. In fact, organizations often ask employees to certify that they have returned all organizational devices and data. Returning company equipment, disabling the departing employee's accounts or removing them, and changing any passwords on shared accounts are all common offboarding practices.

54. D. Neutral risk appetites balance organizational goals against risk. Conservative risk appetites seek to reduce risks over addressing other goals, and expansionary risk appetites will accept risk to achieve goals. Reactionary is not a typical description of risk appetite.

55. C. Known environment tests provide full information to testers, allowing them to use information about the environment without having to discover it. Partially known environment tests provide some, but not all information about the environment for testers. Unknown environment tests simulate what an attacker would encounter and do not provide information; instead, the testers have to discover it themselves. Third-party tests are conducted by external groups or individuals and may be known, unknown, or partial knowledge tests.

56. D. BPAs, or business partners agreements, are used when two organizations want to do business as a partnership. SLAs, or service level agreements, determine service levels and penalties if they are not met. Nondisclosure agreements, or NDAs, are used to protect sensitive data. Master service agreements, or MSAs, are foundational documents determining how organizations will work together as a foundation for specific work covered in SOWs, or statements of work.

57. B. Unknown environment tests simulate what an attacker would encounter and do not provide information; instead, the testers have to discover it themselves. Known environment tests provide full information to testers, allowing them to use information about the environment without having to discover it. Partially known environment tests provide some, but not all information about the environment for testers. Third-party tests are conducted by external groups or individuals and may be known, unknown, or partial knowledge tests.

58. B. Likelihood describes the possibility of a risk occurring. Impact describes what will happen if it does, potential is not a term used in this space, and rate of occurrence is how often a risk occurs on an annual basis.

59. C. Known environment tests provide full information to testers, allowing them to use information about the environment without having to discover it. This means that the testing will be more efficient and will provide more information in most cases. Partially known environment tests provide some, but not all information about the environment for testers. Unknown environment tests simulate what an attacker would encounter and do not provide information; instead, the testers have to discover it themselves. Third-party tests are conducted by external groups or individuals and may be known, unknown, or partial knowledge tests.

60. B. Risk exception recognizes risk areas where an organization may not be in compliance with policies or regulations, and may be acknowledged because they cannot be addressed in a timely manner or are required for the organization to conduct business. Risk transfer options move the costs of risks to another organization such as through insurance. Risk avoidance involves preventing the risk from occurring. Mitigation works to limit the impact of a risk, such as by taking action to prevent further malware spread.

61. C. Regulatory compliance typically requires risk assessment on a regular basis, often once a year. Ad hoc, one-time, and continuous risk assessments are used for other purposes to serve the organization but are not as common for regulatory compliance.

62. A. Partially known environment tests provide some, but not all information about the environment for testers. In this case, knowledge of the systems, IPs, and services is an example of partial knowledge. Known environment tests provide full information to testers, allowing them to use information about the environment without having to discover it. Unknown environment tests simulate what an attacker would encounter and do not provide information; instead, the testers have to discover it themselves. Third-party tests are conducted by external groups or individuals and may be known, unknown, or partial knowledge tests.

63. B. An organization willing to accept significant risk has adopted an expansionary risk appetite. Neutral risk appetites balance risk and other factors, conservative appetites seek to limit risk rather than prioritize other goals or objectives, and limited is not a term used on the Security+ exam objectives in this area.

64. A. Information gathering and scanning together are common elements of reconnaissance. Since this involves both scanning and OSINT gathering, this is reconnaissance instead of passive information gathering via OSINT. Known environment tests provide full information to testers, allowing them to use information about the environment without having to discover it. Unknown environment tests simulate what an attacker would encounter and do not provide information; instead, the testers have to discover it themselves.

65. A. Individuals who use the GDPR's right to be forgotten are data subjects, a person who can be identified by their personally identifiable information. Data controllers determine how data will be used, and processors do the actual data processing. Data owners are responsible for protection, usage, and quality of datasets.

66. C. Exposure factors are the percentage of value of an asset that would be lost due to an incident. ALE is the annual loss expectancy, and the ARO is the annual rate of occurrence. SLE is the single loss expectancy. Calculating these gives the cost of an incident, but EF is the impact of the risk and is not calculated using these, nor does it involve the likelihood of the risk.

67. C. Physical security testing involves testing an organization's physical security defenses and practices, including guards, locks and doors, and other physical security components. Offensive penetration testing involves acting like attackers, while defensive penetration testing seeks to learn as defenders. Integrated penetration testing combines both.

68. D. Integrated penetration testing combines both offensive and defensive penetration testing, and testing guards as well as attempting to make it through access controls is an example of an integrated test. Physical security testing involves testing an organization's physical security defenses and practices, including guards, locks and doors, and other physical security components like access control vestibules. Offensive penetration testing involves acting like attackers, while defensive penetration testing seeks to learn as defenders.

69. B. Offensive penetration testing involves acting like attackers, including nation-state actors with advanced capabilities like those described in this question. Physical security testing involves testing an organization's physical security defenses and practices, including guards, locks and doors, and other physical security components like access control vestibules. Defensive penetration testing seeks to learn as defenders. Integrated penetration testing combines both.

70. B. The GDPR is a regulation, making this a regulatory assessment or audit. There is no penetration testing mentioned, the auditors are not described as internal or external, and no attestation is mentioned.

71. A. Secure, ransomware resistant backups can mitigate the impact of ransomware but cannot stop it from impacting systems like an endpoint detection and response (EDR) tool can. Since Alexandria's focus is on immediate mitigation, her best answer is EDR. Cybersecurity insurance is a means of transferring risk, and simply operating as usual is an acceptance strategy.

72. B. Shane's organization has determined their risk appetite. They are willing to accept some risk, but may also choose to mitigate, transfer, or otherwise deal with their risk to match their appetite. Ad hoc describes risk assessment, not risk appetite or thresholds, and there is no way to determine if this is a conservative, neutral, or expansionary risk appetite.

73. C. Defensive penetration testing seeks to allow the organization to learn as defenders. Offensive penetration testing involves acting like attackers, including nation-state actors with advanced capabilities like those described in this question. Physical security testing involves testing an organization's physical security defenses and practices, including guards, locks and doors, and other physical security components like access control vestibules. Integrated penetration testing combines both.

74. D. Integrated penetration testing combines both offensive and defensive techniques and is often woven into an organization's practices on an ongoing basis. Offensive penetration testing involves acting like attackers, including nation-state actors with advanced capabilities like those described in this question. Defensive penetration testing seeks to allow the organization to learn as defenders. Physical security testing involves testing an organization's physical security defenses and practices, including guards, locks and doors, and other physical security components like access control vestibules.

75. D. Auditors provide a statement about an organization's posture as part of an attestation process. This provides assurance that the auditors have reviewed the organization's practices and have found them suitable or that deficiencies have been identified. Penetration testing is the process of testing the security of an organization and is not an audit. Audit sign-off occurs when management signs an audit to acknowledge their awareness of its results. Regulatory defense was made up for this question.

76. A. Without more information about the specific audits that Joe conducts, all we know is that he is an internal auditor. As an employee of the company that he is working for, he is considered an internal auditor. External audits are conducted by third parties. Regulatory audits assess compliance with laws, whereas compliance audits may look at laws or other compliance targets.

77. D. The Payment Card Industry Data Security Standard (PCI DSS) is an industry standard, not a law, so this is a compliance audit, not a regulatory audit. Third-party auditors make it an external rather than an internal audit.

78. B. Filling out forms attesting to your own organization's compliance status is an example of a self-assessment. This is not an audit activity, PCI DSS is not a regulation, and no third parties were involved to make it external or independent and third party.

79. C. Audit committees are typically part of the organization's board of directors, and they oversee financial reporting–related activities. Audit committees are required for US-traded companies that are listed on stock exchanges. Shareholders, third-party assessors, and the security office are not typical places to find an audit committee.

80. D. Continuous integration/continuous delivery (CI/CD) pipelines deploy software on an ongoing basis, making them a good fit for continuous risk assessment techniques. Ad hoc, one-time, and third-party assessments are not suited to the ongoing, rapid assessment pace needed for a CI/CD model.

81. B. External audits like a SOC 2, Type 2 audit should be conducted by an independent third party to be considered valid. An internal audit, no matter who signs off on it, is not used for this purpose, nor are self-assessments. Penetration tests do not generate an SOC 2 audit report.

82. D. An organization's risk threshold is the level where they will switch from accepting a risk to seeking to handle the risk. In this case, the risk has surpassed the organization's risk threshold, resulting in a plan to avoid the risk. The risk did not drop below the threshold, the risk assessment was successful in helping the organization identify a concern, and no controls failed.

83. A. The Health Insurance Portability and Accountability Act (HIPAA) is a regulation, and organizations that must comply with laws need to conduct regulatory assessments. Offensive testing is a penetration testing model that mirrors actual attackers. Known environment testing leverages full knowledge of an organization as part of a penetration test. Physical testing validates physical security controls.

84. A. Policies are high-level descriptions of an organization's intent and understanding of their topic. Procedures will have descriptions of how a change is made in detailed form, while standards will describe how changes are created, made, and approved. Regulatory requirements are most likely to be part of standards or procedures.

85. C. Marek should follow his organization's change management process to document the change required and to ensure that it is regularly reviewed. This may not require a risk assessment since it may be a simple requirement or may have already been assessed. The type of security variance needed is not described, so it is not clear if removing the system from the network is necessary.

86. A. Business continuity plans address how the organization will respond, including referencing runbooks that may detail how to handle restoration or other efforts on a step-by-step basis, but doesn't itself include that level of detail. Business continuity policies describe the organization's intent at a high level and are likely to reference the business continuity plan. They are not the same, as the policy is a higher-level document than the plan is.

87. C. Policies are distinct from procedures and standards because they include high-level statements of intent rather than specific practices. Procedures document the practices an organization will use, whereas standards set expectations or specific configurations or details about how something is done or set up.

88. C. The EU's GDPR provides the right to be forgotten, which allows Terry to request that organizations remove all of his data from their systems. HIPAA is a US regulation; data stewardship is an organizational role, not a right; and personal data ownership is not a right.

89. B. Risk exposure is calculated by multiplying probability and impact. Cost is measured in currency, time, or other cost metrics; vulnerability is often measured using CVSS scores; and audit findings may have criticality ratings.

90. B. Qualitative risk assessment relies on expertise and staff members who have relevant knowledge to provide a rating based on their experience, skills, and knowledge. A common rating for probability in a qualitative risk assessment might be low, medium, or high, rather than a 0–100 rating based on statistics or large datasets.

91. B. Rules of engagement determine how a penetration tester will conduct an engagement. Passwords may be part of the information provided before the test for a full knowledge or partial knowledge test but are not part of the rules of engagement.

92. D. Rules of engagement are created for penetration testing efforts that include a wide variety of information, including scope, schedules, what to do if a preexisting compromise is discovered, requirements for how to handle third-party-hosted tools and environments, how sensitive data and data related to the penetration test will be handled, and who to contact in emergencies. A right-to-audit clause is included in contracts, allowing audits to occur as part of the contract. SLAs are used to set service levels and penalties if they are not met, and MOUs document organizations' interest and willingness to work together.

93. A. An organization's risk threshold is the level where they will switch from accepting a risk to seeking to handle the risk. Their risk appetite is the amount of risk an organization is willing to accept to achieve its goals. Ad hoc risk level and third-party risk level were made up for this question.

94. D. AUPs, or acceptable use policies, describe how organizational resources, systems, and services can and should be used.

95. C. Large breaches, particularly when the organization has been negligent, can have large impacts on the organization's reputation, resulting in long-term damage. Fines and contractual impacts may be impactful but are often resolved relatively quickly. Due diligence was not shown but is not an impact—rather, it is part of an organization's responsibilities.

96. B. A statement of work (SOW) or work order (WO) is created to list the tasks and deliverables that will be performed under the blanket master services agreement (MSA). An MOU, or memorandum of understanding, declares how two organizations want to work together; a business partners agreement (BPA) establishes a partnership between two organizations; and punch lists are not covered under the Security+ exam outline but are a list of tasks that must be accomplished for a contractor to be paid.

97. D. Jack should use the manufacturer's published mean time between failures (MTBF), which is a measure of the reliability of a system. It is the expected amount of time that will elapse between system failures. While organizations typically replace devices well before their MTBF ratings, knowing how long the devices should last on average can be useful in long-lived applications and for budgetary planning. A recovery time objective, or RTO, is set by organizations to describe how long restoring systems or services to normal function after a disruption can take. Mean time to repair, or MTTR, is the average time it takes to repair a system or device. A recovery point objective, or RPO, describes how much data can be lost in the event of an outage or issue.

98. D. Mean time between failures (MTBF) is a measure of the reliability of a system. It is the expected amount of time that will elapse between system failures, but it is merely an average. Jason should expect that drives will fail, and that their average service life will be 300,000 hours. That means that half of the drives are likely to fail before 300,000 hours, and half will fail after that number.

99. C. A recovery point objective, or RPO, describes how much data can be lost in the event of an outage or issue. A recovery time objective, or RTO, is set by organizations to describe how long restoring systems or services to normal function after a disruption can take. Mean time to repair, or MTTR, is the average time it takes to repair a system or device. The mean time between failures (MTBF) is a measure of the reliability of a system. It is the expected amount of time that will elapse between system failures.

100. A. The Security+ exam objectives list three categorizations you need to be familiar with for anomalous behavior: risky, unexpected, and unintentional. The other terms listed are not ways that the exam categorizes anomalous behavior.

101. A. Greg has conducted an ad hoc assessment by quickly pulling together a team without a formal process or procedure. Instead, he is seeking to quickly assess risk and take action. A one-time assessment typically follows an established methodology but is only conducted once. Third-party risk assessment uses external teams or staff, and continuous risk assessment is done on an ongoing basis.

102. B. Mean time to repair, or MTTR, is the average time it takes to repair a system or device, and Olivia needs to know that to determine what she can promise in her service level agreements that rely on server repair timelines. A recovery time objective, or RTO, is set by organizations to describe how long restoring systems or services to normal function after a disruption can take; it doesn't determine how fast the server can be fixed but sets a goal that needs to take things like repair and recovery time into account as it is determined. A recovery point objective, or RPO, describes how much data can be lost in the event of an outage or issue, and the mean time between failures (MTBF) is a measure of the reliability of a system. It is the expected amount of time that will elapse between system failures.

103. C. The underlying agreement between two organizations that determines how the organizations will work together is a master services agreement (MSA). A MOU, or memorandum of understanding, declares how two organizations want to work together; a business partners agreement (BPA) establishes a partnership between two organizations; SLAs (service level agreements) set service level expectations and penalties if they are not met; and a business partners agreement (BPA) establishes two organizations as partners rather than establishing a working relationship for services as set forth in SOWs.

104. C. A recovery point objective, or RPO, describes how much data can be lost in the event of an outage or issue, and journaling allows recovery of database transactions by replaying them against the database once it is restored. Journaling may slow down recovery time objectives as the actions are replayed. A recovery time objective, or RTO, is set by organizations to describe how long restoring systems or services to normal function after a disruption can take. Mean time to repair, or MTTR, is the average time it takes to repair a system or device. The mean time between failures (MTBF) is a measure of the reliability of a system. It is the expected amount of time that will elapse between system failures.

105. B. A recovery time objective, or RTO, is set by organizations to describe how long restoring systems or services to normal function after a disruption can take. A 12-hour RTO means that recovery from outages should take less than 12 hours. Failing over to a warm site will typically take a while, meaning that starting to fail over after 12 hours will miss the RTO, and MTBF is the mean time between failures, not a recovery timeframe. Failing every 12 hours on average would be unacceptable for almost any technical service or system!

106. B. Valerie should immediately begin a move to the warm site. She knows that moving to her warm site takes half the average time to repair for her datacenter's power infrastructure. That means that in most cases, moving will result in at least a 12-hour shorter outage. If the time to repair proves to be shorter than 12 hours, she can simply stop the move. Waiting does not restore her to operation sooner than 24 hours in the average case, and waiting to make the decision reduces the amount of advantage she gets from moving to the warm site.

107. A. Quantitative risk assessments assign numeric values and calculations to determine relative risk. Qualitative risk assessment uses knowledge and expertise to assess risk. Calculated risk is not a term that is commonly used to describe assessment processes like these, and risk registers list risks that an organization has identified but that don't necessarily involve calculations.

108. B. Risk registers list organizations risks and their ratings, along with additional information that the organization uses to track or describe risks. Risk appetite plans, quantitative registers, and qualitative assessment reports were made up for this question.

109. C. Qualitative risk assessment uses knowledge and expertise to assess risk and are thus typically faster and more likely to be completed than a quantitative risk assessment. Quantitative risk assessments assign numeric values and calculations to determine relative risk. Choosing internal or external risk assessments is not a primary driver of speed compared to choosing quantitative over qualitative risk assessments.

110. D. SLE, or single loss expectancy, uses the asset value (AV) and exposure factor (EF) to determine the SLE. Purchase date, which department manages the server, and its operating system are not part of the calculation.

111. B. Undertaking reasonable steps to meet legal requirements like compliance with regulations is known as due diligence. Data stewardship may be part of those actions, but it focuses on oversight of data and data governance and may not be specifically regulatory focused.

112. B. Single loss expectancy, or SLE, is calculated by multiplying the asset value (AV) by the exposure factor (EF). In this case, that means that the potential loss during a loss event would be $125,000.

113. A. Annualized loss expectancy (ALE) is calculated by multiplying the annual rate of occurrence (ARO) by the single loss expectancy (SLE). If a single loss expectancy for a $1,000,000 asset is $100,000 and the annual rate of occurrence is .5—in other words, it happens every two years on average—then the ALE is $50,000.

114. D. Waylon is a risk owner. He is responsible for ensuring that the risks related to data and the application are managed appropriately. Board members have overall responsibility for an organization. Data processors have a data role, not a risk ownership role, and auditors assess organizations against standards and practices rather than owning risk.

115. B. Without a license to operate, Nathaniel's organization will be unable to conduct business. Reputational damage, fines, and contractual impacts can all be navigated if the organization can continue to do business.

116. C. Susan can calculate the single loss expectancy (SLE) by multiplying the asset value (AV) by the exposure factor (EF), resulting in $25,000. If this loss occurs twice a year, then the annualized loss expectancy (ALE) is $50,000.

117. A. Annual rate of occurrence is calculated by determining how many times in a year the event happens, on average. If it happens less than once a year, the rate is a fraction based on that rate. Here the event happens once every four years, or .25 of the time during a given year.

118. D. Annualized loss expectancy is calculated by multiplying the annualized rate of occurrence (ARO) and the single loss expectancy (SLE). Total cost of ownership (TCO) and recovery point objectives (RPO) are not part of this type of risk calculation.

119. B. Passive reconnaissance is any reconnaissance that is done without actually connecting to the target. In this case, John is conducting a form of OSINT, or open source intelligence, by using commonly available third-party information sources to gather information about his target. Active reconnaissance involves communicating with the target network, such as doing a port scan. The initial exploitation is not information gathering; it is actually breaking into the target network. A pivot is when you have breached one system and use that to move to another system.

120. C. Using default settings is a form of weak configuration and indicates that the organization is not using baselines effectively and may not have appropriate processes and standards in place. Many vulnerability scanners and attack tools have default settings built-in to test with, and default settings are easily obtained for most devices with a quick search of the Internet. Configuring the accounts is not the issue; using default credentials and settings is. Although training users is important, that's not the issue in this scenario. Patching systems is important, but that won't change default settings.

121. D. Active reconnaissance connects to the network using techniques such as port scanning. Both active and passive reconnaissance can be done manually or with tools. Unknown and known environment tests refer to the amount of information the tester is given. Attackers and testers use both types of reconnaissance.

122. B. The rules of engagement for a penetration test typically include the type and scope of testing, client contact information and requirements for when the team should be notified, sensitive data handling requirements, and details of regular status meetings and reports. The remaining options were made up for this question.

123. B. Unlike a disaster recovery plan that is written to help an organization recovery from a person-made or natural disaster, a business continuity plan focuses on how to keep the business running when it is disrupted. Thus, Charlene's BC plan would detail how to keep the organization running when a system outage occurs.

124. C. Many cloud service providers do not allow customer-driven audits, either by the customer or a third party. They also commonly prohibit vulnerability scans of their production environment to avoid service outages. Instead, many provide third-party audit results in the form of a service organization controls (SOC) report or similar audit artifact.

125. D. A disaster recovery plan addresses what to do during a person-made or natural disaster. A flood that completely fills a datacenter would require significant efforts to recover from, and Gurvinder will need a solid disaster recovery plan—and perhaps a new datacenter location as soon as possible! A COOP, or continuity of operations plan, is needed for U.S. government agencies but is not required for businesses. A business continuity plan would cover how to keep the business running, but it does not cover all the requirements in a natural disaster of this scale, and a flood insurance plan is not a term used in the Security+ exam objectives.

126. C. Right-to-audit clauses are commonly accepted as part of service and leasing contracts regardless of location for datacenter co-location and facility rental contracts. Cloud service providers, however, are less likely to sign a right-to-audit contract. Instead, they may provide third-party audit data to customers or even to potential customers.

127. A. Playbooks list the actions that an organization will take as part of a response process. A runbook lists the steps required to perform an action like notification, removing malware, or similar tasks. Playbooks tend to be used to document processes, whereas runbooks tend to be used for specific actions. A disaster recovery (DR) plan is used to recover from disasters, and a business continuity (BC) plan is used to ensure that the organization continues to function.

128. A. Caroline should select ISO 27002. ISO 27002 is an international standard for implementing and maintaining information security systems. ISO 27701 is an international standard security technique for privacy information management systems; NIST 800-12 is a general security standard and it is a US standard, not an international one; and NIST 800-53 is a collection of security and privacy controls for information systems and organizations.

129. C. Change management is the process of documenting all changes made to a company's network and computers. Avoiding making changes at the same time makes tracking any problems that can occur much simpler. Due diligence is the process of investigation and verification of the accuracy of a particular act. Acceptable use policies state what actions and practices are allowed in an organization while using technology. Due care is the effort made by a reasonable party to avoid harm to another. It is the level of judgment, care, determination, and activity a person would reasonably expect to do under certain conditions.

130. A. An acceptable use policy (AUP) is a document stating what a user may or may not have access to on a company's network or the Internet. A clean desk policy ensures that all sensitive/confidential documents are removed from an end-user workstation and locked up when the documents are not in use. Mandatory vacation policy is used by companies to detect fraud by having a second person, familiar with the duties, help discover any illicit activities. Job rotation is a policy that describes the practice of moving employees between different tasks. Job rotation can help detect fraud because employees cannot perform the same actions for long periods of time.

131. C. The PCI DSS, or Payment Card Industry Data Security Standard, is a security standard that is mandated by credit card vendors. The Payment Card Industry Security Standards Council is responsible for updates and changes to the standard. GDPR, or the General Data Protection Regulation, is a standard for data privacy and security in the European Union (EU). COPPA is the Children's Online Privacy Protection Act, a U.S. federal law. CIS is the Center for Internet Security and is not a law or a regulation.

132. D. Quantitative risk assessment is the process of assigning numerical values to the probability an event will occur and what the impact of the event will have. Change management is the process of managing configuration changes made to a network. Vulnerability assessment attempts to identify, quantify, and rank the weaknesses in a system. Qualitative risk assessment is the process of ranking which risk poses the most danger using ratings like low, medium, and high.

133. D. A memorandum of understanding (MOU) is a type of agreement that is usually not legally binding. This agreement is intended to be mutually beneficial without involving courts or money. An SLA (service level agreement) defines the level of service the customer expects from the service provider. The level of service definitions should be specific and measurable in each area. A BPA (business partner agreement) is a legal agreement between partners. It establishes the terms, conditions, and expectations of the relationship between the partners. An ISA (interconnection security agreement) is an agreement that specifies the technical and security requirements of the interconnection between organizations.

134. A. The single loss expectancy (SLE) is the product of the asset value ($16,000) and the exposure factor (.35), or $5,600.

135. A. Risk acceptance is a strategy of recognizing, identifying, and accepting a risk that is sufficiently unlikely or that has such limited impact that a corrective control is not warranted. Risk transfer is the act of moving the risk to hosted providers who assume the responsibility for recovery and restoration or by acquiring insurance to cover the costs emerging from a risk. Risk avoidance is the removal of the vulnerability that can increase a particular risk so that it is avoided altogether. Risk mitigation is when a company implements controls to reduce vulnerabilities or weaknesses in a system. It can also reduce the impact of a threat.

136. D. A parking policy generally outlines parking provisions for employees and visitors. This includes the criteria and procedures for allocating parking spaces for employees and is not a part of organizational security policy. Instead, it is an operational or business policy. An acceptable use policy (AUP) describes the limits and guidelines for users to make use of an organization's physical and intellectual resources. This includes allowing or limiting the use of personal email during work hours. Business continuity policies describe how the organization approaches business continuity efforts, and incident response (IR) policies document the organization's IR intentions and high-level goals.

137. A. Quantitative risk assessment is the process of assigning numerical values like cost and frequency of occurrence to the probability an event will occur and what impact the event will have, and thus directly evaluates the cost of a risk occurring. Qualitative risk assessment is the process of ranking which risk poses the most danger such as low, medium, and high. A business impact analysis (BIA) is used to evaluate the possible effect a business can suffer should an interruption to critical system operations occur. This interruption could be as a result of an accident, emergency, or disaster. Threat assessment is the process of identifying and categorizing different threats such as environmental and person-made. It also attempts to identify the potential impact from the threats.

138. D. A nondisclosure agreement (NDA) protects sensitive and intellectual data from getting into the wrong hands. An NDA is a legal contract between the company and a third-party vendor to not disclose information per the agreement. Encrypted data that is sent can still be decrypted by the third-party vendor if they have the appropriate certificate or the key but does not restrict access to the data. Violating an NDA would constitute unauthorized data sharing, and a violation of privileged user role-based awareness training has nothing to do with sharing proprietary information.

139. C. Sharing of profits and losses and the addition or removal of a partner, as well as the responsibilities of each partner, are typically included in a BPA (business partner agreement). Expectations between parties such as a company and an Internet service provider are typically found in a service level agreement (SLA). Expectations include the level of performance given during the contractual service. An SLA will provide a clear means of determining whether a specific function or service has been provided according to the agreed-on level of performance. Security requirements associated with interconnecting IT systems are typically found in an interconnection security agreement, or ISA.

140. D. Systems should be restored within four hours with a minimum loss of one day's worth of data. The RTO (recovery time objective) is the amount of time within which a process or service must be restored after a disaster to meet business continuity. It defines how much time it takes to recover after notification of process disruption. The recovery point objective, or RPO, specifies the amount of time that can pass before the amount of data lost may exceed the organization's maximum tolerance for data loss.

141. A. A data retention policy defines how long an organization will keep data. Removing sensitive documents not in use is a clean desk policy. A formal process for managing configuration changes is change management, and a memorandum of understanding consists of legal documents that describe mutual agreement between two parties.

142. B. ALE (annual loss expectancy) is the product of the ARO (annual rate of occurrence) and the SLE (single loss expectancy) and is mathematically expressed as ALE = ARO × SLE. Single loss expectancy is the cost of any single loss, and it is mathematically expressed as SLE = AV (asset value) × EF (exposure factor).

143. C. Risk transfer is the act of moving the risk to hosted providers who assume the responsibility for recovery and restoration or by acquiring insurance to cover the costs emerging from a risk. Risk acceptance is a strategy of recognizing, identifying, and accepting a risk that is sufficiently unlikely or that has such limited impact that a corrective control is not warranted. Risk mitigation is when a company implements controls to reduce vulnerabilities or weaknesses in a system. It can also reduce the impact of a threat. Risk avoidance is the removal of the vulnerability that can increase a particular risk so that it is avoided altogether.

144. C. The mean time between failures (MTBF) is a measure of the reliability of a system or component. It is the expected amount of time that will elapse between system or device failures. MTTR (mean time to repair) is the average time it takes for a failed device or component to be repaired or replaced. An RPO (recovery point objective) is the period of time a company can tolerate lost data being unrecoverable between backups. ALE (annual loss expectancy) is the product of the annual rate of occurrence (ARO) and the single loss expectancy (SLE).

145. A. Quantitative risk analysis requires complex calculations and is more time-consuming because it requires detailed financial data and calculations. Quantitative risk assessment is often subjective and requires expertise on systems and infrastructure, and both types of assessment can provide clear answers on risk-based questions.

146. B. Risk acceptance is a strategy of recognizing, identifying, and accepting a risk that is sufficiently unlikely or that has such limited impact that a corrective control is not warranted. Risk mitigation is when a company implements controls to reduce vulnerabilities or weaknesses in a system. It can also reduce the impact of a threat. Risk avoidance is the removal of the vulnerability that can increase a particular risk so that it is avoided altogether. Risk transfer is the act of moving the risk to other organizations like insurance providers or hosting companies who assume the responsibility for recovery and restoration or by acquiring insurance to cover the costs emerging from a risk.

147. A. Data owners assign labels such as top secret to data. Custodians assign security controls to data. A privacy officer ensures that companies comply with privacy laws and regulations. System administrators are responsible for the overall functioning of IT systems.

148. B. ALE (annual loss expectancy) = SLE (single loss expectancy) × ARO (annualized rate of occurrence). SLE equals $750,000 (2,500 records × $300), and ARO equals 5%, so $750,000 times 5% equals $37,500.

149. C. RPO (recovery point objective) specifies the allowable data loss. It is the amount of time that can pass during an interruption before the quantity of data lost during that period surpasses business continuity planning's maximum acceptable threshold. MTBF (mean time between failures) is the rating on a device or component that predicts the expected time between failures. MTTR (mean time to repair) is the average time it takes for a failed device or component to be repaired or replaced. ARO (annual rate of occurrence) is the ratio of an estimated possibility that a threat will take place within a one-year time frame.

150. C. Onboarding is the process of adding an employee to a company's identity and access management system. Offboarding is the process of removing an employee from the company's identity and access management system. A system owner is an individual who is in charge of managing one or more systems and can include patching and updating operating systems. An executive user was made up for this question.

151. D. This is a procedure, which documents what you should do in general terms. A policy lays out an organization's intent, and this is more specific than that. A playbook has specific, detailed action, and this procedure does not include that level of detail. Checklists are a step-by-step guide to accomplishing a task, and this document outlines required steps, not step-by-step detail.

152. B. Organizational policy frameworks typically contain policies, standards and procedures that support and expand on the policy, and guidelines. Risk registers, audit reports, vulnerability scans, and pentest reports are all artifacts organizations generate in support of information security practices. Laws are not part of a policy framework but may influence it.

153. C. The mean time to repair (MTTR) for a system or devices is the average time that it will take to repair it if it fails. The MTTR is used as part of business continuity planning to determine if a system needs additional redundancy or other options put in place if a failure and repair would exceed the maximum tolerable outage. It is calculated by dividing the total maintenance time by the total number of repairs. MTBF is the mean time between failures, MTTF the mean time to failure, and MITM is an on-path attack.

154. A. Helen has created a disaster recovery plan (DRP). RPOs, or recovery point objectives, are set to determine how much data may be lost if an event or incident occurs; incident response plans focus on incidents, not outages or disasters; and MTBF, or mean time between failures, is not a type of plan.

155. B. Personal health information (PHI) may be covered by state, local, or federal law, and Greg's organization should ensure that they understand any applicable laws before storing, processing, or handling health information.

156. D. An individual is most likely to face identity theft issues if their personally identifiable information (PII) is stolen or breached.

157. C. It is common practice to prohibit interactive logins to a GUI or shell for service accounts. Use of a service account for interactive logins or attempting to log in as one should be immediately flagged and alerted on as an indicator of compromise (IoC).

158. D. Emma should categorize this as a supply chain risk. When organizations cannot get the systems, equipment, and supplies they need to operate, it can have a significant impact on their ability to conduct business. That could create financial risk, but financial risk is not the direct risk here. There is no indication that the vendor will not support the systems, nor is there any information about whether there is an integration issue in the description.

159. B. Patching is a form of avoidance because it works to remove a risk from the environment. Acceptance of flaws that need patching would involve leaving the software unpatched; mitigation strategies might include firewalls, intrusion prevention systems (IPSs), or web application firewall (WAF) devices; and transference options include third-party hosting or services.

160. A. The fines that can result from violation or infringement of regulations like the General Data Protection Regulation (GDPR) can have a significant impact on an organization, or could even potentially put it out of business. Due to this, organizations will track compliance with regulations as part of their risk posture.

161. D. Disaster recovery requires forethought and preparation, response to issues to minimize impact during a disaster, and response activities after a disaster. Thus, a complete disaster recovery plan should include actions that may or will occur before, during, and after a disaster, and not just the recovery process after the fact.

162. B. Although data breaches could result in termination of a card processing agreement, the fact that her organization is noncompliant is most likely to result in a fine. PCI DSS, or Payment Card Industry Data Security Standard, is a vendor standard, not a law, and criminal charges would not typically be filed in a situation like this.

163. D. The General Data Protection Regulation, or GDPR, requires a data protection officer (DPO). They oversee the organization's data protection strategy and implementation, and make sure that the organization complies with the GDPR.

164. B. An SLA (service level agreement) defines the level of service the customer expects from the service provider. The level of service definitions should be specific and measurable in each area. An MOU (memorandum of understanding) is a legal document that describes a mutual agreement between parties. An ISA (interconnection security agreement) is an agreement that specifies the technical and security requirements of the interconnection between organizations. A BPA (business partners agreement) is a legal agreement between partners. It establishes the terms, conditions, and expectations of the relationship between the partners.

165. C. The likelihood of occurrence, or probability, is multiplied by the impact to determine a risk's severity.

166. D. Organizations can determine how they want to determine asset value, but consistency is important in many cases. Thus, the original cost, the replacement cost, or a depreciated cost may be used.

167. A. A business impact analysis (BIA) helps to identify critical systems by determining which systems will create the largest impact if they are not available. MTBF is the mean time between failures, an RTO is a recovery time objective, and an ICD was made up for this question.

168. D. The most common means of transferring breach risk is to purchase cybersecurity insurance. Accepting breaches is rarely considered a valid risk process, blaming breaches on competitors does not actually transfer risk, and selling data to another organization is not a risk handling process but may be a business process.

169. C. The cost of a breach is an example of the impact of a breach. Probability is how likely the risk is to occur, and risk severity is calculated by multiplying probability and impact.

170. C. Gathering vulnerability information for a system that isn't scannable from the Internet will require active reconnaissance as part of the penetration testing effort. OSINT and passive reconnaissance do not involve active scans, and known environments provide full knowledge of the environment.

171. B. Olivia should establish a service level agreement (SLA) with her provider to ensure that they meet the expected level of service. If they don't, financial or other penalties are typically included. Olivia should ensure that those penalties are meaningful to her vendor to make sure they are motivated to meet the SLA. An MOU is a memorandum of understanding and explains the relationship between two organizations; an MSA is a master services agreement, which establishes a business relationship under which additional work orders or other documentation describe the actual work that is done; and a BPA is a business partners agreement, which is used when companies wish to partner on efforts and may outline division of profits or responsibilities in the partnership.

172. A. The single loss expectancy (SLE) describes what a single risk event is likely to cost. It is calculated using the asset value (AV) times the exposure factor (EF), which is an estimated percentage of the cost that will occur in damage if the loss occurs. MTTR is the mean time to repair, ARO is the annual rate of occurrence, and RTO is the recovery time objective. These are not part of the SLE equation.

173. B. Annual rate of occurrence (ARO) is expressed as the number of times an event will occur in a year. Wayne has estimated that the risk event that is being assessed will happen three times a year.

174. D. Data processors are service providers that process data for data controllers. A data controller or data owner is the organization or individual who collects and controls data. A data steward carries out the intent of the data controller and is delegated responsibility for the data. Data custodians are those who are entrusted with the data to store, manage, or secure the data.

175. C. Nicole is a data controller, sometimes called a data owner. She determines the reasons for processing personal information and how it is processed. A data steward carries out the intents of the data controller, data custodians are charged with safeguarding information, and data consumer is not a common data privacy role.

176. D. Kirk has mitigated the risk to his organization by increasing the resources targeted by the DoS attack in an attempt to ensure that the attack will not be successful. Acceptance would involve simply letting the attacks occur knowing they are likely to stop, avoidance might involve finding a way to ensure the attacks cannot occur, and transfer could leverage a third-party mirror or anti-DoS hosting service.

177. C. Offboarding processes are conducted to ensure that accounts and access are removed and that materials, computers, and data are all recovered from the staff member when a member of an organization leaves. Exit interviews are an HR process, job rotation helps to prevent an individual from conducting fraudulent activities over time, and governance helps to manage and maintain data by establishing high-level control over the processes, procedures, and classification of the data an organization uses.

178. B. Playbooks provide detailed, step-by-step instructions for how to address specific topics like denial-of-service attacks. Standards describe the settings or requirements that the organization wishes to use. Regulations are law and are not set by the organization, and guidelines provide advice to organizations seeking to comply with the policy and standards.

179. C. Risk trend analysis shows the change in risks over time, allowing senior leadership to quickly and easily understand where risks are being addressed and where they may be increasing or not getting the attention they need. Ad hoc reports are used when risk information is needed in specific areas, typically in response to specific needs. Risk registers list an organization's risks in detail and are not a quick, visual tool. Risk event reports detail specific events related to risks.

180. B. Third-party assessments of an organization's efforts to meet ISO standards is an example of vendor assessment. Internal audit would leverage internal staff to perform an audit, vulnerability scans use technical tools to identify vulnerabilities, and data inventories identify data and its locations and uses.

181. B. Vendors often ask that customers work with them to preschedule the testing so that they are aware of it. They typically do not place limitations on whether customers or third parties conduct the testing, and after-the-fact notification instead of prior notification is not a typical requirement.

182. B. The IP address of the recipient is not a common way of identifying phishing emails. The source system, domain, or IP may indicate a malicious sender, however! Phishing often focuses on creating a false sense of urgency, uses encrypted and password-protected files to bypass filters, and may claim there is a problem with your password.

183. D. Operational security is the practice of educating users on the importance of protecting sensitive information, including security practices, configurations, and other details. Awareness training is a broad term describing all elements of security awareness. Social engineering is used by attackers to leverage human behaviors and practices for their own gain. Insider threats are threats created by those inside the organization.

184. D. An organization operating in the European Union (EU) and selling in multiple countries means that the company needs to assess legal implications on local, national, and global levels.

185. C. Conflicts of interest occur when an organization has a competing interest that could influence their behavior in a way that is not aligned with the best interest of a customer. Insider threats occur because an insider creates a problem or threat, either on purpose or inadvertently. MOU and SOW violations are both contractual violations and could be conflicts of interest but are not limited to that.

186. D. Decentralized governance allows individual business units to manage themselves rather than central organizations doing so. There is no board or committee described in the question.

187. A. The Treasury Department is a government entity, making this governance government entity–based. Shareholders and boards may play a role, but not via the Treasury Department. Centralized governance occurs inside the organization, not from an external entity.

188. C. Requesting evidence of internal audits and then assessing that evidence is the best option Sandra has. While a right-to-audit clause can be important in contracts, it would only be useful after the contract is signed, not prior to engagement. Supply chain analysis can be useful in specific circumstances, but nothing in the question indicates specific supply chain requirements or concerns. Due diligence is performed, not stated.

189. B. Policy handbooks are used to provide information about high-level security practices and goals. Audit reports may not be broadly available in an organization, runbooks are detailed how-to guides for processes or tasks, and user awareness training focuses on security awareness rather than high-level goals and policies.

190. B. Awareness training remains the best protection against social engineering aimed at individual staff members. While awareness won't stop all attacks, protecting individuals requires them to be trained on a regular basis. Endpoint detection and response (EDR) and next-generation firewall (NGFW) are both technical tools that cannot stop social engineering directly, and security policies help the organization establish their approach to security but won't stop individual responses to social engineering directly.

191. A. Examinations are simpler, typically smaller in scope, and less costly than an audit. Both help provide assurance, but the standards applied are different.

192. D. The first step in developing security training programs is to determine what risks and threats the organization faces. Once those are understood, an appropriate program can be created, including obtaining a budget, determining how training will be presented, and ensuring that regulatory requirements, if any, are met.

193. B. Internal governance committees do not typically include external entities like regulators. Subject matter experts (SMEs), management, and counsel are all commonly members of security governance committees.

194. D. Global, national, and local regulations may impact Dana's security policy, but corporations do not set regulations. Instead, they will influence the policy through contractual obligations.

195. C. Feedback on policies from staff, integrating new and changed regulations, and validating reports from security tools are all common elements used to update security policies. Nondisclosure agreements (NDAs) seek to keep data secure through contractual obligations and are not a typical element in policy updates.

196. C. A MOA, or memorandum of agreement, is a formal document that outlines the terms and details of an agreement between two organizations, including the roles and responsibilities each will have. A SOW, or statement of work, describes the specific work that will be under a master services agreement for an engagement. Service level agreements (SLAs) are written contracts that specify the conditions of service that will be provided by the vendor and the remedies available to the customer if the vendor fails to meet the SLA. Business partners agreements (BPAs) are used when organizations agree to do business with each other in a partnership.

197. B. Companies commonly send questionnaires to potential vendors to gather information about security practices prior to acquiring their products or engaging their services. This is a simpler method than requiring audits or penetration tests, and OSINT will not provide organizational answers about practices in most cases.

198. A. External reporting for compliance is most often driven by the need to meet regulations or contractual obligations. Audit assesses compliance rather than driving reporting, board reporting is considered internal, and KPIs are typically internal measures.

199. B. Automated compliance monitoring is a key tool when organizations want to ensure they are consistently meeting compliance targets. Annual audits do not ensure compliance during the year, whether they are internal or external. Compliance KPIs give organizations compliance targets and measures, but without underlying tools they are simply a way to know the state of compliance when they are checked or updated.

200. C. Mistakes like this are classified as unintentional anomalous behavior. Risky and unexpected behaviors are the other two classifications that are part of the Security+ exam outline. Insider attacks or threats are intentional or unintentional malicious activity, which mistyping a password is not an example of.

201. D. NIST no longer recommends requiring password changes on a regular basis, and instead suggests that passwords only be changed when necessary. This helps to prevent password reuse and avoids influencing users to slightly modify passwords. Disabling MFA, reusing passwords, and using passwords hints are all practices that should be avoided.

202. B. Organizations often use multiple formats for awareness training to address learning preferences and styles. Compliance requirements typically do not specify how awareness is accomplished, just that it has occurred and can be validated. Multiple modes of training tend to increase costs rather than decreasing them, and KPIs for security awareness look at impact, not modes.

203. D. Organizations typically establish KPIs (key performance indicators), which may be described in MSAs (master service agreements), SLAs (service level agreements), or SOWs (statements of work). These help to measure and monitor the vendor's performance. MOUs are used to document how organizations want to work together, not to establish performance measures. Compliance audits and regulatory requirements are only part of performance management.

204. B. Staff should be trained to maintain situational awareness by keeping an eye on their environment and the behaviors of individuals around them. Insider threats are internal actors who undertake malicious actions. Social engineering uses human behaviors to conduct malicious activities, and unintentionally risky behavior is typically accidental threats caused by users.

205. C. Data owners are typically the most senior data–related role in an organization and bear broad responsibility for the data, including oversight roles over stewards, controllers, and processors.

206. D. Deploying security cameras is not a common hybrid work environment option. Use of VPNs, secure Wi-Fi, and appropriate physical security are all common options.

207. C. Contracts, regulations, and licensing all drive external compliance reporting. Reputations may be damaged if organizations are not compliant, but it does not drive reporting.

208. A. Work orders (WO) and statements of work (SOWs) are used to document the specific tasks and deliverables that are performed under an MSA. SLAs, MOUs, and MOAs are not used for this purpose.

209. D. MTBF, or mean time between failure, describes the average time before a device will fail, or the average amount of time between failures of a system. A recovery time objective, or RTO, is set by organizations to describe how long restoring systems or services to normal function after a disruption can take. Mean time to repair, or MTTR, is the average time it takes to repair a system or device. A recovery point objective, or RPO, describes how much data can be lost in the event of an outage or issue.

210. C. ISO 27002 describes controls and helps select and implement controls while also providing guidance on developing information security management guidelines. ISO 27001 establishes control objectives for 14 different categories, including things like HR security, asset management, and operations security. ISO 27701 focuses on managing privacy controls, and ISO 31000 provides guidelines for risk management.

211. A. Physical security standards set requirements for physical security controls like fences, locks, doors, and cameras. Access control policies may be logical or physical control–based, but fence height is not an access control. Business continuity and onboarding don't impact fence height, nor do they rely on it.

212. C. Boards are typically elected by shareholders. Employees, the CEO, and non-shareholders typically do not have the ability to elect or name members of the board.

213. B. Until he knows more details, Greg should classify this behavior as unexpected. Sending large volumes of data may be intentional, could be legitimate and thus not risky, and if it is intentional and part of business needs, would not be an insider threat.

214. C. Using existing tools to monitor for changes that would move the organization out of compliance is a common practice to help ensure ongoing compliance. Quarterly audits are point-in-time checks and won't ensure ongoing compliance. Training helps to keep staff aware, but additional actions are required to ensure compliance, and attestation does not provide ongoing compliance, only a statement at a point in time.

215. C. After audits are acknowledged by management, the auditors will attest that the audit is complete and accurate based on their work and knowledge. Compliance and regulatory reporting may or may not happen depending on the reasons for the audit and the organization's needs. Once an audit is complete, further scans and other work may be conducted by the company but are not guaranteed.

216. B. The employee at Latisha's company can be considered an insider threat because they have provided access to a third party. Most organizations will terminate employees who do this due to violations of their acceptable use policy (AUP). The behavior is anomalous, but an insider threat is a better description. No social engineering is evident, nor is a nation-state actor described.

217. B. Using threat feeds to block phishing campaign URLs as they enter the feed is a proactive way to quickly respond. Web application firewalls (WAFs) are used to protect applications rather than as border devices to block outbound traffic. Manual blocks are commonly used but are slower to implement than threat feed–based responses. Conducting user awareness training is a best practice but doesn't directly respond to campaigns.

218. B. Amanda has discovered an insider threat. Insider threats can be difficult to discover, as a malicious administrator or other privileged user will often have the ability to conceal their actions or may actually be the person tasked with hunting for threats like this! This is not a zero-day—no vulnerability was mentioned, there was no misconfiguration since this was an intentional action, and encryption is not mentioned or discussed.

219. A. Behavior like this would be considered risky, as clicking on unknown, unexpected links is a common way to succumb to a phishing attack. Unexpected typically describes behavior that isn't typical for the user, and we do now know if this user typically behaves this way. The Security+ exam outline doesn't use irresponsible as a category, and the click was intentional.

220. B. Establishing a baseline for security awareness is important so that Ben can determine what, if any, impact a program is having. This will drive KPIs as well as influence which actions and steps are taken to evolve the program. Implementing a security program is recommended by many standards, but they don't determine initial awareness state. Penetration tests can provide information about where issues lie but don't provide a broad baseline assessment either.

221. B. Malicious tools like BadUSB can make a USB cable or drive look like a keyboard when they are plugged in. Malicious thumb drives have been used by penetration testers simply by dropping them in a parking lot near their intended target. A Trojan or a worm is a possibility, but the clue involving the keyboard would point to a USB device as the first place Naomi should look.

222. B. A common practice is to report suspicious messages to an internal security team so that they can take action on phishing and other potential security issues. Reporting to third parties will not provide the same visibility, nor will deleting the messages. Asking users to click on messages works against security best practices!

223. A. Establishing security awareness KPIs, including incident rates, training uptake, responses to security awareness surveys, and other measurable indicators, is both the broadest and most useful option listed. Third-party awareness audits are not a typical method for doing this, and conducting surveys and tracking incident rates are both actions that will be part of common awareness KPIs.

224. B. Myles should be concerned about contractual impacts as part of his customer relationships. Noncompliance with regulations is likely to make him unable to fulfill contracts or to be in violation of contractual terms that require his company to be in compliance. Fines, loss of license, and sanctions may also occur, but they are less directly impactful to customers and are not guaranteed.

225. D. An enterprise password manager can help to make it easier to use appropriate passwords without requiring users to memorize them. This results in less reuse, stronger passwords, and the ability to manage them, including preventing password reuse. Biometrics, training, and adopting NIST password complexity and length standards will not have the same broad impact.

226. A. Risk matrices are often used to summarize risk registers for senior management. SLE and ALE reports are not common documents, although ALE and SLE reports are commonly used as part of quantitative risk assessment and reporting. Risk KPIs are used to track progress on risk management, not to provide a summary of a risk register.

227. B. Guidelines provide advice to organizations seeking to comply with policies and standards. Policies outline the principles and rules that guide the execution of security efforts throughout the enterprise. Standards provide mandatory requirements describing how an organization will carry out its information security policies.

Index

Online Test Bank

To help you study for your CompTIA Security+ certification exam, register to gain one year of FREE access after activation to the online interactive test bank—included with your purchase of this book! All of the chapter review questions and the practice tests in this book are included in the online test bank so you can practice in a timed and graded setting.

Register and Access the Online Test Bank

To register your book and get access to the online test bank, follow these steps:

1. Go to www.wiley.com/go/sybextestprep. You'll see the **"How to Register Your Book for Online Access"** instructions.
2. Click "here to register" and then select your book from the list.
3. Complete the required registration information, including answering the security verification to prove book ownership. You will be emailed a pin code.
4. Follow the directions in the email or go to www.wiley.com/go/sybextestprep.
5. Find your book on that page and click the "Register or Login" link with it. Then enter the pin code you received and click the "Activate PIN" button.
6. On the Create an Account or Login page, enter your username and password, and click Login or, if you don't have an account already, create a new account.
7. At this point, you should be in the test bank site with your new test bank listed at the top of the page. If you do not see it there, please refresh the page or log out and log back in.